D1129641

parents aren't supposed to like it

VOLUME 3

parents aren't supposed to like it

Rock & Other Pop Musicians of the 1990s

David P. Bianco, Editor

AN IMPRINT OF GALE

Detroit · New York · Toronto · London

Parents aren't supposed to like it

Rock & Other Pop Musicians of the 1990s

David P. Bianco, Editor

Staff

Sonia Benson, U·X·L Senior Editor
Carol DeKane Nagel, U·X·L Managing Editor
Thomas L. Romig, U·X·L Publisher

Mary Beth Trimper, Production Director
Evi Seoud, Assistant Production Manager
Shanna Heilveil, Production Associate

Cynthia Baldwin, Product Design Manager
Barbara Yarrow, Graphic Services Director
Michelle DiMercurio, Art Director
Jessica L. Ulrich, Permissions Assistant
Marco Di Vita, Graphix Group, Typesetter

Library of Congress Cataloging-in-Publication Data
Bianco, David P., 1947-
    Parents aren't supposed to like it: rock and other pop musicians of the 1990s/David P. Bianco
      p. cm.
    Includes bibliographical references, discographies, and index.
    Summary: Profiles over 100 contemporary musicians and bands in the categories of alternative rock, rap, folk music, and others..
    ISBN 0-7876-1731-8 (alk. paper).—ISBN 0-7876-1732-6 (alk. paper).—ISBN 0-7876-1733-4 (alk. paper).—0-7876-1734-2
    1.Musicians—Biography—Dictionaries, Juvenile. 2. Musical groups—Dictionaries, Juvenile. 3. Popular music—Dictionaries, Juvenile. [1. Musicians.] I. Title.
    ML3929.B5 1997
781.66'0922--dc21
[B]
                    97-34040
                    CIP
                 AC MN

10 9 8 7 6 5 4 3 2

Printed in the United States of America

contents

Green Day

VOLUME 3

Reader's Guide

There's something for just about every young music fan in *Parents Aren't Supposed to Like It: Rock & Other Pop Musicians of the 1990s.* This comprehensive resource contains more than 135 biographical/critical entries on the hottest bands and musicians of the 1990s, from a wide range of musical tastes and genres, including grunge, rap, traditional rock and roll, folk, heavy metal, British pop, ska, art rock, techno, rhythm and blues, and much more.

Perfect for browsing or for research, the three volumes are arranged by general musical categories with an overview of each category preceding the alphabetically arranged profiles of musicians in that genre. Volume 1 is devoted entirely to alternative rock; volume 2 contains Brit pop, dance music, and hip-hop and rap; and volume 3 features folk and folk rock, heavy metal, rhythm and blues and urban soul, rock and roll, and singers/ songwriters.

Portraits and other black-and-white photos of the musicians accompany most entries. Fun facts and fascinating anecdotes ap-

k. d. lang

pear in sidebars throughout the volumes, and pertinent quotes by and about the musicians begin each entry and can be found highlighted within the text. The entries conclude with sections listing awards, selected discographies, further reading sources, and contact information, with web sites for nearly all the musicians. Along with a thorough subject index for the three-volume set, there are three tables of contents to aid the reader, listing entries in the order in which they appear, in alphabetical order by musician, and in a breakdown by specific genres.

Scope

All of the bands and artists selected for inclusion are relevant to current popular music of the late 1990s. Most sold a lot of records in the 1990s, are on the cutting edge of a musical trend, or have been highly influential to music of the 1990s. The bands featured in *Parents* provide a representative cross-section of different styles of pop music, reflecting the wide variety of tastes exhibited by the record-buying public. The musicians included differ greatly not only in musical style, but in attitude, image, political messages, belief systems, and lifestyles.

Placing musicians in general genre sections provides a unique opportunity to compare the stories and experiences of artists with those of their peers. With overviews introducing these sections, a reader can quickly come up with an overall picture of the particular musical scene in which their favorite bands participate. Many modern musicians, of course, play in several genres, or have combined genres for new sounds. The editors of *Parents* have made an effort to place musicians in the category they are generally associated with, knowing that in many cases the musicians could easily fit well into another category. The tables of contents are provided in order to facilitate quick reference.

The profiles in *Parents* present the stories of the lives and careers of the featured artists, revealing childhood and family life and the inspirations and obstacles involved in the rise to stardom. Descriptions of the artists' recorded music and live performances are provided along with views of the critical and commercial response to their work. Beyond this, the entries contextualize the musical scene and the pop music business in the various genres as they relate to the musicians' experiences. Music festivals, major and independent record labels, innovative producers, musical technology, social and political controversy, and many other behind-the-scene aspects of pop music are brought out in the context of the musicians' life stories.

About the Contributors

David P. Bianco, editor of *Parents Aren't Supposed to Like It*, is a freelance writer, editor, and publishing consultant. His longstanding interest in popular music has resulted in the publication of two previous music reference books, *Who's New Wave in Music: An Illustrated Encyclopedia, 1976-1982, The First Wave* and *Heat Wave: The Motown Fact Book*. Other contributors are listed on the following page:

Kathy Bilitzke: freelance writer.

Charity Anne Dorgan: writer and editor with thirteen reference books to her credit, and a classically trained amateur singer and harpist.

Brian Escamilla: former editor of *Contemporary Musicians,* a biographical reference series, and a freelance writer.

Jo-Ann Greene: contributor to a wide variety of music publications in both the United States and the United Kingdom, including *Hits, Goldmine, CMJ Monthly, Alternative Press,* and *NME: New Musical Express.* She is also the author of *The Cure* and co-author of *U2: A Visual Documentary.*

Jill Hamilton: contributor to *Rolling Stone, Entertainment Weekly,* and *Playgirl.* Winner of 1996 award from the National Society of Newspaper Columnists.

Ralph Heibutzki: contributor to *Goldmine, DISCoveries, Bass Player* and *Guitar Player,* among other publications. Author of liner notes for Rhino's *Sugar Hill* CD boxed set and for the *Dub Chill Out* compilation by Music Collectors International.

Tim James: cofounder and active member of the non-profit Detroit Musicians Alliance (DMA). Promoter of music festivals and concerts; manager of several Detroit-area bands. Contributor to *Jam Rag* magazine and *Musiczine,* the newsletter of DMA.

Allison Jones: freelance writer and contributor to various music publications, including *Contemporary Musicians* and *Canadian Newsmakers.*

Peter Schorn: multiple-award winning and nominated record producer, songwriter, guitarist, and performer with the band Red September. A founder and past president of the Detroit Musicians Alliance (DMA), he has worked to educate musicians and promote quality music in southeast Michigan. He is a columnist and reviewer for *Musiczine,* the newsletter of the DMA.

Sue Summers: cofounder and vice president of the Detroit Musicians Alliance (DMA); freelance writer for *Musiczine,* the fanzine of the DMA; manager of the independent label Static Records; music promoter and band manager.

Dave Thompson: author of more than sixty rock books, including biographies of Kurt Cobain, Depeche Mode, Red Hot Chili Peppers, Perry Farrell, and U2; regular contributor to *Alternative Press* and *Goldmine* magazines.

Patricia Whipple: co-owner of recording studio; manager, booking agent, and critic in music industry; freelance music writer.

Suggestions

We welcome any comments or suggestions on *Parents Aren't Supposed to Like It: Rock and Other Pop Musicians of the 1990s.* Please write: Editors, *Parents Aren't Supposed to Like It,* U•X•L, Gale Research, 835 Penobscot Bldg., Detroit, Michigan 48226-4094; call toll-free: 800-877-4235; or fax to 313-961-6348.

ALPHABETICAL LISTING OF MUSICIANS

(Boldface numeral indicates volume number, which is followed by page number.)

Tupac Shakur

musicians by genre

(Boldface numeral indicates volume number, which is followed by page number.)

all-girl groups

american folk rock

art rock

Sheryl Crow

Musicians by Genre

Picture Credits

The photographs appearing in *Parents Aren't Supposed to Like It: Rock & Other Pop Musicians of the 1990s* were received from the following sources:

Cover: Grant Lee Phillips of Grant Lee Buffalo: © **Ken Settle. Reproduced by permission.**

AP/Wide World Photos. Reproduced by permission: pp. 1, 5, 24, 57, 60, 78, 93, 138, 164, 174, 219, 220, 230, 241, 249, 310, 330, 344, 368, 378, 387, 418, 420, 439, 451, 473, 542, 574, 585, 588, 594, 597, 611, 621, 626, 627, 630, 643, 644; © **Larry Hulst/Michael Ochs Archives/Venice, CA. Reproduced by permission:** pp. 4, 27, 75, 584; **Archive Photos. Reproduced by permission:** pp. 6, 178, 180, 257, 314, 468, 504; ©**Ken Settle. Reproduced by permission:** pp. 7, 12, 16, 37, 43, 45, 50, 61, 69, 89, 96, 110, 130, 134, 145, 148, 160, 163, 169, 172, 190, 199, 231, 237, 248, 266, 267, 277, 284, 350, 382, 412, 454, 461, 465, 479, 482, 485, 545, 548, 552, 565, 572, 576, 579, 606, 613, 618, 636, 639, 653; **Photograph by Danny Clinch. Columbia, Sony Music. Reproduced by permission:**

The Fugees

p. 11; © Denise Sofranko/Michael Ochs Archives/Venice, CA. Reproduced by permission: pp. 20, 511; Photograph by Rafael Fuchs. Matador Records. Reproduced by permssion: p. 30; Photograph by Christine Alicino. Corbis. Reproduced by permission: p. 33; Photograph by Tim Mosenfelder. Corbis. Reproduced by permission: pp. 34, 182, 253, 254; Photograph by Timothy White. Arista Records. Reproduced by permission: p. 42; Photograph by Frank Ockenfels. Outline Press Syndicate. Reproduced by permission: p. 46; Photograph by Jeff Christensen. Archive Photos/Reuters. Reproduced by permission: pp. 49, 53, 322; Photograph by Tina Paul. Archive Photos. Reproduced by permission: p. 65; Photograph by Jon Hammer. Archive Photos. Reproduced by permission: p. 70, 196, 222, 270; Photograph by Pauline St. Denis. Courtesy of Rykodisc: p. 81; Photograph by Tibor Bozi. Corbis. Reproduced by permission: p. 84, 291, 443; Michael Ochs Archives/Venice, CA. Reproduced by permission: p. 87, 355, 366, 382, 383, 622; Photograph by Scott Harrison. Archive Photos. Reproduced by permission: pp. 101, 153, 187, 559; Photograph by Sin/Tony Mott. Corbis. Reproduced by permission: pp. 105, 123, 497; Photograph by Scope/John Wallace. Corbis. Reproduced by permission: p. 106; Photograph by James Smolka. Reproduced by permission: p. 111; © Anna Luken/Michael Ochs Archives/Venice, CA. Reproduced by permission: pp. 115, 155, 617; Photograph by Gary Hershorn. Reuters/Archive Photos. Reproduced by permission: p. 117; Photograph by Mike Hashimoti. Corbis. Reproduced by permission: p. 124; Photograph by Lance Mercer. Columbia Records. Reproduced by permission: p. 127; © Joe Hughes/Michael Ochs Archives/Venice, CA. Reproduced by permission: pp. 150, 312; Photograph by Richard Drew. AP/Wide World. Reproduced by permission: p. 192; Photograph by Henry Diltz. Corbis. Reproduced by permission: p. 203; Photograph by Paul Banks. Corbis. Reproduced by permission: pp. 223, 224; Archive Photos/Popperfoto. Reproduced by permission: pp. 227, 516, 541, 634; Archive Photos/Big Pictures. Reproduced by permission: p. 228; Photograph by Mike Segar. Archive Photos/Reuters. Reproduced by permission: pp. 238, 265; © Waring Abbott/Michael Ochs/Archives/Venice, CA. Reproduced by permission: pp. 275, 287, 403, 405, 458, 528; Photograph by Tom Gates. Archive Photos. Reproduced by permission: p. 283; Corbis-Bettmann. Reproduced by permission: 303, 317, 343, 362, 376, 392, 403, 410, 446, 50, 5241, 655; © Al Pereira/Michael Ochs Archives/Venice, CA. Reproduced by permission: pp. 306, 360, 399, 520; © Raymond Boyd/Michael Ochs Archives, Venice, CA. Reproduced by permission: pp. 321, 340, 372, 424, 525; Photograph by Bob Grant. Fotos international/Archive Photos. Reproduced by permission: p. 326; Ruthless Records. Reproduced by permission: p. 338; Photograph by Miranda Shen. Fotos international/Archive Photos. Reproduced by

parents aren't supposed to like it

FOLK MUSIC AND FOLK ROCK

Folk music is people's music, or music for the "folks." Usually created by or for people from the working class, this music was based on traditional songs, traditional arrangements, and traditional instruments.

The folk music boom of the late 1950s and early 1960s followed changes in the social and political life of America. Growing interest in causes like the civil rights movement and opposition to U.S. involvement in the war in Vietnam was fueled by songwriter/singers like Joan Baez, Phil Ochs, and Buffy Sainte-Marie, who strummed at acoustic guitars and railed against injustice. But it wasn't all politics: folk music was well-suited to group singalongs, and it was family-friendly, as demonstrated by the popular *Sing Along with Mitch* TV show and albums hosted by Mitch Miller.

Folk groups, too, achieved popularity, often bringing ancient songs up to date with multi-part harmonies and acoustic pop instrumentation. Among the most popular groups in this mode were the Limeliters, the very political Weavers and the more mainstream Four Freshmen.

Tracy Chapman

In the 1960s folk performers like Joan Baez, Judy Collins, and Bob Dylan started playing on the folk circuit in places like Greenwich Village in New York City. The ideas in the songs fit well with fans' emerging liberal political views. The idea of a person on a guitar singing directly to other people about politics and life also fit in with the 1960s ideals. It was a case of the right music for the right time.

Dylan and the folk revolution

There was a very big moment in the history of folk music when Bob Dylan "went electric" in the mid-1960s. Bob Dylan had been one of folk music's brightest stars at the time. When he went electric, he was showing his support for rock and roll—a big betrayal to folk fans, who were into acoustic instruments and simple, personal songs. Rock and rollers preferred electric guitars and simple lyrics about things like dancing or being in love. Dylan's combination of sounds helped to start a new kind of music called folk rock.

Dylan songs like "Positively 4th Street," "Mr. Tambourine Man," "Blowin' in the Wind," "Subterranean Homesick Blues" and especially "Like a Rolling Stone" turned the songwriter's often abstract images toward social concerns that dominated the period, like war, racial injustice, and the individual's role in a democracy. For listeners used to lyrics about rocking around the clock, dancing in the streets, and falling in and out of love, a Dylan lyric like "Johnny's in the basement, mixin' up the medicine/I'm on the pavement, thinkin' 'bout the government" (from "Subterranean") was startling, new, electrifying—and grown-up. Even several decades later, it has the kind of rhythmic drive and edge that survives in alternative rock and rap. Dylan continued to make influential records through the 1970s. Though his work varied in quality during the 1980s and 1990s, he continued to be a motivating force for thoughtful songwriters in all styles.

Simon and Garfunkel, who started as Tom and Jerry, brought this tradition forward with hipper, more sophisticated songs and splendid harmonies. Paul Simon later went solo and emerged as one of pop music's most consistent and effective songwriters. Another folk star of the 1960s, Richie Havens, achieved considerable success with his deep, powerful voice and percussive guitar sound. Of all the songs he recorded, nothing is better known than his long, improvised version of the traditional song "Motherless Child" at the Woodstock music festival in 1969. Strumming ferociously with his thumb, Havens tapped into a powerful emotion and held a huge crowd of rock fans captive during this mesmerizing performance.

When musicians started mixing the folk and rock music together, each type added something to the sound. Rock gave folk a more uptempo energy, from the faster beats and the electric instruments. Folk gave rock more harmonies plus a greater emphasis on lyrics. Influenced by folk lyrics, rock lyrics became more poetic, personal, and political.

Bands like **R.E.M.** (see entry) or **Indigo Girls** (see entry) are examples of modern bands that came from folk rock.

In the 1970s, most of the public attention that had been centered on folk music went to the singer/songwriter movement when singers like James Taylor, Carly Simon, and Joni Mitchell became popular. It seemed like folk music was going to go back to where it had been before—a small, specialty kind of music that rarely made the charts.

Folk traditions in the 1980s and 1990s

But in the 1980s folk music started making a comeback. In the 1980s MTV started airing their popular *MTV Unplugged*, which featured rock performers playing their songs on acoustic instruments. Many of the new folk artists of the 1980s and 1990s weren't traditional folk artists in the old sense of the word. They often used electric instruments here and there. But many of the basic ideas were the same—stripped-down music, acoustic guitar, and the importance of lyrics.

Michelle Shocked (see entry) is one of the most traditional and untraditional of the latest group of folkies. She was discovered by an English producer at the 1986 Kerrville Folk Festival while she was singing by a campfire. The producer recorded Shocked on his personal recorder and released the tape as *The Texas Campfire Tapes*. The record became a hit and scored Shocked a record deal. Her next record, *Short Sharp Shocked*, stuck with the folk path, and Shocked became known for her folk songs and

Jeff Buckley

her outspokenness. But on the next record, *Captain Swing*, Shocked suddenly did big band tunes in 1940s swing music style. This didn't go over very well with fans, so Shocked went back to her folk roots for her next record, *Arkansas Traveler*. After that record, Shocked and her record company, Mercury, ended their relationship. Now Shocked is truly doing the folk rock thing—making tapes of her music and selling them herself.

In 1988 **Tracy Chapman** (see entry) had her first hit with the Grammy-winning "Fast Car." She rose to fame the folkie way, singing on the street and in coffeehouses. She has many of the traditional folk music elements in her music. Most of the songs on her self-titled debut album simply relied on Chapman's rich, deep voice and her acoustic guitar. In her music, she takes the common folkie stance of social commentary, with songs about racial injustice, domestic violence, and the working class.

Like Chapman, **Indigo Girls** (see entry) are closely related to traditional folk, but are more of a folk-rock band since they use electric instruments and like to rock out occasionally. One way to look at it is that Emily Saliers is the more folk-influenced one, and Amy Ray is the more rock-influenced one. Saliers likes slower, gentler songs, and Ray prefers harder-edged ones. Together they come up with something that's a unique combination of the best of both of their sounds, featuring dual guitars, gently rocking songs, and plenty of harmonies.

Sarah McLachlan (see entry) arrived on the music scene in the late 1980s, at about the same time as the Indigo Girls, Tracy Chapman, and Michelle Shocked, but it took her longer to get widespread attention. Her big break finally came with *Fumbling Towards Ecstasy* and the hit song "Possession." McLachlan grew up in Nova Scotia, Canada, and she uses her background in her music. Her songs are a mix of traditional Irish folk and ambient layers of textured songs. In 1995, she highlighted her folkie roots by putting out a record of stripped-down versions of her *Fumbling Towards Ecstasy* songs.

Michael Penn's (see entry) folk roots are influenced by the folk-rock moments of the Beatles. His first record, *March,* mixed pop melodies and intricate lyrics. The almost retro-sound of the record helped propel Penn to the record charts.

No one will ever know what different kinds of music **Jeff Buckley** (see entry) would have explored in his career, because Buckley died young in a tragic drowning accident. While he was alive, Buckley experimented with all kinds of sounds. Critics heard everything from Led Zeppelin to Van Morrison to Buckley's musician father, Tim Buckley, in Buckley's two records, *Live at Sin-é* and *Grace.* Buckley himself was a fan of all kinds of music, including French singer Edith Piaf and poet/folk rocker Leonard Cohen. The result of all this was a sound that mixed folk, jazz, and rock with equal importance on each.

JEFF BUCKLEY

American folk singer and songwriter

Born in Orange County, California, in 1966; died May 29, 1997

As the son of 1960s folk legend Tim Buckley, there has been the unavoidable comparison of singer-songwriter Jeff Buckley to his father. According to David Galens in *musicHound! rock,* "As the inheritor of such a legacy, Buckley must endure comparisons to his late father and the expectations of fans eager for the progeny [children] to take up where the sire [father] left off. Like his father, Buckley does possess an ethereal [otherworldly] voice capable of dramatic sweeps of range; his singing uncannily evokes Tim's." It was, in fact, Buckley's mother, a classically trained pianist and cellist, who first inspired him with music. His father died of a drug overdose when Jeff was quite young, and a stronger influence was his stepfather, who was an auto mechanic and an ardent rock fan.

Buckley found his grandmother's guitar when he was five years old and taught himself to play. He left home at seventeen and moved to Los Angeles, where he played with what he called "a lot of weird bands," which included a number of jazz, funk, rock, and

"To do something that will just fly away is kind of special. Every time somebody tells you they love you, that 'I love you' flies away, and you wait until the next one." –Jeff Buckley

reggae groups. He also did some studio session work to support himself.

Part of New York folk scene in the 1990s

New York became Buckley's home in 1990. He worked with some hardcore and avant-rock bands, then formed Gods & Monsters with experimental guitarist Gary Lucas. The band proved popular but didn't last long, so Buckley decided to go solo in 1992. He hung out on the Lower East Side of New York and felt very much at home there. "More than any place," Buckley claimed, "this is where I felt I belonged. I prefer the Lower East Side to any place on the planet. I can be who I am here ... I couldn't do it any place I lived as a child. I never fit in in California, even though my roots are there."

His solo shows on the Greenwich Village club circuit gained Buckley a considerable following. His music was recorded at the East Village coffeehouse where he played frequently. The mini-LP, *Live at Sin-é,* was released by Columbia Records in 1993. The four-song CD contained two original songs and two covers. Buckley has stated, "I'm trying to learn from the great teachers, and trying to pay tribute to them. But now I have to burn away all these others and get down to what I really am inside." On his cover versions of Edith Piaf's "Je N'en Connais Pas Le Fin" and Van Morrison's "The Way Young Lovers Do," Buckley improvised around the melody, scat singing in a jazz/folk style for a full ten minutes.

Debut album released in 1994

Buckley's first full-length album, *Grace,* was released in 1994. The record included seven original and three cover songs. In his first recording effort with a band, Buckley surrounded himself with musicians on *Grace* who successfully enhanced his voice. Talking about the collaboration, Buckley said, "The experience of creating and performing with a band was different from my solo work. All the spontaneity and attention to the dynamics of the moment is extended four times and maybe beyond."

Buckley's vocals were recognized by critics as the highlight of *Grace.* David Galens noted, "The unifying principle is Buckley's versatile singing; his voice can sinuously twine itself around a beautiful melody, hover with growling menace and swoop to startling falsetto heights, often within the same song." Reviewer Stephen Holden put *Grace* in the "Exceptional" category in a *New York Times* round-up: "Jeff Buckley reveals a voice of astonishing emotional fire.... Mr. Buckley's songs ... express the same burning mysticism, and his voice, which shades from an ethereal [otherworldly] soprano of heart-rending delicacy into a transported yowl worthy of Robert Plant, makes them indelible [unforgettable]."

As his debut album earned Buckley more popularity, as well as critical acclaim, he and his group began touring in the fall of 1994. Before the recording of *Grace,* he'd toured North America and Europe, playing solo electric shows and then returning later in the year for gigs with his band.

Buckley's 1997 efforts included a collaboration with Inger Lorre. They performed together on *Kerouac-Kick Joy Darkness*, a spoken word album tribute to Beat writer, Jack Kerouac. Buckley played guitar, sitar, and mouth saxophone on their track, "Angel Mine." In 1997 Buckley also contributed the lead vocals on the song, "I Want Someone Badly," which appeared on the soundtrack to the film *First Love-Last Rite*.

While his recording career blossomed, Buckley still loved the feel of performing live. "I'll probably play live till the day I die," he proclaimed. "It's cool to have a CD, with a condensed moment that's been worked over for weeks, but to do something that will just fly away is kind of special. Every time somebody tells you they love you, that 'I love you' flies away, and you wait until the next one."

Jeff Buckley drowned in Memphis Harbor

In the spring of 1997 sad news came that singer Jeff Buckley had accidentally drowned in the harbor of Memphis, Tennessee. Missing since May 29, 1997, Buckley's body was found on June 4. He had gone to Memphis with his band in late February to begin rehearsals. As of March 31, he was performing every Monday night at Barrister's nightclub in Memphis. His last show was on Monday, May 26.

Selected Discography

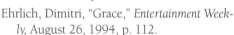

Live at Sin-é (Columbia), 1993, (EP).

Grace (Columbia), 1994.

"Angel Mine" (with Inger Lorre) on *Kerouac-Kick Joy Darkness* (Rykodisc), 1997.

Further Reading

Diehl, Matt, "Fighting Hype and the Weight of His Father's Legend, Jeff Buckley Finds His Own Voice on `Grace'," *Rolling Stone*, October 20, 1994, p. 68.

Ehrlich, Dimitri, "Grace," *Entertainment Weekly*, August 26, 1994, p. 112.

Evans, Paul, "Live at Sin-E," *Rolling Stone*, March 10, 1994, p. 65.

"Jeff Buckley," *People Weekly*, May 8, 1995, p. 92.

Rogers, Ray, "Jeff Buckley" (interview), *Interview*, February 1994, p. 97.

Schruers, Fred, "River's Edge," *Rolling Stone*, August 7, 1997, p. 21.

Contact Information

Columbia Records
550 Madison Ave.
New York, NY 10022-3211

Web Sites

http://www.music.sony.com/Music/ ArtistInfo/JeffBuckley.html

http://www.goodnet.com/~gkelemen/ jeffhome.html

Tracy Chapman

American folk singer and songwriter

Born March 30, 1964, in Cleveland, Ohio

"It's wrong not to encourage people to hope or dream or even to consider what's thought to be impossible. That's the only thing that keeps people alive sometimes." –Tracy Chapman in *Rolling Stone*

From the street corners and coffeehouses of Boston to sold-out arenas throughout the world, Tracy Chapman has delivered homespun tales of social inequality, lost love, and her self-described "hopeful cynicism" with the same unwavering voice and lingering folk-pop melodies. Her 1988 debut album, *Tracy Chapman,* made her an international star virtually overnight due to the overwhelming response to the first single, the emotionally gripping "Fast Car." Grammy Awards and high-profile performances followed, as well as a string of well-received albums. In 1996 *New Beginning* gave Chapman a renewed sense of purpose, a fresh outlook on her success, and another Grammy.

Early love of music

Born in Cleveland, Ohio, in 1964, Chapman's parents divorced when she was four years old. With her older sister, Aneta, Chapman was raised by her mother, who made ends meet by working a series of low-paying jobs and occasionally relying on welfare. "We always had food to eat and a place to stay, but it was a fairly bare-bones kind of thing," she recalled to *Rolling Stone*'s Stephen Pond in 1988. Watching her mother, who refused alimony following her divorce, struggle to raise her kids left a lasting impression on the already politically-minded Chapman. "As a child, I always had a sense of social conditions and political situations," she told Pond. "I think it had to do with the fact that my mother was always discussing things with my sister and me—also because I read a lot."

Chapman also developed an interest in music, listening to the songs her mother and sister liked—mostly 1970s soul and gospel—and plucking out tunes on a ukulele. A battered acoustic guitar soon replaced the ukulele, and while still in grade school Chapman began to explore the complexities of the instrument as well as songwriting. "I've been singing ever since I was a child," she explained to Richard Harrington of the *Washington Post*. "I think I just picked up a guitar because my mother had played it at some point—started teaching myself things and writing my own songs."

The Wooster School and Tufts

While in high school, Chapman's focus on her studies earned her a scholarship to the Wooster School, a progressive Episcopalian prep school in Danbury, Connecticut. It was at Wooster that Chapman first heard the style of music with which she'd later be identified. This included the songs of Crosby, Stills and Nash; Neil Young; and Bob Dylan.

Teachers and classmates would later recall Chapman sitting on the white fence outside her dorm strumming her beat-up guitar. During her first year at Wooster, the school's chaplain and soccer coach, Reverend Robert Tate, organized a collection to buy Chapman a better guitar. (She later thanked Tate in the liner notes to her first album.) So often was she seen with her new guitar—on the fence, at the school coffeehouse, or in the chapel—that the Wooster yearbook for the Class of 1982 predicted, "Tracy Chapman will marry her guitar and live happily ever after."

After leaving Wooster, Chapman headed to Tufts University in Boston to study to be a veterinarian, a dream she'd had since she was six years old. She soon switched her major to anthropology, however, and continued to play her guitar on the street corners and in the coffeehouses of Boston. Classmate Brian Koppelman went to a Chapman performance to see if she'd be willing to play at a campus rally he was putting together. Koppelman was so impressed with the singer/songwriter he offered to introduce her to his father, Charles Koppelman, the chief executive officer of SBK, the largest independent music publishing company in the world. "And she didn't really seem interested," Koppelman recalled to *Rolling Stone*'s Pond. "Tracy genuinely was not interested in money." After father Charles heard her play, he immediately offered her a contract. She refused to sign for six months, since she wanted to graduate from college first.

"Fast Car"

The senior Koppelman then brought Chapman to the attention of Robert Krasnow of Elektra Records, who signed her to a recording contract immediately upon meeting her. Producer David Kershenbaum, who has produced records for folksinger Joan Baez and new wave singer Joe Jackson, was then recruited to set up the recording and hire a studio band. "She was so stable and balanced as a person," Kershenbaum told Pond about recording the first album. "She just really had her head on straight, knew exactly who she was and what she was trying to say and trying to do."

Although Chapman had a vast collection of songs from which to choose, they only recorded the eleven songs that make up the album. Following the recording, Chapman signed a management contract with Elliot Roberts, the manager of Neil Young and Bob Dylan. Roberts convinced her to abandon her idea of touring with a band and play solo acoustic shows instead.

> **"I think people are foolish to believe that there won't be major social changes in this country before we possibly, ultimately, destroy ourselves. There's only so far you can push people before they start to push back, and I've seen that in my life."**

Released to rave reviews, *Tracy Chapman* was an immediate hit. "Fast Car" raced to the Top Ten while the album hovered in the Top Five for months.

"Confrontational rather than confessional," Pond wrote in his *Rolling Stone* review, "pointed rather that poetic, hers is the sound of a smart black woman growing up in the city with her eyes wide open."

For the first time in years there was a hit album that openly discussed the lives and problems of the disenfranchised. Songs like "Why?" and "Talkin' bout a Revolution," delivered in Chapman's clear, husky alto, warned of the growing resentment among those in the inner city and the consequences of a future without social change.

"I think people are foolish to believe that there won't be major social changes in this country before we possibly, ultimately, destroy ourselves," she declared to Pond. "There's only so far you can push people before they start to push back, and I've seen that in my life.... It's wrong not to encourage people to hope or dream or even to consider what's thought to be impossible. That's the only thing that keeps people alive sometimes. For me and my family, that was one of the only things that kept us going."

Overnight success

Within five months of the album's release, the former street-corner troubadour performed before a television audience of millions at London's FreedomFest on June 11, 1988, to honor Nelson Mandela. Then she was headlining Amnesty International's tour, Human Rights Now!, alongside **Bruce Springsteen** (see entry), Sting, Peter Gabriel, and Youssou N'-Dour. In February 1989 Chapman performed "Fast Car" at the Grammy Awards and took home three trophies for Best New Artist, Best Album, and Best Song. The album went on to sell ten million copies worldwide.

Later in 1989 Chapman released *Crossroads*. Although it sold nearly as fast as her debut—four million copies during the first five months of release—critical response was not as high. Most critics contended that, while *Crossroads* was a good album, it was too similar to the debut, thus appearing to be a shadow of the original. "I don't know what it is people want from me," Chapman lamented to Alan Light of *Rolling Stone*. "It seemed like on the first album they were willing to take what it is I have to give. I'm willing to take that gamble and hope that if people like and appreciate what you do, they'll let you choose your direction."

Matters of the Heart

It would be three years before Chapman returned with a new album, 1992's *Matter of the Heart*. Between albums Chapman moved from Boston to San Francisco and contemplated the whirlwind success she'd lived through the previous few years, although the songs on the album weren't directly about that. "Of course you're influenced by your experiences," she explained to Light, "but if anything, (the success) just makes you sit down and reevaluate your life and the things that are important to you." The songs carried the same social weight as Chapman's two previous efforts, especially on such tracks as "Woman's Work" and "Bang Bang Bang." Critical response

The resurgence of women in rock in the late 1980s

Tracy Chapman was the most successful singer/songwriter to emerge from the so-called "new trend" of women performers who emerged in the late 1980s. At that time the mainstream music press took note of an unprecedented number of women in the music scene. Musician magazine devoted an issue to "The Women's Movement of 1988." Generally thought to have begun with Suzanne Vega's hit single "Luka" in 1987, the roster of women who'd be mentioned in this collective breath included Natalie Merchant (then of 10,000 Maniacs), **Michelle Shocked,** the **Indigo Girls, Sinead O'Connor, Melissa Etheridge,** (see entries), and Chapman.

Though there have always been women hitmakers, MTV-styled synth rock of the mid-1980s was not very open to women. Roberta Peterson, a vice president and general manager at Warner Bros. Records told Gillian Garr, author of She's A Rebel, that she wanted to sign Vega to the label around that time, "but they wouldn't have any part of it." Instead Vega signed to A&M Records, but Nancy Jeffries, an Artist and Repertoire (A&R) representative for A&M told Musician magazine in 1988 that they were concerned as well. "We all had some doubts because you're scared about signing a folk singer in 1985." For her part, Chapman praised Vega, telling Musician, "She opened the minds and ears of radio programmers to a kind of music that had gone ignored for quite a while."

lacked enthusiasm however, and it would be Chapman's lowest selling album.

New Beginning

Following the tour to support *Matters of the Heart,* Chapman took some time off to travel to Africa, Mexico, and the southern United States. In August 1994 she put a band together in San Francisco that could both tour and record. The band did a quick tour of the United States to develop as a playing unit and then headed into the studio. When they emerged they had *New Beginning,* Chapman's 1996 release that contained the bluesy "Give Me One Reason." The song became an anthem for the summer of 1996 and went on to win Chapman her fourth Grammy for Best Rock Song.

The rest of the album was filled with the kind of emotional and social subject matter audiences have come to expect from Chapman. "Some of the songs are dealing with issues we are facing in the world right now, like the degradation of the natural environment and the lack of freedom, justice, love and honesty," she said in her Elektra press release. "We're at a place right now, approaching the new century, where we could find new solutions to old problems that are still plaguing society."

Selected Awards

Grammy Award winner for 1) Best New Artist; 2) Best Album, for *Tracy Chapman*;
and 3) Best Pop Performance, Female, for "Fast Car"; 1989.

BRIT Awards for 1) Best International Artist, Female; and 2) Best International Newcomer, 1989.

Grammy Award for Best Rock Song, Female, for "Give Me One Reason," 1997.

Selected Discography

Tracy Chapman (Elektra), 1988.

Crossroads (Elektra), 1989.

Matter of the Heart (Elektra), 1992.

New Beginning (Elektra), 1996.

Further Reading

Billboard, August 24, 1996, p. 1.

Cannon, Bob, "Give Me the Reason," *Entertainment Weekly,* April 26, 1996, p. 58.

Gates, David, "Three Lines, 12 Bars, No Frills," *Newsweek,* July 1, 1996, p. 62.

Nash, Alanna, "New Beginning," *Stereo Review,* January 1996, p. 101.

Thigpen, David E., "Cashing a Reality Check," *Time,* May 13, 1996, p. 101.

Torres, Richard, "New Beginning," *Rolling Stone,* November 16, 1995, p. 111.

Contact Information

Elektra Records
75 Rockefeller Plaza
New York, NY 10019

Web Sites

http://www.rrze.uni-erlangen.de/~sz1526/tracy.html

http://www.elektra.com

InDiGo GiRLS

American folk-rock group

Formed in 1983 in Atlanta, Georgia

Indigo Girls—Amy Ray and Emily Saliers—are a popular folk harmony duo known for their beautiful, yet clashing, voices and for their political consciousness. Saliers's dusky soprano voice and Ray's harmonies stir their audience's spirits while their emotional lyrics raise important contemporary issues, especially Native American concerns.

Old Friends

Ray and Saliers first met in elementary school. Both were poets; both sang in the school choir. While they were undergraduates at Emory University they formed Indigo Girls, and in 1983, Ray and Saliers began to sing in various clubs. They earned their following in the mid-1980s from performances in Atlanta and the southeastern United States.

Ray and Saliers's first album, *Indigo Girls,* debuted in 1989 and launched their careers as popular folk singers. The album sold more than a million copies and was certified platinum by the

"We feel that the way to save our environment is to save the cultural diversity." –Amy Ray

451

Record Industry Association of America. Later albums were equally well received. *Rights of Passage* also earned platinum certification, while *Nomads-Indians-Saints* and *Swamp Ophelia* both received gold record status. Indigo Girls' single releases were applauded as well. A *Billboard* reviewer said that their "Power of Love" was "not to be missed," and their version of Buffy Sainte-Marie's "Bury My Heart at Wounded Knee" also was praised by *Billboard.*

The Music and the Message

Overall, Indigo Girls' harmonies are the hallmark of the duo, the sound that enthralls both critics and audiences. According to a *Billboard* reviewer, "Emily Saliers's and Amy Ray's voices remain a source of endless delight as they harmonize with deceptive ease." But their political voices also capture attention. Their song lyrics often promote social activism regarding animal rights, women's and children's issues, gay rights, and the environment. "I'll Give You My Skin," for example, appeared on the *Tame Yourself* album in 1991 in support of People for the Ethical Treatment of Animals. Later Indigo Girls contributed to *Women to Women 2,* an album promoting breast cancer awareness. They also offered a previously unreleased, acoustic version of "This Train" to the Gay Human Rights Commission's album *Out Loud* in order to raise the public's consciousness about gay and lesbian rights.

Native American concerns—particularly the environment—are perhaps the Indigo Girls's favorite issues. The duo donated the proceeds from their "Bury My Heart at Wounded Knee" single to the Honor the Earth Campaign to benefit Native rights. In 1995, Indigo Girls also performed with the Honor the Earth tour to raise money and awareness regarding Native American environmentalism. They visited five reservations on the month-long tour, which was the largest benefit of its kind. In total, the tour grossed $300,000, and was an uplifting experience for Indigo Girls. As Amy Ray explained: "This tour is something I had been looking forward to for two years. I think it's one of the most important things we've done as far as our personal growth goes." Issues involved in the Honor the Earth Campaign included Native American homelands, sacred sites, and religious freedom; nuclear waste and testing; uranium, coal, and gold mining; clear cutting of timber forests; and the recovery of Native language that had been slipping from use.

With their beautifully braided harmonies, eloquent lyrics, and social concern, Indigo Girls is a good folk-rock group that is doing good things. Their "modern-day Simon & Garfunkel sound" has been embraced by critics and audiences alike, while their commitment to social concerns allows the group to pursue their convictions openly and benefit causes close to their hearts. As one critic noted, there are two good reasons to buy much of the material by Indigo Girls: the music and the opportunity to contribute to worthy causes.

Selected Awards

Grammy Awards, Best Contemporary Folk Recording Award, for *Indigo Girls,* 1990.

Grammy Awards, Best Contemporary Folk Album nomination, for *Swamp Ophelia,* 1995.

Grammy Awards, nomination, for "Hammer and a Nail," 1996.

Selected Discography

Indigo Girls (Epic), 1989.

Nomads-Indians-Saints (Epic), 1990.

Live: Back on the Bus Y'All (Epic), 1991.

Rites of Passage (Epic), 1992.

Swamp Ophelia (Epic), 1994.

1200 Curfews (Epic), 1995 (double live CD).

4.5 (Epic), 1995.

Further Reading

Boehler, Eric, "The Modern Age," *Billboard,* September 10, 1994, p. 105.

Dougherty, Steve, "Out of the Blue," *People Weekly,* August 8, 1994, p. 43+.

Farley, Christopher John, "Indigo Girls: Swamp Ophelia," *Time,* May 23, 1994, p. 70.

Utz, Heidi, "Honoring the Earth: The Indigo Girls Tour to Benefit Native American Environmentalism," *E: The Environmental Magazine,* September-October 1995, pp. 25-26.

Contact Information

Epic Records
51 West 52nd Street
New York, NY 10019

Web Site

www.music.sony.com/music/ArtistInfo/ IndigoGirls.html

Sarah McLachlan

Canadian folk-rock singer and songwriter

Born in Halifax, Nova Scotia, Canada, on January 28, 1968

"It just took me a long time to realize I should feel pride for what I do. That may show a big lack of confidence, but ultimately I was pleased I came to understand things on my own terms." –Sarah McLachlan

Sarah McLachlan, a "lost, screwed up little kid," as she described herself to *Maclean's*, mostly hung out with punks and dropouts when she was growing up in Halifax, Nova Scotia. She studied voice and guitar as a teen, but preferred improvisation to classical training. Her early work experience included washing dishes and serving as counter help at such establishments as Mother Tucker's restaurants until she negotiated a record contract at the age of nineteen. From then on, McLachlan was on her way to becoming an international celebrity as a singer and songwriter.

McLachlan wrote her first song, "Out of the Shadows," in 1987, when she was about twenty. She quickly developed a style of stark, confessional songs that earned her recognition as a composer. Her folk-rock tunes are elegantly simple. Her words are witty and literate, reflecting a maturity that belied her age. "For someone so young," said Chris Mayo, a programming manager at an album alternative radio station in Seattle, "the depth is incredible."

Ambiguities and earnestness

McLachlan writes in a narrative style that is sometimes hard to follow, creating songs with uncertain meanings and curious interpretations. "Good Enough," for example, explored the situations of people out of touch with themselves or those they love. The resulting song is somewhat cryptic [unclear]. "It just kind of happens that way," McLachlan explained to Billboard. "Part of it is meant to be [unclear] because I don't want to be too obvious. Sometimes, unfortunately, I become too unobvious. But I do that when I'm not sure what I'm trying to say, at least when I'm writing it."

McLachlan's songs, basically romantic explorations of one's self and the universe, became known for their emotional honesty. Initially she composed romantic, introspective material about extreme conditions of the heart—like unrequited love or longing. Progressively McLachlan became more external, considering topics such as abortion, animal rights, poverty, or prostitution. McLachlan even began to work out some of life's lessons in her songs. "Possession," for example, referenced one male fan's obsession with the singer. The man went so far as to move to Vancouver just to be near her, and she ultimately had to secure a restraining order to keep him at bay. McLachlan explained in Maclean's that "Possession" "was a kind of therapy, putting myself in the shoes of someone like that. It helped me deal with a very unnerving situation."

In addition to her honest emotional expression and narrative style, McLachlan's remarkable vocal instrument contributes to the overall presentation of her material. "Her voice is just mesmerizing [hypnotic]," explained Leslie Fram, a member of an Atlanta, Georgia, radio station's programming staff. According to Timothy White of Billboard, McLachlan has a skilled balance between her vocal strength and her use of material that goes beyond autobiography.

Securing her place

Following in the footsteps of another notable Canadian singer and songwriter, Joni Mitchell, McLachlan continued in the musical traditions of the Great White North. She was able to achieve domestic and international recognition without receiving a lot of radio airplay. At the time of her debut in 1989, radio was flooded with female performers, which made competing for airplay fierce. Frequently, radio-programming directors considered McLachlan's music too soft for modern rock stations.

Nevertheless, McLachlan established a secure place on album alternative airplay stations. Starting in 1991, she achieved "Heatseekers Impact" status as a new or developing artist, and Fumbling towards Ecstasy gave her an album on the Billboard 200 in 1994.

McLachlan's debut album, Torch, was released in 1988. It sold 200,000 copies. Solace, released in 1991, sold even better and commanded attention for a number of reasons. First, it brought recognition to McLachlan's songwriting abilities. Critics such as Maclean's Nicholas Jennings praised McLachlan's songs—including

Folk technology

Sarah McLachlan is one performer who utilizes modern technology to its fullest capacity. She frequently promotes her material through on-line services such as America Online, CompuServe, and other Internet avenues.

In 1995 McLachlan introduced a multi-media CD-ROM version of her album, The Freedom Sessions. The album featured alternate versions of previously released songs, especially earlier material from the Torch and Solace albums. Since they were not remixes, the new version allowed listeners to hear the experimenting that went into the songs. Not polished or perfect, these versions clearly showed how McLachlan's songs evolved.

McLachlan then worked with Nettwerk Records, pioneers in multimedia technology, to produce a computer CD to complement The Freedom Sessions album. The CD included thirty minutes of video footage, photos, audio clips, and personal narration to provide McLachlan's audience with an opportunity to meet her on a more personal level than conventional media interviews provided. McLachlan even set up computers on tour for concertgoers to preview the CD.

McLachlan's CD-plus-multimedia effort marked the highest profile release of a mixed-media product in the record industry. Dick Wingate, a senior vice president at Arista, viewed the multimedia CD as a bonus. "It is a 'Sarah unplugged' type of set that will appeal to core Sarah fans for the music alone.... And those core fans with computers will want it for the very private look at Sarah they get through the home movies, pictures, and video clips they get in the multimedia part." McLachlan revealed to Billboard that at first she "was very skeptical" of the idea, but in the end was "thrilled with the result."

"Path of Thorns"—because she seemed to bare her soul with the confessional lyrics.

Fumbling towards Ecstasy: McLachlan's breakthrough album

Fumbling towards Ecstasy appeared in 1994. It sold 20,000 copies in its first week in the United States and more than one million units worldwide. The album earned platinum certification in 1995 for selling one million copies in the United States and spent twelve weeks that year on the top video sales charts.

Critics found much to like about *Fumbling towards Ecstasy. Time* music writer David E. Thigpen wrote, "Rather than indulge in emotional bloodletting [emptying], McLachlan creates exquisitely poised songs that resist anger or pathos [pity]." Timothy White of *Billboard* observed, "McLachlan has made a record unlike any one will hear this year, oddly ancient in its serene earthiness, utterly fresh in its patient inquiry."

The album featured lush folk-pop songs, each intelligent and sensual.

Parents Aren't Supposed to Like It

Rolling Stone writer Elysa Gardner noted, "Longing is the prominent theme on the album, both the romantic kind and the longing for self-knowledge and cosmic [universal] awareness." Much of the material McLachlan included reflected images from the dark side of life that the singer saw while visiting Cambodia in 1992. "I came away with a broader understanding of the world, of the darkness that exists out there," McLachlan told *Maclean's*. "I've tried to express that as honestly as I could."

As a result of her honesty, the difficult to grasp songs of passionate dignity included on *Fumbling towards Ecstasy*—though stark, confessional, and difficult to interpret as always—contained lyrics even truer to life. Her efforts were rewarded by a Juno nomination (the Canadian equivalent of a Grammy) for songwriter of the year in 1994.

Though young, McLachlan nevertheless shows remarkable maturity in her songwriting. She is able to take what she sees of life and the world and reveal her heart and soul through music. "It's what honest music has always given me," she explained to *Billboard*, "and what I wanted to give back."

Selected Awards

Canadian Music Video Awards, Favorite Female Video and Best Adult Contemporary Video Awards, for "Possession," 1994.

Juno Awards, Best Female Vocalist nomination and Songwriter of the Year nomination, for *Fumbling towards Ecstasy*, 1994.

Fumbling towards Ecstasy, certified platinum (for U.S. sales of one million copies) by the Recording Industry Association of America, 1995.

Grammy-award nomination, for *Fumbling towards Ecstasy*, 1995.

Selected Discography

Torch (Arista), 1988.

Solace (Arista), 1991.

Fumbling towards Ecstasy (Arista), 1994.

The Freedom Sessions (Arista/Nettwerk), 1995.

Surfacing (Nettwerk), 1997.

Further Reading

Borzillo, Carrie, "Radio, Retail Ecstatic over McLachlan," *Billboard*, March 19, 1994, p. 10.

Gardner, Elysa, "Fumbling towards Ecstasy," *Rolling Stone*, June 16, 1994, p. 109.

Gillan, Marilyn A., "A Different McLachlan Seen on Arista Mixed-Mode Set," *Billboard*, February 4, 1995, p. 10.

Jennings, Nicholas, "Heart on Her Sleeve," *Maclean's*, March 28, 1994, p. 59.

White, Timothy, "Sarah McLachlan: Irony and 'Ecstasy,'" *Billboard*, January 8, 1994, p. 5.

Contact Information

Arista Records
6 West 57th St.
New York, NY 10019

Web Site

www.nettweb.com\artists\sarmc.html

MICHAEL PENN

American folk singer and songwriter

Born Michael Penn, August 1, 1958, in New York, New York

Singer-songwriter Michael Penn "is a thinking person's pop musician," according to critic Parke Puterbaugh in *Stereo Review*. Though Penn is the older brother of actors Sean and Christopher Penn, the critical consensus is that his talent is more than strong enough to stand on its own merits. As reviewer Jeffrey Ressner put it in *Rolling Stone:* "Yeah, Penn is the brother of you know who, but who cares? It's a moot point." David Wild, writing in the same publication, echoed that just "one listen" to the singer's debut album, *March,* "is sufficient evidence that Penn's music warrants attention in its own right."

Born into a show-business family

Penn was born into a show-business family; aside from the fact that his brothers Sean and Christopher would eventually become actors, his father is actor-director Leo Penn and his mother is actress Eileen Ryan. But Michael Penn was interested in music rather than acting from an early age. As Wild reported, one of Penn's best early memories was of receiving the Beatles' album

Something New from a family friend when he was five years old. Penn learned to play the guitar by the time he was in junior high; he even belonged to a band that played songs made famous by the likes of David Bowie, Cream, and the Rolling Stones in school talent shows.

"I really wanted to make a record that utilized the benefits of technology, but still retain a real warmth and earthiness."

By the time he attended high school in Santa Monica, California, Penn's musical tastes had become more eclectic, and he had begun to write what Wild described as "earnest, downbeat songs." Penn himself recalled to Wild that he "leaned towards the gloomy and pretentious back then.... Everyone told me I should see [the black comedy film] *Harold and Maude*, because I was Harold." During the early 1980s, Penn became involved with a band called Doll Congress. Though the recording they made was unsuccessful, they established something of a local cult following in Los Angeles, California, clubs; once Doll Congress even served as the opening act for rock group R.E.M. But the band's work did not provide Penn with enough to live on, and he did other jobs to support himself, such as working as a customer services representative for a photography firm. He also appeared as an extra on the television show *St. Elsewhere*.

Eventually Penn realized that Doll Congress, as Wild put it, "wasn't going anywhere," and left the group in 1986. Sometime afterward, he was invited to perform a musical number on the television comedy/variety program *Saturday Night Live* when his brother Sean was serving as guest host. But Michael found the experience uncomfortable. He told Wild: "I was scared.... I have no idea how I came off, and I certainly haven't gone back to find out." Following this, he and former Doll Congress keyboardist Patrick Warren began working on some of the material that would become part of the album *March*. Penn said of the recording in an RCA publicity release: "I really wanted to make a record that utilized the benefits of technology, but still retain a real warmth and earthiness. We spent a long time trying to find a way to make the drum machine feel and sound good ... and trying to find ways to integrate it with the sound of acoustic guitars. Most of the sounds on the record are acoustic sounds, even if they're sampled; everything has its footing in real life."

Signed with RCA Records in 1989

After RCA Records signed Penn to a contract, *March* was recorded. The video for the single, "No Myth," received lots of airplay on the video channels MTV and VH-1, helping Penn's album up the charts and making it successful enough to merit a 1990 concert tour. *March* also received much praise from the critics. Ressner claimed, "Penn maintains a delicate balance between rhythmic pop and sensitive folk music, pulling off the perilous feat with surprising clarity." Puterbaugh liked *March* also, citing the tracks "Brave New World," "Half Harvest," "Bedlam Boys," and "Evenfall" as particularly noteworthy. He concluded that Penn had "real soul" and "real daring."

Penn's second album, *Free-for-All,* was released by RCA in 1992. It was recorded after extensive touring, something Penn found a bit disorienting. He told *Rolling Stone*'s David Wild, "All I learned from being on the road was that hotels with gyms are better than hotels without gyms and that I absolutely cannot write on the road." This helped explain the title of the album, which originated in a phrase from the song "Bunker Hill." Penn was quoted in *Musician* as saying, "It describes the time we're living in, that we're this nickel someone's flipped, it's up in the air spinning around and we're not quite sure where it's going to land yet."

With this recording effort, Penn indeed landed on his feet. The progressive sound on *Free-for-All* goes in both folk and rock directions. Gary Leboff stated in *VOX*, "His freeform songwriting creates tracks of startling shape and originality, offering literate reflections on the human condition while tipping a musical hat to the Beatles and Bob Dylan."

Penn's next album, *Resigned,* was released on Epic Records in 1997. The album's Beatlesque flavor featured eleven orginial pop-rock songs.

Selected Discography

March (RCA), 1989.

Free-for-All (RCA), 1992.

Resigned (Epic), 1997.

Further Reading

Musician, October 1992.

Richardson, Ken, "I'm with Stupid," *Stereo Review,* May 1996, p. 92.

Rotondi, James, "Michael Penn: Trial by Fire," *Guitar Player,* October 1993, p.52.

Rolling Stone, November 30, 1989; February 22, 1990; August 1992.

Stereo Review, February 1990.

VOX, March 1993.

Contact Information

Epic Records
550 Madison Ave.
New York, NY 10022-3211

Web Site

http://www.proex.com/t-bone/m_penn/

MICHELLE SHOCKED

American folk singer and songwriter

Born Karen Michelle Johnson,
February 24, 1962, in Dallas, Texas

Michelle Shocked is a performer known for her staunch independence, her folksy tales of Americana, and her troubadour spirit. After finding a cult audience with the *Texas Campfire Tapes,* an album released without her knowledge or permission in 1986, she went on to mainstream success with three albums for Mercury Records that combined folk, swing, and country blues with Shocked's blend of heartfelt, emotional, and sometimes humorous lyrics.

Following the last of those albums, 1992's *Arkansas Traveler,* Shocked and Mercury had a falling out, with Shocked refusing to record and eventually initiating a lawsuit to release her from her contract, citing the 13th amendment—the abolition of slavery. After a long battle she was released from Mercury and resurfaced in 1996 with *Kind Hearted Woman* on the smaller Private Music label.

Early rebel

Born Karen Michelle Johnson in Dallas, Texas, to strict Mormon parents, Shocked found her rebellious streak at an early age.

"Playing in a musical league of her own, Michelle Shocked is one of America's very few pop performers who are truly graced by inspiration." –Tony Scherman, *People Weekly*

Unable to cope with her smothering upbringing in East Texas, Shocked ran away from home in her teens. Upon her return, Shocked's mother promptly had her institutionalized, not once but twice. Preferring the life of a homeless vagabond to an unwilling hospital patient, Shocked left home again and went to live in the various squatter communities of San Francisco, Amsterdam, and New York. (Squatting is the act of living, illegally, in an uninhabited building, often on public land.)

Throughout this time Shocked was learning the guitar and writing songs that were influenced by the punk rockers she was living with. However, she still maintained a strong current of folk and country influences from her Texas roots. While playing around a campfire at the Kerrville Folk Festival in Kerrville, Texas, in 1986, Shocked was asked by a man named Pete Lawrence if he could record her on his Sony Walkman. Shocked obliged and months later heard that those recordings—complete with chirping crickets and passing trucks—were released in England under the title, *The Texas Campfire Tapes* on the Cooking Vinyl label. The album was successful, reaching number one in England and bringing Shocked to the attention of the major labels in the United States. However, since it was released without her permission and with no contract for fair payment, it led to her first lawsuit with a record company.

Troubadour swing

Shocked soon signed with Mercury, who released *Campfire Tapes* in the U.S.,

which was then followed by her studio debut, *Short Sharp Shocked,* in 1988. "Michelle Shocked is simply the brightest new voice unearthed from the American roots-music landscape in a long while," *Rolling Stone* declared, adding that the album contained "songs richly seasoned by the singer's acoustic heritage in electric roadhouse rock." Anyone who doubted the depth of Shocked's social activism, having signed to a major label, needed to look no further than the album's cover, which featured a newsphoto from the *San Francisco Examiner* of Shocked in a police chokehold during a mid-1980s squatter's rights demonstration.

Break from Mercury

Captain Swing, a rousing set of tunes set to a jump-swing beat, was Shocked's second studio album, released in 1990. She then set out on her most ambitious project, 1992's *Arkansas Traveler.* For this album Shocked traveled around the country recording a different song in each locale. She was joined by different artists in each place, including blues legend Taj Mahal, members of the classic rock group The Band, Pops Staples (of the gospel/rhythm and blues vocal group The Staple Singers), blues artist Clarence Gatemouth Brown, and relative newcomers to the music scene such as members of Hothouse Flowers and Uncle Tupelo and Alison Krauss.

For the cover of this album Shocked wanted to appear in black-face to make a point about black musicians who've been ripped off by white performers. Mercury wouldn't let her. The label also disapproved of her ideas to record gospel and funk albums, saying they were out of character for her. Eventually they landed in a four-year stand-off that effectively ended their working relationship.

For her part, Shocked said she learned a lot about herself through her troubles with Mercury, and that will help her music. "To me, that's what [this experience] has been," she told Steve Hochman of the *Los Angeles Times,* "giving less time to my records and taking time to figure out what my resources are for putting so much guts into what I have to say."

In 1996 Mercury released *Mercury Poise,* a Shocked-titled "Best of" collection that ended up competing with *Kind Hearted Woman,* the first album of new music from Shocked in four years. Released by her new label, Private Music, the album caused Tony Scherman of *People Weekly* to proclaim Shocked as "one of America's very few pop performers who are truly graced by inspiration."

Selected Discography

The Texas Campfire Tapes (Mercury), 1986.

Short Sharp Shocked (Mercury), 1988.

Captain Swing (Mercury), 1990.

Arkansas Traveler (Mercury), 1992.

Kind Hearted Woman (Private Music), 1996.

Mercury Poise (Mercury), 1996.

Further Reading

Interview, November 1988, p.72; March 1992, p. 114.

Los Angeles Times, October 6, 1996, p. C3.

Nash, Alanna, "Kind Hearted Woman," *Stereo Review,* January 1997, p. 100.

People Weekly, November 7, 1988, p. 79.

Rolling Stone, November 3, 1988, p. 28, 112.

Scherman, Tony, "Kind Hearted Woman," *People Weekly,* November 4, 1996, p. 36.

"Still Shocked," *New Yorker,* June 13, 1994, p. 38.

Contact Information

Private Music
8750 Wilshire Blvd.
Beverly Hills, CA 90211

Web Site

http://www.shellshock.com

Heavy Metal

The *All Music Guide to Rock* traces the first heavy metal moments to the British Invasion, specifically the two-chord opening to the Kinks' "You Really Got Me." According to the book, "'You Really Got Me' didn't swing, it pounded, laying the groundwork for the simplistic hard rock of AC/DC and the scores of boogie bands in the mid-'70s." Generally, though, the Kinks are not really thought of as a heavy metal band. Probably the two major forefathers of heavy metal are Led Zeppelin and Black Sabbath. Led Zeppelin took the blues and played them at top volume with a heavy guitar sound and pounding drums. They also combined their blues with folk and rock and roll, adding hippie-influenced mystical lyrics to the mix.

Black Sabbath took a different approach to the music. They shunned the hippie imagery and went for more scary subject matter on songs like "Warpigs." They didn't play fast, but they played loud and ominously. Like Led Zeppelin's singer Robert Plant, Black Sabbath singer Ozzy Osbourne had a high-pitched wail. This piercing style of vocals would become the standard to

Axl Rose of Guns N' Roses

which future heavy metal bands would aspire.

Other early pioneers in metal were Cream (a late 1960s supergroup that included Eric Clapton) with the guitar-heavy and bluesy "Sunshine of Your Love" and "Strange Brew"; Blue Cheer, a San Francisco band that gave a metal treatment to the song "Summertime Blues;" and British group Judas Priest, a band that was big on leather clothes. Jimi Hendrix also helped define the metal sound with his loud playing and intricate guitar techniques.

By the early 1970s several long lasting heavy metal elements were already in place: high-pitched singing style (Robert Plant, Ozzy Osbourne), lyrics dealing with forbidden subjects like the occult (Black Sabbath), volume (Blue Cheer, plus others), and intricate guitar playing (Jimi Hendrix, Led Zeppelin's Jimmy Page).

Glam metal combined make-up, costumes, and drama

Another element arrived with Alice Cooper—make-up and drama. Although earlier heavy metal bands certainly relied on theatrics to get their music across, Alice Cooper (a character created by Michigan-based musician Vincent Furnier) took it to a whole new level. At the time, it was shocking enough that he adopted a girl's name, but even more shocking, he wore dramatic stage make-up and included snakes, electric chairs, and plenty of fake blood in each of his shows.

Kiss took this one step further and dressed all four of its members in cos-

tumes and make-up. Kiss's shows took heavy metal to an extreme in a cartoon-like way. They embraced all the cliches, like playing big guitar solos, blowing things up and spewing fake blood, to an absurd extent, and found the audiences loved it.

Meanwhile Aerosmith was making an important contribution to heavy metal by scoring a hit with the slow song "Dream On." With that, they helped plenty of future metal bands score hits of their own using the "power ballad" technique, that is, releasing a slow, moody, more accessible song to get airplay and attract fans.

The 1980s was a decade of ups and downs for heavy metal. Van Halen helped make metal more accessible to a wider audience with their more pop-oriented sound. Eddie Van Halen's fast and complicated-sounding guitar playing was in the tradition of past heavy metal bands, and helped influence future metal guitarists.

Probably the biggest event for heavy metal in the 1980s was the release of Metallica's record "Kill 'Em All." **Metallica** (see entry) took traditional metal elements (loud guitars, big drums, scary subject matter) and sped the whole thing up, making a sound that was even louder and faster (speed metal). Although the record wasn't a widespread hit, it was influential on the underground metal scene.

What did become widespread hits in the 1980s were pop-metal bands. It started with Quiet Riot, continued with Def Leppard, and eventually led to the rise of bands like Motley Crue, Poison, and Bon Jovi. These 1980s bands were big on spandex, big hair, and girlish looks, and took glam metal to an extreme. Critics called them "hair bands" and dismissed them as silly.

Guns N' Roses find wider audience

Later in the 1980s, harder, grittier metal started getting more attention. This was metal that wasn't as concerned with pretty looks and nice clothes. One of the first of these bands, **Guns N' Roses** (see entry), was sort of a transitional band. They were halfway between the darker, later bands like **Slayer** (see entry), and the more image-conscious bands like Poison. Guns 'N Roses blues-based metal was highlighted by Slash's heavy riffs and Axl Rose's extremely high-pitched screechy voice. The popular heavy metal combo of big riffs plus big screech helped make songs like "Welcome to the Jungle" and "Sweet Child O' Mine" huge hits.

Although Jimi Hendrix had obviously played metal quite well decades before, **Living Colour** (see entry) entered the fray billed as a "black" heavy metal group. Regardless of the absurdity of this being considered unusual, Living Colour did at least expand some horizons on what heavy metal could be. Living Colour showed that color didn't matter when it came to rocking hard.

Speed metal gained momentum

In the late 1980s bands like Metallica, **Megadeth** (see entry), and Slayer—

groups that sped up the pace and increased the aggression—started gaining wider popularity. Metallica was the pioneer in this movement. The guys didn't wear make-up or spandex and weren't even slightly pretty. They brought the music to its basics—loud volume, dark lyrics, and big guitars. Their fast and furious sound was called "thrash metal" and turned out to be one of the new directions in metal. Megadeth, led by former Metallica member Dave Mustaine, also started playing thrash-metal. Although not as influential as Metallica and plagued by Mustaine's personal problems, Megadeth helped to spread the popularity of thrash-metal.

Danzig (see entry) takes a light approach to their sound, which combines elements of previous heavy metal bands. There are the bluesy sounds of traditional heavy metal, subject matter about Satan and evil, and leader Glenn Danzig's tattooed hardcore looks. It was a winning combination for the band in 1994 when the song "Mother" (helped by plenty of airings on MTV) became a hit.

Slayer started out influenced by the pop metal bands, wore eye make-up, and were very dramatic. But then, influenced by producer Rick Rubin, they went for a grittier approach. Trying hard to shock audiences, Slayer filled their songs with ultra-graphic lyrics about Satan and the dark side. Slayer also helped start the death-metal movement, a disturbing branch of metal that takes Slayer's approach to a greater extreme.

Tool achieved success on MTV as well as the metal underground with its

James Hetfield of Metallica

commercial brand of hard rock that was even more successful than the band's first incarnation—though disappointed Roth fans dubbed the group "Van Hagar." But Hagar was ejected in the late 1990s for a brief reunion with Roth, who was in turn jilted for former Extreme frontman Gary Cherone. Hagar, undaunted, came back with a hit solo album in 1997.

Aerosmith, meanwhile, just kept cranking out hit albums.

Selling metal

Like Slayer, **Pantera** (see entry) also started off influenced by pop metal bands. But then, guitarist Darrell Abbott changed his nickname from "Diamond" to "Dimebag," and the band pursued the more lucrative world of harsher-sounding, more aggressive metal. It paid off. Pantera was virtually unknown in the wider music world when their record *Far Beyond Driven* debuted at number one on the charts in 1994.

This was a common pattern for many metal bands who could not get airplay on radio or MTV. The bands would build up a following on the heavy metal underground by constant touring and word of mouth, then suddenly burst onto the sales charts with fast-selling new records. (As a rule, sales of metal records tend to drop off drastically after the initial fast-selling first week or two.)

While thrash-metal was coming to the forefront of the metal scene, another kind of metal was developing. The new brand was influenced by the grunge sound coming out of Seattle, Washington.

passionate songs and arty style. A whole underground of hardcore metal styles, such as "grindcore," tried to avoid the comic-book aspects of metal. Brazil's Sepultura provided some of the hardest, most relentless metal around, and such bands as Life Of Agony, Godflesh, Brutal Truth, and punk-metal survivors like Napalm Death let their names provide a clue to what listeners could expect.

Van Halen's saga continued into the 1990s; after singer David Lee Roth parted ways with the group to pursue a checkered solo career, the band recruited 1970s survivor Sammy Hagar. With Hagar in tow, Van Halen produced a sleek,

Seattle bands combined heavy metal and grunge

Soundgarden (see entry) was from Seattle and played a grunge/metal hybrid. The band was influenced by old time heavy metal bands like Black Sabbath and Led Zeppelin. Singer Chris Cornell's high shriek and guitarist Kim Thayill's big minor key riffs were the centerpieces of the group. The band was a missing link of sorts between metal and grunge. They played metal (previously considered uncool by the "alternative" crowd), but their Seattle roots and apparent intelligence helped grunge fans accept them as one of their own. Soundgarden explored much more melodic, Beatlesque territory before breaking up in 1997. One of their finest songs, "Black Hole Sun" (from *Superunknown*), was even covered in a jazzy "lounge" version that made it sound like a pop standard.

Similarly, **Alice in Chains** (see entry) became part of alternative rock's grunge movement, but was initally considered even more metal than Soundgarden. The harshness of their music came from their sound, which is heavy, slow, and menacing, and also from the depressing lyrics that talk about the band's problems with drugs and despair. Queensryche, meanwhile, while not a "grunge" band, hailed its Seattle roots in "Jet City Woman" and generally offered a thoughtful alternative to the typical "hair band" hard rock.

White Zombie takes it "over the top"

Instead of wallowing in gloom and doom, **White Zombie** (see entry) takes a different approach to metal. White Zombie goes for the fun approach. They wear crazy, bright-colored clothes and sing about stuff like fast cars and B-movies. Following in the footsteps of bands like Alice Cooper and Kiss, they continue the tradition of heavy metal as over-the-top, showy, and sort of silly.

The 1990s also saw the return of hard-rock bands of the past, such as horror-punk-metal veterans The Misfits and chainsaw-wielding rockers Jackyl.

As of the late 1990s there is no one movement in the heavy metal scene. There are several directions, including the campy approach taken by bands like White Zombie, the gloomy grunge approach of Alice in Chains, and the anti-social direction of Slayer. And other bands are combining elements of metal and coming up with something new. Alternative bands like **Marilyn Manson** (see entry) are combining the shock rock of heavy metal with goth rock to create something new. And Prodigy combines the shock value and fury of metal with techno dance music. Meanwhile, 1997's hit "Spawn" movie soundtrack saw metal-alternative bands like Filter and Korn teaming up with techno/electronica and rap artists.

Danzig

American heavy metal band

Formed 1986 in Los Angeles, California

Twenty years after starting the Misfits in 1977, Glenn Danzig started his fourth band. Each of his bands so far have been innovative. The Misfits helped pioneer hardcore rock. Next, the short-lived Samhain went for an experimental punk/rock sound. Then Danzig's band named Danzig delved into dark, bluesy metal. Now with his new band, Glenn Danzig is going for a more technological, noisy sound.

This latest band is named, guess what, Danzig. "Danzig has always been set up, from the beginning, so that I would never have to change the name of the band again," explains Danzig in a record company press release. "It would be my name and if people came and went, then that's the way it was."

Stormy upbringing

In *Musician,* Danzig described his upbringing in Lodi, New Jersey, as "stormy." "I wasn't a nice kid, but I wasn't the worst kid. The worst kids I knew are now dead or in jail. I could have been one of them if I'd made the wrong decision. I ended up on that road on a number of occasions and had to steer myself back," he said. Danzig spent a lot of time listening to music, reading comic books, and getting in trouble. When he was eleven he got his first gig being a drum roadie. At thirteen he got a spot singing for a local Black Sabbath cover band.

In 1976, after playing in a couple bands, he founded the hardcore band, the Misfits, a band that had such scary tunes as "Mommy, Can I Go Out and Kill Tonight." Although that band is now considered influential, at the time, the band was just broke. Danzig doesn't like to talk about the Misfits now. "It should have been discussed when it was pertinent," he said in *Musician*. Feeling his creativity was being held back in the Misfits, he formed Samhain.

"We were called a metal band, a thrash band, a speed-metal band, a death metal band. Nobody knew what we were."

One night after Samhain played at the New Music Seminar in 1986, a stranger came into their dressing room. "This wild card shows up saying, 'You guys were incredible! I want to sign your band!' I didn't know who he was. He looked like somebody from ZZ Top," said Danzig in *Musician*. The guy turned out to be producer Rick Rubin, the head of American Records (then called Def American) who signed the band that became Danzig.

Control freak

In the studio Danzig controlled everything. He wrote the songs and told everyone how to play. "You might see that as control. I see it as more of a producer's role," he said in *Musician*.

The first record named *Danzig* came out in 1988. "We were called a metal band, a thrash band, a speed-metal band, a death metal band," said Danzig in *Rolling Stone*. "Nobody knew what we were." *Musician* said the band's music occupied a space between "punk and pop, metal and melody." "As the players grind out brusque, bluesy hard rock, (Danzig) conjures a spectre of blood, vengeance and supernatural possession in a deep, authoritative voice that prompts comparisons with Jim Morrison." Other common voice comparisons are Roy Orbison and Elvis Presley.

"No trick or treaters come to my house for Halloween."

Danzig, both the band and the guy, has been accused of Satanism, a charge Danzig denies. It's easy to see how people get that impression. Explained *Entertainment Weekly* in 1994: "Elaborate demons-and-dragons sagas unspool in his lyrics; his band revels in gothic spectacles; and he resides in a forbidding 1905 mansion that his L.A. neighbors have dubbed 'the Addams Family house.'" Or as Danzig put it in *Rolling Stone*: "No trick or treaters come to my house for Halloween."

Danzig put out *Danzig II: Lucifuge* and *Danzig III: How the Gods Kill* (Def American), but it wasn't until MTV started airing a video for "Mother" that Danzig broke through. Ironically, "Mother" was just a new live version of a song from the first Danzig record.

Danzig after Danzig

After the follow-up, *4,* Danzig left the band, got some new bandmates, and found a new label. This new Danzig record *Blackaciddevil* came out on Halloween 1996. "I wanted to do something that nobody else was doing," Danzig is quoted as saying on the Hollywood Records' Danzig web page. "So I took an element of industrial that I like here and an element of techno there, then mixed it with what I normally do. Then I'd experiment with the different directions—which I wanted to do anyway—and then watch what happened when I mixed it together."

Why did he form yet another band? On the web site, Danzig says it's because his old bandmates wanted to stick with a retro sound. "I wanted to just keep expanding," he said.

Selected Awards

Danzig, certified gold.

Thrall: Demonsweatlive, certified gold.

Selected Discography

Danzig (Def American), 1988.

Danzig II: Lucifuge (Def American), 1990.

Danzig III: How the Gods Kill (Def American), 1992.

Thrall: Demonsweatlive (Def American), 1993.

4 (American), 1994.

Blackaciddevil (Hollywood), 1996.

Further Reading

Hajari, Nisid, "Sympathy for the Devil," *Entertainment Weekly,* October 14, 1994, p. 28.

Obrecht, Joe, "Danzig: Dark Magick or Day Gig?" *Guitar Player,* February 1995, p. 73.

Simels, Steve, "Danzig 4," *Stereo Review,* December 1994, p. 142.

Wild, David, "The Devil Inside," *Rolling Stone,* March 24, 1994, p. 41.

Young, John, "Danzig Knows the Power of the Dark Side," *Musician,* August 1994, p. 38.

Contact Information

Hollywood Records
500 S. Buena Vista
Burbank, CA 91521

Web Site

http://www.hollywoodrec.com/Hollywood Records/Musicians/Danzig/

GUNS N' ROSES

American heavy metal/hard rock band

Formed in 1985 in Los Angeles, California

One of the enduring roles that rock musicians have played through the years is that of the "bad boy." From the earliest days of rock, the bad boy has caused fear among "polite" society. The black-leather-jacket-clad, motorcycle-riding "juvenile delinquent" as typified by Marlon Brando in the 1950s motorcycle film, *The Wild Ones,* was readily adopted by rockers looking to shock sensibilities. As The Rolling Stones in the 1960s and Aerosmith in the 1970s had done before them, Guns N' Roses were the bad boys of the 1980s. They frequently behaved in a way that unmistakably said, "This is not just an image, but the way we really are."

Welcome to the jungle

While the band came together in Los Angeles and reflected the seamier side of that city, its co-founders, Axl Rose and Izzy Stradlin, hailed from the American Midwest. Rose was born William Rose, on February 6, 1962 in Lafayette, Indiana. He was adopted by L. Stephen Bailey when his mother remarried while he

"We're like a ... grenade, and it's like everybody's struggling to hold the pin in!" –Slash

Guns N' Roses

was a baby (he legally changed his name to W. Axl Rose in 1986). Stradlin was born Jeffrey Isbelle on April 8, 1962, also in Lafayette. After knocking around in local bands (including one called Axl, which he adopted as his name), Rose hitch-hiked to Los Angeles, where Stradlin had already been a struggling musician for several years.

After several variations of bands with musicians that would eventually split to become L.A. Guns, Guns N' Roses' line-up settled down to include lead guitarist Slash (born Saul Hudson, July 23, 1965, Stoke-on-Trent, Staffordshire, England), bassist Michael "Duff" McKagen (born February 5, 1964, Seattle, Washington) and Steven Adler (born January 22, 1965, Cleveland, Ohio) on drums.

The band made their debut at Los Angeles's Troubadour Club after just two days of rehearsals. They rapidly developed a cult following of fans who were drawn to their potent mix of punk attitude and bare-knuckled hard rock. They released a four-song EP on their own Uzi/Suicide label in February 1986. All 10,000 copies sold out in four weeks, attracting the attention of the major labels. After some competition, they signed with Geffen for the relatively paltry sum of $75,000 in March 1986. The money didn't last long, since the band reportedly used the advance to settle debts and buy drugs.

At first they had some difficulty finding management and a producer. They weren't able to start work on their major label debut until late in the summer of 1986 with producer Mike Clink behind the board. Geffen re-released their EP in

January 1987 as an appetizer for what was to come. The band spent early 1987 touring as an opener for heavy metal bands like Iron Maiden, and Slash was dispatched to Hawaii to deal with his substance abuse problems. (The band was very open about its drug and alcohol use and abuse.)

Appetite for destruction

The hard-rock/heavy-metal genres in the mid-1980s were dominated by glammish-pretty boy bands like Poison, Cinderella, and Bon Jovi. Guns N' Roses was grittier and louder than those bands. From the opening notes of "Welcome to the Jungle," the album's leadoff track and single, Guns N' Roses announced their presence to the world … loudly. Their songs were filled with the desperate grit of Los Angeles life: the drugs, the booze, the trouble to be found. "Mr. Brownstone" dealt with heroin, and "Night Train" referred to the cheap wine favored by people on the skids.

The video for "Jungle" had Rose made-up with moussed hair and eyeliner, a cliched glam-metal look that was quickly ditched for their breakthrough hit "Sweet Child O' Mine." The song, inspired by Rose's girlfriend, allowed the band to cross over and attract a legion of female fans. It also hinted at the sensitive soul that lurked behind the macho facade. The album went on to sell over 13 million units, the most ever for any band's debut release and one of the top 10 sellers in history.

You wouldn't have known that there was a sensitive side to the band based on

Parents Aren't Supposed to Like It

their antics during the marathon tour in support of *Appetite for Destruction*. Their alcohol and drug consumption was so legendary that when they opened for the then-newly-rehabbed Aerosmith, they were told to keep it in their dressing rooms so as not to tempt the headliners back into their own old ways. During the Monsters of Rock Festival in England in August 1988, two people died in the mosh pit, even though the band had repeatedly stopped playing in an attempt to calm the crowd down. They were unaware that anyone had been hurt until after their set. Some band members also got into minor scrapes with the police for offenses generally committed while drunk and disorderly.

One in a million

For Christmas 1988, Geffen released the eight-song EP, *G N' R Lies*. Consisting of the band's 1986 live EP and four new acoustic-based songs, it delivered a hit with the sweet ballad "Patience." It also delivered more controversy.

The song "I Used to Love Her (But I Had to Kill Her)" received protests from women's-rights groups who were offended by the black-humor lyrics, which were interpreted as condoning domestic violence. Greater condemnation was targeted towards "One in a Million" because of the use of slurs against homosexuals and minorities. Rose tried to explain that he wasn't a bigot; rather, he was trying to express how he felt as a naive Midwestern kid arriving in the dog-eat-dog urban jungle of Los Angeles. Slash (who is partially black) also defended Rose, but an-

other batch of marks were added to the group's ever-controversial reputation.

Bad apples

Much of 1989 and 1990 was spent acting out the drama of their fame. Rose married long-time girlfriend Erin Everly (daughter of Everly Brother Don) in April 1990, but then filed for divorce less than a month later. They reconciled, but then split for good. She revealed to *People Weekly* in July 1994 that Rose constantly abused her. Rose was subsequently linked to Victoria's Secret model Stephanie Seymour.

The band claimed that Adler's drug use had affected his drumming to an unacceptable degree and gave him the sack in September 1990. He was replaced by journeyman skin-basher Matt Sorum, ex-The Cult and Y Kant Tori Read (a rock band fronted by a then-unknown **Tori Amos**). Adler filed suit a year later, claiming that he was wrongly removed and stripped of his partnership interest in the group. He also claimed that it was the others who introduced him to hard drugs. The case was settled out of court and Adler was paid a reported $2.5 million. The new lineup of Guns N' Roses (including new keyboardist Dizzy Reed) debuted before 120,000 people at the Rock in Rio II Festival in Rio de Janeiro, Brazil, in January 1992.

Riots

The band always had a confrontational stance toward the audiences that sometimes resulted in Rose challenging hecklers to fight. However, past brawls were eclipsed by the riot that occurred on July 2, 1991, in Maryland Heights, Missouri. Distracted by a fan with a camera, Rose demanded that security take the camera away. When security didn't react quickly enough for Rose's taste, he dove off the stage and went after the fan himself. More then fifty people, including fifteen police officers, were injured in the ensuing melee and fifteen were arrested. Over $200,000 in damage was done to the newly-opened venue. Charges were filed against Rose for assault and property damage. A fan sued the band, venue, and promoters, claiming that he was assaulted. The promoters sued the band. The lawyers were very busy. The venue was so damaged that a show two days later had to be canceled, and the Guns N' Roses show in Chicago was canceled.

Just seven days later at a show in Colorado, Rose stopped the band in the middle of the fifth song and demanded that a heckler be removed. During a four-date stint later that month at the Forum in Los Angeles, police stopped Rose's limousine for making a prohibited turn. Rose threatened to cancel the show if a ticket was issued. Police decided the 19,000 potential rioters at the Forum were not worth a ticket and let the incident slide.

Platinum illusions

While the band was tearing up the world (literally), they also had been hard at work on their next release with Mike Clink co-producing with the band. Rose was unhappy with the job that superstar engineer Bob Clearmountain had done and the mix had to be redone from scratch. The results were the simultaneously released albums *Use Your Illusion I & II* in September 1991. With thirty songs spread over two discs and clocking in at nearly two-and-a-half hours, it was a monumental achievement. It shipped a record 4.2 million units and debuted in the top two slots of the charts (ironically, *I* was at #2 and *II* was #1). It was the first time in seventeen years that any artist had held the top two positions. Both albums went triple-platinum in less than two months.

The albums contained an amazing spread of material, as the band experimented with songs that ran to ten minutes in length with multiple sections. The epic ballad "November Rain" (from *I*) had choirish backing vocals, piano, and synth strings. Detractors thought the band was selling out, but that charge was readily countered by the other tracks. On "Get in the Ring" (*II*), Rose breaks into a rant in the middle of the song in which he taunts rock magazines and editors by name. While attacking one's detractors from the stage is commonplace, committing such attacks on record for posterity is another matter entirely.

While there were more ballads (including a different version of "Don't Cry" on each disc), there was also an abundance of the twin-guitar, Marshall-stack-powered riff-mongering that was their stock-in-trade. Their horizons may have been broadening, but they hadn't forgotten their roots.

The apparent growth shown on the *Illusion* albums was dealt a serious blow when Stradlin announced that he was leaving the band the week after the dou-

Parents Aren't Supposed to Like It

ble-album's release. Rose confirmed Stradlin's exit a month later, saying that he was tired of touring and making videos. He was replaced by Gilby Clarke. Stradlin released a solo album in October 1992 that failed to crack the top 100 album chart. With the departure of the group's principal songwriter went the focus that the band desperately needed to overcome their personal demons. The fact that there has been no new original GNR material in the six years following *Use Your Illusion* bears this view out.

Punk roots

In December 1993, Guns N' Roses released an album of punk covers entitled *The Spaghetti Incident.* Containing songs originally performed by punk rock bands such as the Sex Pistols, the New York Dolls, the Stooges, and the UK Subs, the album also included a song written by convicted murderer Charles Manson. Recorded by Rose with his gardener playing guitar, the track caused much debate inside the group. Critics blasted the inclusion of the song, saying it was a cheap stunt and questioning whether Manson was going to profit from royalties (he didn't). None of the renditions captured the impact that made the originals relevant. To the band's credit, however, they encouraged listeners to seek out the originals in the liner notes. Of note was the inclusion of "Since I Don't Have You," the classic 1959 hit by the do-wop group The Skyliners. Performed straight, it showcased Rose actually singing in a voice other than his trademark shriek.

Aftermath

The last recorded effort from Guns N' Roses was a remake of the Rolling Stones' "Sympathy for the Devil," which appeared in the 1994 film adaptation of Ann Rice's *Interview with the Vampire.* Slash voiced his displeasure with how the track turned out and started a side project called Slash's Snakepit to fill his time while Rose figured out what he was doing. He also signed an endorsement deal with Marshall amplifiers for his own signature model amp. He was the first personal endorsee in Marshall history; not even Jimi Hendrix, who popularized their amps in the 1960s, was given this treatment. In October 1996 it was announced that he had left the band over differences with Rose concerning the band's direction. Reportedly, Rose wanted to move in an industrial direction, while Slash wished to stick with the blues-rock formula they had mastered.

Sorum and McKagen formed a project called Neurotic Outsiders with ex-Sex Pistols guitarist Steve Jones and Duran Duran bassist John Taylor. The Neurotic Outsiders released a self-titled album in 1995, which showcases Steve Jones's material. The album gives a taste of what the Pistols might have sounded like if they were from Los Angeles.

Rumors continued to swirl as to the status of the band. With only Rose and McKagen left from the original line-up, there were unconfirmed reports that former members of **Nine Inch Nails** (see entry) were in, and that techno godfather **Moby** (see entry) would produce the next Guns N' Roses album. Ex-**Pearl Jam** (see entry) drummer Dave Abbruzzese was reported to be drumming with the others.

As the end of the century approaches, Guns N' Roses has sold well over 20 million albums of fine hard rock. However, when dealing with volatile personalities in the pressure-cooker of a band, it is sometimes unavoidable that an explosion may occur. At this time, it is best to examine what they did before the blast, because a future for Guns N' Roses is unforeseeable.

Selected Awards

MTV Video Awards: Best New Artist Video, for "Welcome to the Jungle," 1988; Best Heavy Metal Video, for "Sweet Child O' Mine," 1989; Best Cinematography, for "November Rain," Video Vanguard, 1992.

American Music Awards: Favorite Hard Rock Single, for "Sweet Child O' Mine," 1989;

Favorite Heavy Metal/Hard Rock Artist, 1992.

Billboard Music Awards: Top Pop New Artist, 1988; Favorite Heavy Metal/Hard Rock Artist and Album for "Appetite for Destruction," 1990.

Rolling Stone Readers Poll: Worst Male Singer and Worst Dressed Male Rock Artist for Axl Rose, Best Heavy Metal Band for GNR, 1990.

World Music Awards: Best-Selling Hard Rock Artist of the Year, 1993.

Selected Discography

Live ?!@ Like A Suicide* (Uzi/Suicide), 1986.

Appetite for Destruction (Geffen), 1987.

G N' R Lies (Geffen), 1988.

Use Your Illusion I & II (Geffen), 1991.

The Spaghetti Incident (Geffen), 1993.

Further Reading

Browne, David, "Step Three: Publicity; Slash Press N' the Flesh," *Entertainment Weekly,* March 17, 1995, p. 36.

Gill, Chris, "Punk Days Revisited: Slash Returns to His Roots," *Guitar Player,* January 1994, p. 104.

Gitter, Mike, "Guns N' Roses," (concert review), *Rolling Stone,* April 29, 1993, p. 25.

Turman, Katherine, "Coiled and Ready," (Slash interview), *Rolling Stone,* April 20, 1995, p. 53.

Contact Information

Geffen Records
9130 Sunset Blvd.
Los Angeles, CA 90069-6197

Web Site

http://www.teleport.com/~boerio/gnr/trailer.html

Living Colour

American heavy metal band

Formed in 1983 in Brooklyn, New York; disbanded in 1995

It's hard to believe that in the 1980s a band could be considered to be breaking new ground just by being a group of African Americans playing hard rock. But that was the case with Living Colour. They had a really hard time getting signed for that very reason. Record companies seemed confused by the concept and claimed they wouldn't be able to market such a band. Once Living Colour did get signed, marketing them was no problem. Thanks to a popular video for "Cult of Personality" on MTV, the band scored a hit right away with *Vivid,* their 1988 debut album. Still, they were considered a black rock band instead of just a rock band.

If there was going to be a band to be saddled with such a label, Living Colour was the right band. The members were outspoken and intelligent on race issues and were graceful spokespeople. Although the band members were happy to speak about race issues, they sometimes felt uncomfortable with all the attention that one factor got. "I would go to interviews where, literally, not a song was mentioned," said guitarist Vernon Reid in *Rolling Stone.*

"What's cool about Living Colour is you don't have to be a certain way to be down with the band. You don't have to be a white man, a black man—you don't have to be anything but open to check the music out." –Vernon Reid, guitarist

"And I realized some people were not interested in our music but just Living Colour as a symbol."

City kids

Living Colour founder and guitarist Vernon Reid was born in London, England. His parents are West Indian. He moved to Brooklyn, New York, where his dad worked as an air-traffic controller and his mom worked at a hospital workers union. Reid first started getting attention as a guitar prodigy when he was a teen playing in an avant-garde band called the Decoding Society. He became very involved in the New York City music scene, writing rock reviews and playing in various bands.

Reid co-founded the Black Rock Coalition in the mid-1980's, a group devoted to creative freedom that helps promote African American rockers. He started looking for people to join his band Living Colour, named for an old NBC-TV announcement "The following program is brought to you in living color." Reid recruited singer Corey Glover after seeing him sing "Happy Birthday" at a mutual friend's party. Glover was studying to become a pilot and was an actor appearing in television commercials and the movie, *Platoon*. Then, drummer William Calhoun, a Berklee School of Music graduate, met Reid in the Bronx and joined up. Bassist Muzz Skillings signed up and the band was ready.

The Jagger edge

Reid, who had played guitar on Mick Jagger's solo record, *Primitive Cool,* got Jagger to produce the band's demo. Even with this advantage, the band still had problems getting a record deal. "They said 'We don't have the time or the energy to make this happen,'" Reid said in *Newsday*. They finally did get a deal with Epic and put out the funk-metal record *Vivid*. After a single "Middle Man" didn't do much, the band broke through with "Cult of Personality." Another single, "Glamour Boys," hit the Top Forty, and the band was suddenly famous. The record ended up staying on the charts for a year.

Jagger signed the band up for the high-profile opening slot on the Rolling Stones' Steel Wheels tour (1989-90). At one point during the tour, the band got into a public verbal battle with Guns 'N Roses over Axl Rose's derogatory remarks against homosexuals and "immigrants." "We basically said we didn't dig it because the labeling of people is not cool. It reduces people," said Reid in *Rolling Stone*.

They released *Time's Up* in 1990. It was a more diversified record, according to *Rolling Stone*. "They skid all over the black-rock map, zigzagging from the fusion meltdown in the midsection of 'Information Overload' to the bedrock Memphis soul of 'Under Cover of Darkness' and the sweet Soweto hop of 'Solace of You.'" (Note how even *Rolling Stone* characterized Living Colour's territory as "black-rock.")

As usual, the band was outspoken in their lyrics, like the line "A black man taught him how to sing / And then he was crowned king" from "Elvis Is Dead."

Parents Aren't Supposed to Like It

The band said they were just calling it as they saw it. "Part of what we're doing is just dealing with the fabric of our lives, the things we see happening around us," explained Reid in *Rolling Stone*.

Less fame, more acclaim

After releasing an EP of covers, playing Lollapalooza, and switching bassist Skillings for Doug Wimbash, the band came back with *Stain* in 1993. By this time, the band had become a critics' favorite. "Vernon Reid is the most inventive, eclectic and stimulating rock guitarist around right now," raved *Guitar World* in a review calling *Stain* "wicked." *Rolling Stone* said the band "plays at its hardest" and gave the record four out of five stars.

But Living Colour's heyday was over. The band members stopped feeling a strong sense of purpose and unity. "It wasn't fun anymore. The magic was no longer there," Reid said in *Performance*. In 1995 Living Colour broke up.

Selected Awards

Vivid double platinum.

Time's Up gold record.

1989 MTV Award, three awards, including Best New Artist for "Cult of Personality."

1990 Grammy Award, Best Hard Rock Performance.

1991 Grammy Award, Best Hard Rock Performance.

Selected Discography

Vivid (Epic), 1988.

Time's Up (Epic), 1990.

Stain (Epic), 1993.

Pride (Greatest Hits) (Epic), 1995.

Further Reading

Ahearn, Charlie, "Living Colour Rock 'n' Soul," *Interview*, September 1990, p. 32.

Breskin, David, "Voodoo child: The 'Rolling Stone' Interview with Living Colour's Vernon Reid," *Rolling Stone*, July 8, 1993, p. 87.

Fricke, David, "Living Colour's Time Is Now," *Rolling Stone*, November 1, 1990, p. 50.

Gore, Joe, and Chris Jisi, "Livelier Colours," *Guitar Player*, November 1990, p. 30.

Light, Alan, "A 'heavier, funkier' Living Colour," *Rolling Stone*, January 21, 1993, p. 18.

Contact Information

Epic Records
2100 Colorado Ave.
Santa Monica, CA 90404

Web Site

http://www.willamette.edu/~cwick/lc/

MEGADETH

American heavy metal band

Formed 1983 in Los Angeles, California

"It's like you invented the first golf club, and now they've got these graphite shaft jobs and the ball goes 300 miles into space." –Dave Mustaine on other bands copying Megadeth

Although not many people noticed it at the time, 1983 marked an important split in metal history. It was when Dave Mustaine was kicked out of **Metallica** (see entry). At the time, Metallica was working on a new style of music, which would change the face of heavy metal from the popular glam-pop style to a harder, more serious kind of thrash metal. When Mustaine formed his own band, Megadeth, the question was: which band will be at the forefront of metal? The answer: both.

Mr. Revenge

Mustaine grew up in Southern California, a child of abuse. His parents divorced, and he moved in with his sisters. He became inspired to play music after fighting with his brother-in-law over the metal band Judas Priest. "I decided then that I was going to play this music," he said in *Rolling Stone*. "That would be my revenge." He played in a few bands before meeting James Hetfield and Lars Ulrich in Norwalk, California. The three started Metallica, which quickly started working on a new, harder kind of metal.

Dave Mustaine

Mustaine was in the band three years. Although Mustaine helped write many of the songs, he was making the rest of the band angry with his drug use. Finally, he was kicked out. One rumor had Mustaine being asked to leave because of his drug abuse. Another said Mustaine was ejected after he kicked James Hetfield's dog. Megadeth, named after a military term for nuclear war casualties, put out their first record *Killing Is My Business ... And Business is Good!!!* in 1985. Mustaine called his brand of music speed-metal.

Major label success, major personal life failure

Megadeth signed with a major label and put out *Peace Sells ... But Who's Buying?* Though the record became a bestseller, Poland and Samuelson left the band. They were replaced by guitarist Jeff Young and drummer Chuck Behler. The new line-up put out 1988's *So Far, So Good.... So What?* which was a big success, too. *Rolling Stone* called the album "spectacular." However, Young and Behler left, or were kicked out, soon after. Mustaine replaced them with guitarist Marty Friedman and drummer Nick Menza, who played on 1990's *Rust in Peace. Rust in Peace* sold well and got good reviews, too. *Rolling Stone* gave it four out of five stars, complimenting the record's "nasty speed thrash with an almost jazzlike intricacy [complexity] and drive."

Despite all the critical and public approval, Mustaine's drug use became completely out of control. "I became like a dope-seeking missile, and after awhile I was losing my mind," he said in *Rolling Stone*. "I got to the point where I just could not play anymore. I knew that I was going to die if I didn't get sober, and even that didn't make me stop. I would have done anything for coke or heroin." It wasn't until Mustaine was stopped by police for driving under the influence that he quit. He was given the choice between giving up drugs and jail. He chose giving up drugs.

Megadeth un-drugged

Mustaine turned to music. "I become a lot stronger when I put on my guitar," he said in *Guitar Player.* "It's like Sinbad putting on his belt, or Wonder Twin power, or Popeye eating Spinach. When I don't have my guitar, I feel vulnerable—people can see the man behind the guitar." On 1992's *Countdown to Extinction,* Mustaine slowed the music down a little and came up with the hit song, "Symphony of Destruction." The rehabilitated Mustaine wrote a song for the movie, *Bill and Ted's Bogus Journey,* and ended his feud with Hetfield when Megadeth was invited to open for Metallica.

"I got to the point where I just could not play anymore. I knew that I was going to die if I didn't get sober, and even that didn't make me stop."

Some applauded Megadeth's new maturity; others thought the band was getting too commercial. Whichever, the band was still controversial. The cover art on the 1994 record *Youthanasia,* showing an old woman hanging babies on a clothesline, got the record banned in Chile. *Entertainment Weekly* gave the record a "B-" saying Mustaine's "tortured lyrics and virtuoso [skillful] guitar clichés are still with us, making this the sort of musical speedball that might impress but won't impact."

June 17, 1997, marked the arrival of *Cryptic Writings*. In it, Megadeth took some steps away from their fast and furious metal. One song, "Use the Man," is completely acoustic, while another, "Trust," has string arrangements. Although there is some of the familiar hard and heavy metal, Mustaine defended the calmer sounds on Capitol Records' web page: "We made this record for not only our hard-core fans, but did what we wanted as music fans. To thine own self be true."

Selected Awards

So Far, So Good ... So What! certified gold, 1990.

Peace Sells ... But Who's Buying? certified platinum, 1992.

Genesis Awards, Doris Day Music Award, for anti-hunting message on *Countdown to Extinction*, 1993.

Countdown to Extinction, certified double platinum, 1994.

Rust in Peace, certified platinum, 1994.

Youthanasia, certified platinum, 1995.

Selected Discography

Peace Sells ... But Who's Buying? (Combat/Capitol), 1986.

So Far, So Good ... So What! (Capitol), 1988.

Rust in Peace (Combat/Capitol), 1990.

Countdown to Extinction (Combat/Capitol), 1992.

Youthanasia (Capitol), 1994.

Hidden Treasures (Capitol), 1995.

Cryptic Writings (Capitol), 1997.

Further Reading

Palmer, Robert, "Rust in Peace," *Rolling Stone,* November 15, 1990, p. 149.

Pike, Jeff, "Clash of the Titans," *Billboard,* June 22, 1991, p. 37.

Rotondi, James, "Megadeth's Mustaine and Friedman Aim Higher and Wider," *Guitar Player,* December, 1994, p. 45.

Sinclair, Tom, "Youthanasia," *Entertainment Weekly,* November 4, 1994, p. 74.

Contact Information

Capitol Records
1750 North Vine St.
Hollywood, CA 90028

Fan club:

Megadeth CyberArmy
Dept. Net
PO Box 883488
San Francisco, CA 94188

Web Site

http://hollywoodandvine.com/megadeth/megadeth.html

metallica

American heavy metal band
Formed 1981 in Los Angeles, California

Metallica has always done things differently. When their fourth record, *...And Justice For All,* made it into the Top Ten, it wasn't because of a hit song or video. Metallica had never even made a video at the time, and finding a Metallica song on the radio was nearly impossible. They did it on their own, through constant touring and word-of-mouth. "We always wanted to be different from the rest of the music business," said drummer Lars Ulrich in *People Weekly.*

Metallica is a different kind of metal band. Coming on the music scene in the 1980s when cartoony glam metal (a performing style typified by heavy make-up and outrageous costumes) was at its peak, Metallica played a new, more serious metal, with a harder, thrashier sound and a lack of frills. "No glam rockers, they dress in T-shirts, jeans and sneakers, (and) are 100 percent mousse-free," reported *People Weekly* in 1988. "Instead of hook-rich, cliché-ridden pleas to party girls, [guitarist and singer James] Hetfield writes punk-like lyrics that rage at death, drugs, war, conformity, pollution and any authority figure who comes to mind."

"Wow, we're kind of hated again. I like that."–James Hetfield in *Entertainment Weekly*

In the late 1990s Metallica changed the rules again. They made the surprise move of headlining the 1996 Lollapalooza, a music festival generally not associated with metal. Then the band started experimenting with new sounds, like the blues, and slower songs on 1996's *Load*. This alienated some fans of their old thrash and burn. Metallica even cut off their long heavy metal hair. The guys in the band said they just needed to grow as musicians. As for the criticism, if people don't like the latest Metallica, then maybe they just aren't getting it.

"Are we mainstream? Are we alternative? Are we a Swedish polka band?" said Ulrich in *Entertainment Weekly*. "It's just one big pile of music, and either you survive or you don't."

Metallica, as kids

Lars Ulrich grew up in Copenhagen, Denmark, with parents who were free spirits. His father was a professional tennis player and big music fan. Ulrich was left to fend for himself a lot in an upbringing he described as "pretty open" in *Rolling Stone*. According to him, he could have anything he wanted as long as he got it himself. "As far as my parents were concerned, I could go see Black Sabbath twelve times a day. But I had to find my own means, carrying the paper or whatever, to get the money to buy the tickets. And I had to find my own way to the concert and back." Ulrich planned to be a tennis pro until he moved to Los Angeles, California, and discovered he was "not even in the top ten on the block," as he put it in *People Weekly*. Ulrich got into

drumming and started meeting other metal players.

After going to London and touring with a new wave British metal band, Ulrich returned to the United States. Through an ad in the paper, Ulrich met James Hetfield, who was a veteran of several bands. Hetfield was the son of strict Christian Scientists. When he was a teenager, his mom died. By the time he met Ulrich, he was working in a factory. The two recruited guitarist Dave Mustaine and Hetfield's roommate, bassist Ron McGovney, and Metallica was born.

The band got a house together in El Cerritos, California. "We had the old garage converted into a rehearsal room with egg cartons. It was the refuge, the sanctuary for everybody in the neighborhood. People would come over and live there, hang there. It was a lot of fun—when you're nineteen," said Ulrich in *Rolling Stone*.

The word spreads

The band recorded a demo tape that was passed around in underground circles and gave the band notoriety. After the tape, McGovney quit and Cliff Burton took over bass duties. There was another line-up change the next year, in 1983, when the band got sick of Mustaine and his drug abuse and kicked him out. Kirk Hammett replaced him. Mustaine went on to form his own heavy metal band, **Megadeth** (see entry).

"We were living very, very meagerly," said Hammett in *Rolling Stone*. "I remember, on our first tour, we got ten bucks a day on days off and seven bucks on a show day because we could always eat free at the gig." The band recorded their first two records, *Kill 'Em All* and *Ride the Lightning,* on a minor label. Three months after its release *Ride the Lightning* got picked up by major label Elektra. Although the record only made it to #100 on the charts, it sold a half million copies in six months.

Things continued to improve for the band. They played on a Monsters of Rock tour, then released *Master of Puppets.* Although the record had no video or even a single, it made #29 on the charts.

Metallica's stripped-down, no-frills metal had caught on with head-bangers. "Bands like us and Slayer started selling records," said Ulrich, who is considered the business-oriented member of Metallica, in *Rolling Stone.* "We were appealing to the kids in a way that everything didn't need to be so prefabricated and product oriented. With us it was constant touring and constantly being in people's faces. And it showed all the people in the high rise buildings—the record companies—that there were kids out there who wanted more than what they were getting through FM radio."

Moving beyond tragedy

In 1986 Burton was killed in a bus accident. The band dealt with the blow by getting back to work. They hired Metallica fan and ex-Flotsam and Jetsam bassist Jason Newsted, then went back on tour. The new line-up kicked out an album of covers, *The $5.98 EP—Garage Days Revisited.*

Metallica proved the dominance of their brand of metal when *...And Justice For All* came out in 1988. Although marred by poor sound quality, the Grammy-nominated record became an instant metal classic. The record stayed on the charts for over a year. 1991's *Metallica* cemented the band as the most important metal band around. "Their most successful (and best) album to date," raved the *All Music Guide to Rock.*

Throughout the early 1990s Metallica kept up a rigorous touring schedule, collected awards, and saw their records sell millions. (*Metallica* has stayed in the top 200 for years.) They finally took a break after the touring got to be too much. "It almost killed us—we almost killed each other," said Hammett in *Entertainment Weekly.*

Back with a new direction

When the band reunited, they came out with 1996's *Load,* a record that moved away from the typical Metallica sound. Then there was the matter of the new haircuts. Some fans were not pleased. "You can only be what the public thinks you are for so long before it becomes boring. A lot of people get fixated on what they *need* us to be—appearance-wise, how we should sound," said Hammett in *Entertainment Weekly.* Said Ulrich: "'Why don't you make another record like *Master of Puppets?*' We already made it! There is a percentage of people who think they own Metallica, and this is what Metallica is to them."

Metallica plans to ignore what the fans think and stick with doing what they want to do on their next record. By the end of 1997, they'll release a new record based on songs from the same batch from which the *Load* songs came. Meaning no new *Master of Puppets.* Meaning fans could be angry.

But Metallica is sticking with their instincts and making the kind of music they want to make, regardless of what the fans think. "We knew it could take months, even years, for it to sink in with people," said Newsted in the non-union version of the *Detroit Free Press.* "It's always going to be a mixed reaction ... But we have more to offer than just going 220 miles an hour."

Selected Awards

Grammy Award for Best Metal Performance, for "One," 1990.

"One," certified gold, 1990.

The $5.98 EP—Garage Days Revisited, certified platinum.

Grammy Award for Best Metal Performance, for "Stone Cold Crazy," 1991.

Bay Area Music Awards, Outstanding Album and Outstanding Metal Album, for *Metallica,* 1992.

Bay Area Music Award, Outstanding Song, for "Enter Sandman," 1992.

Bay Area Music Award, Outstanding Drummer/Percussionist, to Lars Ulrich, 1992.

Grammy Award, Best Metal Performance with Vocal, for *Metallica,* 1992.

MTV Video Music Award, Best Metal/Hard Rock Video, for "Enter Sandman," 1992.

Bay Area Music Awards: 1) Outstanding Group, 2) Outstanding Guitarist (Kirk Hammett), 3) Outstanding Bassist (Jason Newsted), and 4) Outstanding Drummer/Percussionist (Lars Ulrich), 1993.

American Music Award, Favorite Artist, Heavy Metal/Hard Rock, 1993.

Rolling Stone's Music Awards, Readers' and Critics' Picks, Best Heavy Metal Band, 1993, and Readers' Picks, 1994.

Master of Puppets, certified triple platinum, 1994.

Metallica, certified for sales of eight million copies, 1995.

Kill 'Em All, certified double platinum, 1995.

Ride the Lightning, certified triple platinum, 1995.

...And Justice for All, certified quadruple platinum, 1995.

Selected Discography

Kill 'Em All (Elektra), 1983.

Ride the Lightning (Elektra), 1984.

The $5.98 EP—Garage Days Revisited EP (Elektra), 1987.

Master of Puppets (Elektra), 1986.

...And Justice For All (Elektra), 1988.

Metallica (Elektra), 1991.

Load (Elektra), 1996.

Further Reading

Dougherty, Steve, "Metallica, Unapologetic Avatars of Transuranic Metal Find Success in a Spandex, Moussed-up World," *People,* November 21, 1988, p. 73.

Fricke, David, "Married to Metal," *Rolling Stone,* May 18, 1995, p. 72.

Fricke, David, "Pretty Hate Machine," *Rolling Stone,* June 27, 1996, p. 32.

Ratliff, Ben, "Metallica," *New York Times,* March 4, 1997, p. C16.

Rotondi, James, "Write the Lightning: James Hetfield's Stormy Songcraft," *Guitar Player,* October, 1996, p. 48.

Parents Aren't Supposed to Like It

Contact Information

Elektra
75 Rockefeller Plaza
New York, NY 10019

Fan club:

The Metallica Club
PO Box 18327
Knoxville, TN 37928-2327

Web Site

http://www.elektra.com/metal_club/
metallica/metallica.html

pantera

American heavy metal band

Formed in 1982 in Arlington, Texas

 "We've grown into a monster!" –from Pantera's "Strength Beyond Strength"

From left: "Dimebag" Darrel Abbott, Paul Abbott, Rex, Philip Anselmo

I n April 1994, Pantera hit the number one spot on the charts with *Far Beyond Driven*. The main reaction from many music fans was "Pantera? Who?" Pantera is a band that hasn't followed the usual music industry path. Pantera's songs are too harsh and abrasive to get much play on the radio. And most critics don't like their hyper-aggressive speed metal, describing it as brutal, foul-mouthed, menacing, sinister and anti-social. And the band members are bad interview subjects. "What the band members have to say often borders on the incomprehensible, not to mention the unprintable," said *Texas Monthly*.

So Pantera had to figure out a different way to get attention. They slowly developed a fan base by playing countless shows, becoming known on the heavy metal circuit. It was a good thing for the band, since live shows are their forte. The live Pantera onslaught includes deafening volume, unrelenting music, and singer Philip Anselmo stalking the stage like a mad animal.

"It's a 100 percent pure energy release from both the band and the audience," said drummer Paul Abbott in a record company press release for *Far Beyond Driven*. In *Texas Monthly* Abbott elaborated, "It's a way for people to come and vent their frustrations or whatever they want to get out of their systems. They smash and slam into each other. Everybody who comes to a Pantera show knows what they're coming to see. It's not four pretty guys playing pretty music. It's an emotion. It moves you."

Pantera's past

The Abbott brothers, Paul and Darrell, had gotten into music because their father owned a recording studio and encouraged them to experiment with the equipment and with music in general. "I can remember one birthday of mine where (their dad) said 'Son, you can either have a BMX bike or you can have this,' and he pointed to a guitar. I ended up taking the bike, but he did plant a seed in my mind," said Darrell Abbott in *Guitar World*.

Paul Abbott formed Pantera in high school in Pantego, Texas, with brother, Darrell, and their high school jazz band friend, bassist Rex "Rocker" Brown. (At the time, Darrell Abbott called himself "Diamond"; later he changed his name to "Dimebag.") Terry Glaze joined as singer/guitarist. They named themselves after the Spanish word for panther. The band was into glam rock, had big hair, wore spandex, and copied bands like Bon Jovi and Motley Crue. "We were the best cover band in the world. We could play any cover tune you could name, as long as it was rock and roll," said Paul Abbott in *Texas Monthly*. This early version of Pantera put out glam records on the Metal Magic label throughout the 1980s.

Changes in attitude

When new singer Phil Anselmo joined, the band's sound started changing. They put out one last 1980s-style metal record, *Power Metal,* then got signed by a major record label. On their major label debut, *Cowboys from Hell,* the band was starting to develop their harder sound. They started playing heavier, harsher music and set it to Anselmo's maniacal vocals. The new aggressive image worked. *Cowboys From Hell* went gold, and Pantera played the high-profile European tour Monsters of Rock with AC/DC, **Metallica** (see entry), and the **Black Crowes** (see entry).

When *Vulgar Display of Power* came out, the cover showed a fist smacking into a face. It was an appropriate image for the band, since Pantera's music was getting more brutal with each record. Anselmo "roars with larynx-bruising vehemence," said *Texas Monthly*. The record hit number one. 1994's *Far Beyond Driven* and 1996's *The Great Southern Trendkill* kept up the trend toward nastiness, each record getting even heavier than the last. *People Weekly* said *Far Beyond Driven* "makes one wonder how Judas Priest was ever considered dissonant."

And it's all just going to get harsher. "We're into topping ourselves," said Darrell Abbott in *Guitar Player*. "Most bands come out with a heavy record, then it gets lighter and lighter. You're stuck listening to the first record, wishing and dreaming. That ain't what we're about, though."

Selected Awards

Cowboys from Hell gold

Vulgar Display of Power platinum

Selected Discography

Cowboys From Hell (Atco), 1990.

Vulgar Display of Power (East-West), 1992.

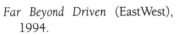

Far Beyond Driven (EastWest), 1994.

The Great Southern Trendkill (EastWest), 1996.

Further Reading

Darzin, Daina, "Rebel Yellers," *Rolling Stone,* June 30, 1994, p. 24.

Gill, Chris, "Pantera," *Guitar Player,*, May 1994, p. 20.

Jackson, Devon, "The Great Southern Trendkill," *Entertainment Weekly,* May 10, 1996.

Levitan, Corey, "Far Beyond Driven," *People,* May 9, 1994, p. 24.

Rubiner, Michael, "Rage On," *Texas Monthly,* June 1994, p. 72.

Contact Information

EastWest
75 Rockefeller Plaza
New York, NY 10019

Web Site

http://www.elektra.com/metal_club/pantera.html

Slayer

American heavy metal band
Formed in 1982 in Los Angeles, California

Slayer is the kind of band that people either really, really love or really, really hate. In an article on guitarist Kerry King, *Guitar Player* seemed to be taking the second position. The magazine said the Slayer record *Divine Intervention* was "full of repulsive, socially irresponsible lyrics on subject matter such as murder, rape, torture and religion bashing. Fortunately, bassist Tom Araya screams out the lyrics in an unintelligible manner, and some Slayer fans can't read the lyrics sheet, while they cruise their trucks through the trailer park with the record blasting," said the magazine.

It's common that Slayer fans take much of the brunt of anti-Slayer sentiment. In a story in the *Voice Rock & Roll Quarterly,* even the band's producer Rick Rubin put down Slayer fans, calling them the "nothing-to-live-for-Slayer audience."

By now, Slayer and their fans are used to it; after all, being unacceptable is kind of the whole point of the band. "We dig being Slayer. We dig having our reputation, and we just feed off of it," said guitarist Kerry King in *Guitar Player.*

"Slayer is about the dark cloud that hangs over the world and that's the image and intensity that I want people to understand." – Slayer's Tom Araya.

Tom Araya

Young Slayer

Kerry King was fourteen years old when he met guitarist Jeff Hanneman at an audition in 1981. The two shared an interest in demonic thrash-metal. King met drummer Dave Lombardo when Lombardo delivered a pizza to his neighborhood. The fourth member was Araya. His family had fled political unrest in their native country, Chile, and had moved to the Huntington Beach, California, area. When he joined the band, Araya was a healthcare worker, studying to become a nurse.

They came up with an evil-enough-sounding name and stole some lumber and lights to use for shows. Their first performance was in a rented high school gym. They got some better gigs, which led to their first single, "Aggressive Protector," getting released on a 1983 metal compilation, *Metal Massacre III* on Metal Blade Records. Metal Blade liked the cut and signed the band. When Slayer put out 1984's *Show No Mercy* and 1985's *Hell Awaits,* they wore eye make-up and took an almost ridiculous approach to their "evil" by wearing upside down crosses and writing bizarre lyrics about death, murder, and what ever else bad they could think of. "Many in metal circles considered the band a joke at the time, but they found a small following among metal listeners looking for something new, different, and extreme," reported the *All Music Guide to Rock.*

They find their sound

Rick Rubin helped change the band's career. Rubin, a producer and owner of American Records (then called Def American), saw potential in the band and signed them to his label, even though at the time the label was mostly a rap label. Rubin advised Slayer to try a more stripped-down sound on *Reign in Blood.* They did and were rewarded with their first chart showing at number ninety-four. At first, the distributor refused to put the record out because of references to Satan. Eventually another distributor took over. The *All Music Guide to Rock* called the record "Slayer's masterpiece" and noted the record's "very fast bursts of aggression that change tempo or feel without warning, keeping the listener off balance and producing a very wild, disjointed, barely controlled effect."

Rubin, a man who understands promotion, told the band to increase the satanic references on their next record. They did and came out with 1988's *South of Heaven.* The big controversy on this record was about the song "Silent Scream," an anti-abortion tune. How does the band find the kind of subject matter that always seems to make someone mad? By writing about things that makes *them* mad. "I've seen a lot of stuff that pissed me off, so I wrote about it," said King in *Guitar Player.*

Slaying it again

Slayer put out what many critics consider to be their most accessible record with 1990's *Season of the Abyss.* Of course, "accessible" means different things to different people. Lines like "dying terror, blood's cheap, it's everywhere, mandatory suicide, massacre on the front line," obviously weren't going to appeal to everyone. *Entertainment Weekly* gave it a "B+" and called it "very heavy metal of the thrash kind." The record helped cement Slayer's reputation as a top metal band, and Slayer played with their cohorts **Megadeth** (see entry), Anthrax, and **Alice In Chains** (see entry) on the 1991's Clash of the Titans tour.

After putting out the double record *Live—Decade of Aggression,* Lombardo quit the band and started work with his own band, Grip. New drummer Paul Bostaph, who had been with metal band Forbidden, came onboard. The new quartet recorded *Divine Intervention* which debuted at number eight on the charts. "The song remains the same and it's an ugly one," said *Entertainment Weekly,* giving the record a "B." "Still, the music's headlong charge toward the apocalypse demonstrates why Slayer is the speed metal band against which all others will be forever judged."

New record, yet another new drummer

Slayer got a new drummer, Jon Dette, for the next record *Undisputed Attitude.* "Now we're on our third drummer. We burn 'em out," said King in press materials for the record. The record was recorded in a month and has one new original plus covers of Slayer's favorite punk songs. The bands they covered included Verbal Abuse, Minor Threat, and T.S.O.L. "We're exposing kids to what the new 'punk' sound should be, as opposed to what **Green Day** (see entry) sound like now," said King. "Or Rancid. Or Offspring. The big thing these days is geek music. The guy you beat up in high school. My idea was that this record was what made Slayer what we are." The idea came to King when he was listening to the radio. "The Offspring was on, and I had my Minor Threat tape with me, so I was like, let's just take a test. Offspring? Minor Threat? Night and ... day." *Entertainment Weekly* gave the record a "C-" and said "Slayer seem to think that playing as fast and rigidly as possible makes for harder rock, but it's just lazy schtick."

The future of Slayer? As long as there are disaffected kids around who like hearing songs about evil, there's going to be a Slayer around. Or at least a band like Slayer. "Obviously, a lot of our fans do identify with evil—or at least they think they do," said Hanneman in *Rolling Stone.*

Selected Awards

Divine Intervention, certified gold, 1994.

Seasons In The Abyss, certified gold, 1993.

Reign in Blood, certified gold, 1992.

South of Heaven, certified gold, 1992.

Selected Discography

Reign in Blood (Def Jam) 1985.

South of Heaven (Def American), 1988.

Seasons in the Abyss (Def America), 1990.

Decade of Aggression Live (Def American), 1991.

Divine Intervention (American), 1994.

Undisputed Attitude (American), 1996.

Further Reading

Eddy, Chuck, "Undisputed Attitude," *Entertainment Weekly,* June 21, 1996, p. 66.

Gill, Chris, "Slay Anything: Slayer's Kerry King Goes Off the Record," *Guitar Player,* December 1994, p. 49.

Masuo, Sandy, "Undisputed Attitude," *Rolling Stone,* May 30, 1996, p. 49.

Palmer, Robert, "Divine Intervention," *Rolling Stone,* February 9, 1995.

Pike, Jeff, "Clash of the Titans," *Billboard,* June 22, 1991, p. 37.

Contact Information

American Recordings
3500 W. Olive Ave., Suite 1500
Burbank, CA 91505

Web Site

http://american.recordings.com/American_
Artists/Slayer/slayer_home.html

Parents Aren't Supposed to Like It

WHite ZOMBiE

American heavy metal band

Formed in New York, New York, in 1985

Rob Zombie loves horror movies, he always has, even when he was little. He was always fascinated by dead bodies and other gruesome things. One of the first grisly memories is of the pictures in his Mom's copy of *Helter Skelter,* a book about the Manson family. He loved looking at the photos of the chalk out-lines of the dead bodies. "I was in kindergarten;" he says, "other kids loved baseball." But Zombie loved horror, that's why he named his band White Zombie and called himself Rob Zombie.

Back in the mid 1980s, America was swept away by the New Wave. Most of the bands came from England, played synthesizers, made great videos, and had pretty silly names like Duran Duran, Spandau Ballet, and Haircut 100. Zombie hated those groups and what he thought were their boring, silly pop songs. He liked bands with lots of guitars, who made lots of noise onstage, and whose performances were more than fashion shows.

"Riveting deep grooved, slamming industrial tunes.... It's brutal, calibrated monster-metal excess. Cool, heh-heh." – *USA Today*

Let's get zombified

So, Zombie formed his own band with his then girlfriend, bassist Sean Yseult. Of course, there were a few other bands playing metal as well, but they weren't much different from those New Wave bands. They were all pretty, wore make-up, and their sound was based on glam. Zombie didn't want to be like that either. But America seemed to like those kind of groups. And so, throughout the 1980s, White Zombie played grotty little clubs and released singles, EPs, and an album, *Soul Crusher*. But nobody cared.

You Said Zombie, heh, heh, heh, heh

In 1991 the band recorded *La Sexorcisto: Devil Music Volume One*. White Zombie were not your typical metal band, and they wanted to be creative. So, on the album, they included lots of samples (short little bits of sounds and dialogue) mostly taken from movies. The problem was, it was only after they had finished the record, that the band realized they needed permission to use the samples. Most of the people who were sampled were happy to let White Zombie use these bits. But some people, including the actor Robert De Niro, were not, and so the band couldn't use them. So the group had to go back into the studio and take out all those samples, a very time-consuming process. This held up the release of the record for almost a year. But in the end, it was worth the wait, because *La Sexorcisto* was a hit. The single from the record, "Thunderkiss

'65," was a smashing success. Beavis and Butthead, the MTV cartoon characters, became instant fans, playing the video over and over.

I walked with a zombie

Times had changed since White Zombie had formed, and a new generation of kids had come along who loved rock. And nobody rocked harder and better than Zombie. They were asked to appear many times on MTV's *Headbangers Ball,* and their live shows kept getting bigger and bigger. The band spent a lot of time on the road touring. That helped them find more and more fans, and most of them bought *La Sexorcisto.* It took about a year, but finally the album entered the charts. By early 1994, the record had sold over a million copies, earning the group a platinum disc.

When White Zombie finally entered the studio to record their new album, they were careful not to make the same mistake they had done on their last. Instead of sampling movies, the band decided to create their own samples. They spent a whole week just making up and recording fake dialogue and recording cool, weird noises.

In fact, *Astro-Creep 2000: Songs of Love, Destruction, And Other Synthetic Delusions Of The Electric Head* is almost drowning in layers of music, noise, and samples. Rob Zombie actually hears how the finished song will sound in his head, and then piece by piece, the band will put it all together to create the jigsaw that is White Zombie's music.

Parents Aren't Supposed to Like It

It's brutal

"Riveting deep grooved, slamming industrial tunes ...." *USA Today* wrote. "It's brutal, calibrated monster-metal excess. Cool, heh-heh." The album went straight into the Top Ten and stayed on the chart for over a year. This time, Zombie's record went platinum in just two months. The album and the single, "More Human Than Human," earned the band two Grammy nominations, and won them a MTV Video Music Award.

Remixes from the crypt

Later in 1996, *Supersexy Swingin' Sounds* appeared. The album contained remixes of the songs from *Astro-Creep 2000*, done by a host of famous music people. These included Nine Inch Nails (NIN) member Charlie Clouser, super mix masters The Dust Brothers, and the great producer John Fryer, who produced albums for both NIN and Gravity Kills.

White Zombie have remained a band apart, their songs are scary, and their music even scarier. Horror movies are still Zombie's main influence, although the songs aren't about real movies. They're more about the frightening things that Zombie sees in his own head. And that's what creativity and Zombie are all about, putting onto record the sounds and visions one can only imagine.

Selected Awards

"More Human Than Human" nominated for Grammy for Best Hard Rock Performance.

Astro-Creep 2000 nominated for Grammy for Best Engineered Album (Non-Classical).

"More Human Than Human" won MTV Video Music Award for Best Hard Rock Video.

Voted Best Metal Band in Rolling Stone's 1996 Music Awards in both the Readers' and Critics' polls.

Selected Discography

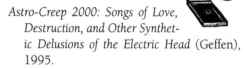

La Sexorcisto: Devil Music Vol. 1 (Geffen), 1992.

Astro-Creep 2000: Songs of Love, Destruction, and Other Synthetic Delusions of the Electric Head (Geffen), 1995.

Supersexy Swingin' Sounds (Geffen), 1996.

Further Reading

Christie, Ian, "White Zombie," *Alternative Press*, April 1995, p. 53.

Duff, S. L., "White Zombie," *RIP*, April 1995, p. 44.

Gardner, Elysa, "It's Hard Work Being a Zombie," *Los Angeles Times*, June 27, 1995.

Wiedenbum, Marc, "That Creeping Feeling," *Pulse*, June 1995, p. 57.

Contact Information

Geffen Records
9130 Sunset Blvd.
Los Angeles, CA 90069

Web Site

http://carbon.cudenver.edu/~enielsen/zombie/

RHYTHM AND BLUES AND URBAN SOUL

In the mid-1940s, when African American veterans were returning home from World War II, they found not only a new gospel sound, but an exciting blues style, called jump blues, being played by small combos. With its roots in boogie woogie and the blues-swing arrangements of Count Basie, Cab Calloway, Louis Jordan, and others, this new blues style acquired an enormous following in black urban areas across the country. Unlike the swing-era big bands, jump blues featured fewer horns and a heavy rhythmic approach marked by a walking boogie bass line, honking saxophone solos, and a two-four drum pattern. Among the greatest masters of postwar jump blues were guitarist T-Bone Walker, saxophonist Eddie "Cleanhead" Vincent, and blues shouter Big Joe Turner.

Soon many jump blues ensembles began to feature singers versed in a smooth, gospel-influenced vocal style. In 1949 the popularity of this style led *Billboard* to change its black pop chart title to rhythm and blues, thus coining the name of this new music. Rhythm and blues drew upon gospel, electric urban blues,

Ray Charles, R & B pioneer

and swing jazz to create a vibrantly modern sound appealing to the younger generation of postwar blacks. Some of the early recordings illustrating the gospel influence on rhythm and blues were Cecil Grant's 1945 hit "I Wonder," Roy Brown's 1947 classic "Good Rocking Tonight," and Wynonie Harris's 1949 disc "All She Wants To Do Is Rock."

With the increased number of rhythm and blues recordings, a handful of black radio disc jockeys became locally famous as the first promoters and salesmen of this music. Bringing their colorful street language to the airwaves, pioneer black DJs such as Al Benson and Vernon Winslow not only helped popularize R & B, but also set the trend for modern pop radio.

R & B and the Black Church

In the early 1950s numerous gospel quartets and street corner singing groups set out to establish careers in the black popular music scene. Influenced by gospel music and such mainstream groups as the Inkspots, vocal groups appeared performing complex harmonies in a capella style. Urban street corners became training grounds for thousands of hopeful African American artists. This music, known as doo-wop, first arrived on the scene with the formation of the Ravens in 1945.

Shortly after there came a great string of doo-wop "bird groups" including the Orioles who, in 1953, scored a nationwide hit with "Crying in the Chapel"—a song which, for the first time in black popular music, walked an almost undistinguishable line between gospel and mainstream pop music. In the same year Billy Ward formed the Dominoes, featuring lead singer Clyde McPhatter.

In the wake of the success of these vocal groups, numerous gospel singers left the church to become pop music stars. In 1952, for example, the Royal Sons became the Five Royales, the Gospel Starlighters (with James Brown), and finally the Blue Flames. Five years later a young gospel singer named Sam Cooke landed a number one pop hit with "You Send Me," which achieved popularity among both black and white audiences.

The strong relationship between gospel and rhythm and blues was evident in the music of more hard-edged R & B groups, including Hank Ballard and the Midnighters. Maintaining a driving blues-based sound, Ballard's music featured gospel harmonies and everyday themes, as evidenced in the 1954 hit "Work with Me Annie." However, the capstone of gospel R & B appeared with Georgia-born pianist and singer Ray Charles, who in 1954 hit the charts with "I Got a Woman," which was based upon the gospel song "My Jesus Is All the World to Me." Charles's 1958 recording "What I'd Say" is famed for its call-and-response pattern that directly resembled the music sung in Holiness churches.

Urban soul

Soul music came to the forefront in the 1960s. It added gospel and pop influences to rhythm and blues to create a distinctive sound. Although mainly concerned with love and romance, soul music treated the subject in a more mature and complex way. Arrangements and harmonies became more intricate than the straightforward R & B songs. And the gospel influence found soul singers more pleading and jubilant in their singing than their R & B counterparts. As soul evolved in the 1970s, it became more middle-of-the-road; its arrangements added more pop sounds to go with its gospel and R & B influences.

Funk was another important development in R & B from the 1960s. Pioneered by James Brown and George Clinton's Parliament/Funkadelic groups, funk added a new dimension to R & B. Funk emphasized repetitive, churning rhythms, and the short, choppy lyrics seemed to become part of the beat. As funk evolved in the 1970s into a form of dance music, the lyrics became less and less important.

Two trends in contemporary urban soul and R & B

Like other contemporary musical forms, soul and R & B borrow heavily from each other and from other musical forms such as rap. Yet they remain distinct, too. On the R & B side, for example, many influences can be heard in the pioneering work of **Prince (The Artist Formerly Known As)** (see entry). Not content with middle-of-the-road soul or intricately arranged R & B, he experimented with new combinations of funk, soul, gospel, R & B, pop, and rap to create his own unique sound.

The charts: pop, R & B, and crossover

Billboard, the weekly trade magazine of the record industry, compiles weekly charts of the top-selling singles in the United States. Two of the major charts are the so-called pop chart ("Hot 100"), which ranks the top pop singles, and the R&B chart ("Hot R&B Singles") which ranks the top R&B singles. The rankings are based on two factors, sales and radio airplay.

A single becomes a crossover hit when an R & B single does well on the pop chart, or when a pop single does well on the R & B chart. Such chart performance indicates a song has broad appeal to both the pop and R & B audiences. Crossover hits are played on both pop and R & B radio stations, and they sell well to both audiences.

Artists like **Babyface** (see entry), **Boyz II Men** (see entry), and **Bobby Brown** (see entry), on the other hand, were more influenced by soul than by R & B. Theirs is the world of romance, of men pleading with women, all made modern by original, up-to-date arrangements. **Tevin Campbell** (see entry), a young artist at the beginning of a very promising career, fits into the soul tradition, but as he grows older his songs may develop along different lines.

Women in soul

The tradition of girl groups in soul and R & B dates back to the 1960s.

The Artist Formerly Known As Prince

Groups such as the Supremes, the Marvelettes, and Martha and the Vandellas recorded for Motown and succeeded in scoring hits on the pop as well as the R & B charts. Their songs reached a wider audience than traditional R & B hits, a phenomenon known as crossing over, because they crossed over from one audience to another. Their influence in the 1990s can be seen in groups such as **En Vogue** (see entry).

En Vogue and other modern girl groups, though, are different in many

Parents Aren't Supposed to Like It

ways from the groups of the 1960s. In the earlier groups, members were expected to submerge their own identities for the good of the group. There were no solo outings by group members. And members were expected to be well-mannered and polite at all times. They performed strict, well-rehearsed routines. And when one of the members became famous enough for a solo career, as in the case of Diana Ross and the Supremes, the group was unable to continue its same level of popularity without its lead singer.

With the advent of New Jill Swing (a mix of rap, R & B, and pop) in the 1990s, groups like En Vogue helped to redefine the image of girl groups. Members of the group were expected to have a powerful voice and behave boldly, from singing sexy songs to wearing revealing clothing to establishing themsevles as successful solo artists. The individual personality of each member was not to be subordinated to that of the group. They were to stand out individually as funky divas.

TLC (see entry) developed along slightly different lines, incorporating more rap and hiphop into their music. They chose to reject the "funky diva" image, refusing at first to wear revealing clothes, for example. They sang about assertive women and, in general, their songs took on a broader range of subjects. While they did sing about love, they also sang about safe sex.

BABYFACE

American rhythm and blues singer, songwriter, and producer
Born Kenneth Edmonds, April 10, 1959, in Indianapolis, Indiana

"Without real love there's no music, no songs, no stories worth singing about."

—Babyface

Kenneth "Babyface" Edmonds has turned a simple talent for writing love songs into a remarkable songwriting, producing, and performing career. His instincts for creating hit songs for other artists have resulted in more than one hundred top ten R & B (rhythm and blues) and pop hits, including forty number one R & B hits. The list of artists for whom he has written and/or produced hits is long and impressive: Michael Jackson, **Boyz II Men** (see entry), **TLC** (see entry), Madonna, Whitney Houston, Mariah Carey, Toni Braxton, Gladys Knight, Eric Clapton, and more.

What is it about Babyface that made him one of the hottest hitmakers in R & B? Andre Harrell, president of Motown Records, explained it to *Time,* "He says everything a woman wants to hear. He's the best male interpreter of romance there is." Edmonds remains modest in the face of such praise and the numerous awards that he's won. His method is to study each artist that he writes for, tailoring his work for each individual style. "You have to listen and kind of know where they are," he told *Ebony.*

Even though some of the biggest names in pop music wanted to work with Babyface, sometimes they don't always agree with him. Boyz II Men, for example, was reluctant at first to record Edmonds's "I'll Make Love to You." He told *Ebony*, "They were very reluctant to do it. You have to explain things when people are reluctant. But if I have a feeling about something, I'll stand strong and tell them, 'You're not getting it.'" In this case, "I'll Make Love to You" went on to set a record by staying at number one on the pop chart for fourteen weeks in a row in 1994, breaking the thirteen-week record Babyface and Boyz II Men had set with "End of the Road" in 1992.

Dues were paid before success struck

Born April 10, 1959, in Indianapolis, Indiana, Kenneth Edmonds was one of six brothers. He got his first taste of show business in the sixth grade when he sat in with his brother Melvin's band at a high school dance. By the time he was in high school he was performing with bands in clubs and lounges throughout the Midwest.

His first recording session took place in Cincinnati, Ohio, with an R & B group called The Deele. It was there he met Antonio "L.A." Reid, with whom he would team to form one of the most successful songwriter/producer teams in the business. But that would come later. For now, Kenneth Edmonds was simply Babyface, a nickname that funk superstar Bootsy Colling of Parliament-Funkadelic gave him.

Relocating to Los Angeles, California, Babyface recorded three albums with The Deele between 1984 and 1988. These were lean years with Babyface struggling just to pay the bills. As he recalled in *Ebony*, "I had been trying to get things placed forever. I had tons of songs that nobody would take." Things started to turn around, though, in 1988 when he co-wrote the group's biggest hit, "Two Occasions." That was also the year he left the group to pursue a solo career, while continuing to write and produce for other artists with partners L.A. Reid and later Daryl Simmons.

Became a hitmaker with L.A. Reid

Reid and Babyface began scoring hits in the late 1980s, first with "Rock Steady" for the long-established Los Angeles vocal group The Whispers. Then in 1988-89 they wrote two number one R & B hits ("Dial My Heart" and "Lucky Charm") for the new group, The Boys, as well as "The Lover in Me" for Sheena Easton, among others. In 1990 they wrote two number one R & B hits ("Ready or Not" and "Can't Stop") for After 7, a group that included two of Babyface's brothers, Melvin and Kevon.

At the same time, Babyface's solo performing career took off when his second solo album, *Tender Lover* (1989), struck double platinum. Sales of the album were driven by the number one R & B hits, "It's No Crime" and the title track. Two other singles from the album, "Whip Appeal" and "My Kinda Girl," were also major hits. Babyface was reaching the broader pop market, too, as two of the four singles cracked the top ten on the pop chart.

Achieved biggest success with Boyz II Men

Babyface and L.A. Reid cemented their reputations as the number one hit-makers in R & B when they co-wrote and produced "End of the Road" for Boyz II Men in 1992. The record became one of the biggest-selling singles of all time, breaking a record set by Elvis Presley's "Heartbreak Hotel" back in 1956 when it stayed atop *Billboard*'s pop chart for thirteen weeks. For "End of the Road," Reid, Babyface, and Daryl Simmons shared a Grammy Award for the Best R & B Song (Babyface's first Grammy), and Reid and Babyface also won a Grammy for Producer of the Year.

Two years later Babyface wrote and produced "I'll Make Love to You" for Boyz II Men. The song shattered their previous record by staying atop the pop chart for an amazing fourteen weeks. The song won Babyface a Grammy for Best R & B Song.

Meanwhile, Babyface's third solo album, *For the Cool in You* (1993), was spinning off four top ten R & B hits: the title track, "Never Keeping Secrets," "And Our Feelings" (with After 7 on backing vocals), and "When Can I See You?" The album itself was certified double platinum by November 1994.

Co-headlining with Boyz II Men, Babyface launched his first concert tour on December 27, 1994, in Minneapolis, Minnesota. Describing Babyface's performance, *USA Today* wrote: "Kenneth 'Babyface' Edmonds has established himself as the premier songwriter in the pop/R & B world. He's now revealing himself as a consummate [skilled and accomplished] performer.... Babyface stole the show with a classy, crafty set."

Holding your breath, waiting to exhale

The November 1995 release of the soundtrack album to the film, *Waiting to Exhale*, marked Babyface's debut in the world of motion picture scores. He called the project "one of those once-in-a-lifetime opportunities that you dream about as a songwriter/producer." The soundtrack contained sixteen songs performed by an all-female vocal cast that included Whitney Houston, Toni Braxton, Aretha Franklin, Brandy, TLC, Mary J. Blige, SWV, Patti LaBelle, and others. Babyface wrote fifteen of the sixteen songs, including the title track.

The album went on to sell more than five million copies and was the number one pop album for five weeks, topping the R & B chart for ten weeks. The project resulted in twelve Grammy nominations for Babyface at the 1997 ceremonies, where he took home Grammys for Best R & B Song for "Exhale (Shoop Shoop)," which was a hit for Whitney Houston, and for Producer of the Year.

Now is the day

Babyface continued his solo recording career with the 1996 album, *The Day.* The album featured many guest artists in addition to ten new songs written or co-written by Babyface. Highlights from the album included "Every Time I Close My Eyes," a ballad with background vocals by Mariah Carey and a saxophone solo by Kenny G.; "Talk to Me," a bluesy number with Eric Clapton on guitar; "How Come, How Long," a song that addresses domestic abuse in a duet with Stevie Wonder, who co-wrote the song; and the title track, "The Day (You Gave Me a Son)," which celebrated Babyface's feelings about his step into fatherhood.

Reviewing *The Day* in *Time,* Christopher John Farley said "*The Day*'s lyrics have a solid moral core: the family unit is revered, love comes with respect, and men do a lot of crying." And as Andre Harrell pointed out, "The thing that makes Babyface special is the way he talks about love."

Selected Awards

Tender Lover, certified double platinum.

For the Cool in You, certified double platinum, 1994.

Essence Award, 1996.

Grammy Award for Best R & B Song, for "End of the Road," (performed by Boyz II

The Boarder Baby Project

In 1994 Babyface volunteered to serve as national spokesperson for the Boarder Baby Project, a charity dedicated to helping thousands of newborns left each year in maternity wards. As part of his role he made his first-ever live performance as a solo artist at a benefit for The Little Blue House (which provided transitional housing for abandoned children) at a black-tie gala in Washington, D.C., on November 12, 1994. The concert, which also featured R & B groups After 7 and El DeBarge, raised a record amount for the charity.

Men; songwriter award, also given to co-writers L.A. Reid and Daryl Simmons), 1993.

Grammy Award for Producer of the Year, 1993. (Production team of L.A. Reid and Babyface tied with the team of Daniel Lanois and Brian Eno.)

Grammy Award for Album of the Year, for *The Bodyguard,* Original Soundtrack Album, 1994. (Award given to all producers on the album and Whitney Houston.)

Grammy Award for Best Male R & B Vocal Performance, for "When Can I See You," 1995.

Grammy Award for Best R & B Song (songwriter award), for "I'll Make Love to You," (performed by Boyz II Men), 1995.

Grammy Awards for Producer of the Year, 1996 and 1997.

Grammy Award for Best R & B Song (songwriter award), for "Exhale (Shoop Shoop)," (performed by Whitney Houston), 1997.

Has won 38 BMI (Broadcast Music Industry) Awards.

Selected Discography

Lovers (Solar), 1987, and (Epic), 1989.

Tender Lovers (Epic), 1989.

A Closer Look (Epic), 1991.

For the Cool in You (Epic), 1993.

The Day (Epic), 1996.

Further Reading

Collier, Aldore, "Babyface! Top Hit-maker Has It All," *Ebony*, April 1996, p. 26.

Farley, Christopher John, "A Hitmaker and a Gentleman," *Time*, November 11, 1996, p. 90.

Helligar, Jeremy, "Babyface Boom," *People Weekly*, February 27, 1995, p. 73.

Randolph, Laura B., "Babyface Shows Off His New Home and Opens Up about His Bride and His Split with L.A.," *Ebony*, July 1994, p. 36.

Smith, R. J., "Soul Man of Suburbia," *New York Times Magazine*, January 5, 1997, p. 22.

Contact Information

Epic Records
2100 Colorado Ave.
Santa Monica, CA 90404

Web Site

http://www.wallofsound.com/artists/babyface/index.html

BOYZ II Men

American rhythm and blues group

Formed in Philadelphia, Pennsylvania, in 1988

Boyz II Men is one of the top record sellers of all time. They have sold twenty-seven million records—twenty-one million albums and six million singles—ranking the group as number six on the list of top U.S. record sellers after releasing just three albums. They have made history by outselling Elvis Presley and the Beatles. Boyz II Men's success rejuvenated the Motown label and earned the group a contract valued somewhere between twenty and thirty million dollars. What makes Boyz II Men so special—in addition to their ability to create hit music—is their romanticism and their wholesomeness in an era of grunge and gansta rockers.

That Philly Sound

Influenced by Motown and Philadelphia groups of the past, Boyz II Men offers traditionally styled material to rhythm and blues audiences, but the group appeals to pop fans as well. Growing up in Philadelphia, the members of Boyz II Men—Michael McCary, Nathan Morris, Wanya Morris, and Shawn Stockman—

"Our music makes you feel good. We know life isn't all peaches-and-cream, but sometimes you just want to relax and forget about all that." –Shawn Stockman

were predisposed to *a capella* "street-corner" harmonies known as the Philly sound. "One of the things we want is to bring back that Philly sound," explained Shawn Stockman in the *Philadelphia Daily News*. "In the past, there was a time when Philadelphia was nonexistent as far as the music industry was concerned. Nothing was happening. We saw that Philly has all this talent. We were around it and we had a little something going on, so we said, 'Let's bring back that Philly sound and try to put Philly back on the music industry map.'" The group also incorporated the Motown sounds of such pop greats as the Temptations, Diana Ross, and Stevie Wonder into their singing as well.

Big voices

Each member of Boyz II Men has a strong, robust voice. "There's not a weak link in the bunch," record producer Jimmy Jam told *Time*. With their incredible singing skills, Boyz II Men refined the close four-part harmonies of doo-wop and laid the vocal foundation for the next generation of singing groups.

"We saw that Philly has all this talent. We were around it and we had a little something going on, so we said, 'Let's bring back that Philly sound and try to put Philly back on the music industry map.'"

McCary, Morris, Morris, and Stockman trained together at the High School of Creative and Performing Arts in Philadelphia. In 1988 they performed as the Unique Attractions until New Edition's Michael Bivins discovered them at a Philadelphia talent show. Within six years they became stars. In 1992, Boyz II Men toured with **Hammer** (see entry) to promote their first album *Cooleyhighharmony*.

Big sellers

Their debut effort, *Cooleyhighharmony*, combined dance tunes with soulful ballads. The album entered the U.S. charts at number three and remained in the Top Twenty for six months. It initially sold nine million copies—eleven million in follow-up sales—making *Cooleyhighharmony* the all-time best selling rhythm and blues record by a group to date.

"End of the Road," a single from *Cooleyhighharmony*, commanded considerable attention in its own right. Written by renowned composer **Babyface** (see entry), this single topped *Billboard*'s chart for thirteen weeks, breaking Elvis Presley's long-standing record for "Don't Be Cruel." The individual sales of "End of the Road" earned it certification as a platinum record, and it became one of the biggest selling singles in history.

Boyz II Men released their second major album, *II*, in 1994. This album distinguished itself as the first record from the Motown label to debut at number one on the charts since Stevie Wonder's *Songs in the Key of Life*. *II* sold twelve million copies, putting it at number four on the list of all-time best selling records.

"I'll Make Love to You," a single from *II*, debuted at number eight on the charts and remained at number one for fourteen historic weeks. (Boyz II Men's "On Bended Knee" replaced it when "I'll Make Love to You" fell from the number one spot.) A certified platinum record, "I'll Make Love to You" became the fastest-selling single of 1994.

In 1996 Boyz II Men released the single "One Sweet Day" with singer Mariah Carey. The song debuted at number one on the Hot 100 and as number two on the Hot Rhythm and Blues charts. "One Sweet Day" stayed on the charts for sixteen weeks—six weeks longer than The Beatles' "Can't Buy Me Love"—making it the record with the longest run in chart history. In total, the double platinum single sold more than two million copies.

Like their albums and singles, Boyz II Men's videos sold extremely well. *Us II U,* released in 1993, earned platinum certification for its sales, as did *Then II Now* two years later.

Ah! Romance

One reason for the success of Boyz II Men—in addition to their great vocal style—was their wholesomeness. While many of their contemporaries promoted violence, lust, or despair, Boyz II Men promoted just one thing: romance—pure and simple love. "America right now is being bombarded with reality, whether it's talk shows or rap or trials on TV or C-SPAN," noted Motown president Jheryl Busby. "This is the group that once again is introducing us to fantasy. Love affairs. Romance."

Truly tasteful

Their wholesomeness reflected the group's positive attitudes toward life in

general. Recognized as performers with positive values, Boyz II Men received honorary doctorates in humane letters from Drexel University for being role models to youth. Group members credited God with their success and said that religion plays a major role in their lives. With this value system supporting their work, Boyz II Men's videos frequently appeared on Z Music Television, a Christian-based channel available in twenty million homes. "Boyz II Men are not on a Christian label," explained Suzanne Holtermann, manager of marketing for Z Music Television in *Billboard,* "but certainly their music videos would go very well on our network, and they are a very popular, well-known act."

Since the group's appeal spanned generations, Boyz II Men has been invited to perform for a variety of dignitaries and at important events. In 1995, for example, they sang both for Pope John Paul II and for President Bill Clinton at the White House. In 1996, Boyz II Men performed the national anthem at the closing of the Olympic Games held in Atlanta, Georgia. "Even old guys like me can appreciate what they're doing," said Harry Ellis Dickson, retired conductor of the Boston Pops in *Time*. "That's one reason I think they're going to be around for a long time."

Indeed, Boyz II Men has ambitions for the future. "We have a long way to go as far as achieving the kind of success we want," Stockman said. "You know, like the Beatles—that kind of longevity. That's what we're trying to establish."

Selected Awards

American Music Awards, Favorite New Rhythm and Blues/Soul Artist, 1992.

Billboard Music Awards, 1) Top Duo or Group Singles Artist, 2) Top Singles Artist, 3) Top Single for "End of the Road," and 4) Top 40 Radio Monitor Tracks for "End of the Road," 1992.

Grammy Awards, Best Rhythm and Blues Performance with Vocals by a Duo or Group, for *Cooleyhighharmony*, 1992.

NAACP Image Awards, Best New Artist, 1992.

Soul Train Music Awards, Best New Rhythm and Blues/Soul Artist, 1992.

American Music Awards, 1) Favorite Pop/Rock Single, and 2) Favorite Soul/Rhythm and Blues Band, 1993.

Grammy Awards, Best Rhythm and Blues Performance with Vocals by a Duo or Group, for "End of the Road," 1993.

NAACP Image Awards, Best Vocal Group, 1993.

Soul Train Music Awards, 1) Best Rhythm and Blues/Soul Group Single, 2) Rhythm and Blues Song of the Year, and 3) Rhythm and Blues Music Video of the Year, 1993.

World Music Awards, International New Group of the Year, 1993.

American Music Awards, 1) Favorite Pop Rock Single, and 2) Favorite Rhythm and Blues Single, both for "I'll Make Love to You," and 3) Favorite Rhythm and Blues Band, Duo, or Group, 1995.

Blockbuster Entertainment Awards, 1) Top Rhythm and Blues Group, and 2) Top CD, 1995.

Grammy Awards, 1) Best Rhythm and Blues Performance by a Duo or Group for "I'll Make Love to You," and 2) Best Rhythm and Blues Album for *II*, 1995.

Soul Train Music Awards, 1) Best Rhythm and Blues/Soul Single by a Group, Band, or Duo for "I'll Make Love to You," and 2) Best Rhythm and Blues/Soul Album for *II*, 1995.

American Music Awards, 1) Favorite Band, Duo, or Group, and 2) Favorite Soul/Rhythm and Blues Album, 1996.

Soul Train Music Awards, Sammy Davis, Jr., Award for Entertainer of the Year, 1996.

Selected Discography

Cooleyhighharmony (Motown), 1991.

Christmas Interpretations (Motown), 1993.

II (Motown), 1994.

Further Reading

Farley, Christopher John, "No Grunge, No Gangstas," *Time,* September 5, 1994, p. 70.

Light, Alan, "Motown's Baby Boyz," *Rolling Stone,* March 5, 1992, pp. 21-22.

McQueen, Mari, "Just One of the Boyz," *People Weekly,* November 13, 1995, pp. 99-100.

Townsel, Lisa Jones, "At Home and in Harmony with Boyz II Men," *Ebony,* February 1996, pp. 86-88.

Contact Information

Motown Records
6255 Sunset Blvd., 17th Fl.
Los Angeles, CA 90028

Web Site

www.polygram_us.com/polygram/motown/
    artists/boyz2men/

BOBBY BROWN

American rhythm and blues singer

Born Robert Baresford Brown in Roxbury, Massachusetts, (near Boston) on February 5, 1969

"I love it! There's something about being in front of a crowd that just hypes me up and makes me want to be the center of attention."

—Bobby Brown

For a while Bobby Brown was the hottest rhythm and blues star around. He won all the major music honors. His records dominated the charts in America and abroad, and fans rioted just to get his autograph.

Big dreams began in Boston projects

Since he was a child, Brown aspired to greatness in the music industry. His big dreams began in Boston in the tough neighborhoods of the Orchard Park projects. He first performed publicly at age three when his mother put him on stage during intermission at a concert by soul-singer James Brown. But his real chance at stardom came in 1981 when he co-founded the New Edition, one of the most popular rhythm and blues groups of the 1980s. "I was the one always saying we can sing our way out of Boston and onto 'Soul Train,'" Brown recalled in *Newsweek*. "The others would laugh at me because I had these really big dreams, but I knew we had what it took."

Indeed, New Edition—Brown, Ronnie DeVoe, Ricky Bell, Michael Bivins, Ralph Tresant, and Johnny Gill—became a huge success. As teen idols, they sold more than twenty million records, including their certified platinum *All for Love* album. New Edition's music featured an urban beat, romanticism, and dancing—lots of fancy dance moves, especially by Brown.

Brown clearly commanded the most attention in the group. His singing and dancing talents marked him as New Edition's strongest performer. "He's ... got the most style and charisma," wrote Allison Samuels and Karen Schoemer in *Newsweek*. "When it's time to get down on the dance floor, the others go part way down; Bobby goes way, way down."

New Jack Swing

Brown left New Edition in 1986 for a solo career. His first album, *King of Stage,* reached number eighty-eight on the U.S. charts and resulted in two singles: "Girlfriend" and "Girl Next Door." Brown's second album, however, established him as a star, independent of New Edition.

Don't Be Cruel, released in 1988, defined New Jack Swing—a swank, macho form of hip-hop rhythm and blues. The album, according to *Time* magazine, "marked 'new jack swing' as a creative hotbed of black pop." Produced by Los Angeles-based hitmakers L. A. Reid and **Babyface** (see entry), *Don't Be Cruel* combined hip-hop, soul, and dance music and met with wide popular appeal. The album stayed on the charts for ninety-seven weeks, ultimately reaching number one in the United States and number three in the United Kingdom. Its sales totaled eight million copies.

Applauded as a daring and exciting album, *Don't Be Cruel* showed Brown's versatility as an entertainer. He effectively performed funk, rhythm and blues, and dance numbers as well as soulful ballads. The first single released from the album, "Don't Be Cruel"—a certified gold record—topped the U.S. rhythm and blues charts in 1988. "My Prerogative," Brown's second single from *Don't Be Cruel,* became his first solo number one hit on *Billboard's* charts. "My Prerogative" earned certification as a gold record in 1989 and was frequently seen as a video—featuring Brown's dancing—on MTV. "Roni" served as Brown's third consecutive U.S. Top Ten hit.

The singer issued three more gold records in 1989—the dance video hit "Every Little Step," "On Our Own" from the *Ghostbusters II* soundtrack, and "Rock Wit' Cha."

The 1990s began strongly for Brown. He released *Dance ! ... Ya Know It!,* an album of remixed hits, as well as *His Prerogative,* a collection of videos issued by MTV. Both received platinum certifications for topping the one million mark in sales. Brown's 1992 album, *Bobby,* reached number two in the United States and sold two million copies. Despite being called overcalculated and underinspired, the album included two certified gold singles: "Humpin' Around" and "Good Enough."

Two sides of the coin

"He has a temper from hell," explained Whitney Houston about her husband Bobby Brown, the reputed "bad boy" of rhythm and blues. With a history of combativeness, womanizing, and partying to excess, Brown earned his notoriety.

Growing up in a rough neighborhood taught Brown to fight, and fight he frequently does. "If a man disrespects me," the singer told People Weekly, "then he better be prepared to defend himself. My father taught me that if I was ever disrespected by another man, then that man has to apologize to me as a man or I'll have to make him apologize." Some examples of Brown's altercations include being charged with his bodyguards in the 1992 beating of Lee Ruckan in Atlanta. In 1994 Orlando, Florida, police also arrested Brown in the beating of a nightclub patron. A year later Brown faced misdemeanor battery charges in Los Angeles for kicking a hotel security guard.

Besides fighting, Brown is known for his womanizing. Before marrying Houston, Brown fathered three children by two different women. The singer then was involved in a paternity suit regarding a child born after his marriage.

Brown also has been sanctioned for his overtly sexual performances on stage. In 1989, for example, the singer was arrested and fined $652 for sexually suggestive dancing during a concert in Georgia. Later in 1995 he was arrested and fined $850 for lewd acts during a performance at the Augusta-Richmond County Civic Center.

Finally, the singer has had problems with alcohol. After years of hard partying and at least one arrest in 1996 for driving under the influence, Brown underwent treatment for alcohol abuse at the Betty Ford Center in the mid-1990s.

Looking back, Brown told Newsweek. "I had my fun. I did what any young person does on their own with money. I was never out to hurt anybody. I was just having a good time."

Problems, problems

When Brown married superstar Whitney Houston in 1992, his aspirations seemed endangered by her skyrocketing career. Was Brown becoming "Mr. Whitney Houston"? His 1992 album was a commercial disappointment, and his finances were quickly deteriorating. By 1994, Brown sued his business affairs managers, charging negligence in handling his affairs. Though the singer earned about $27.7 million between 1989 and 1993, he faced financial ruin. With his Atlanta mansion—valued between $1.3 and 1.5 million—at auction due to tax liens, Brown nearly lost his home. Nippy, Inc. (Houston's management company) purchased the estate.

After two tumultuous years together—and one daughter, Bobbi Kristine—Brown and Houston separated in 1994 amid tabloid claims that Brown battered his wife. The parting was brief, however. "I don't want to talk about my personal life except to say I've been blessed," Brown told *People Weekly* in 1996. "We're together. We love our little daughter."

New(er) edition

With order restored at home, Brown returned to New Edition to rebuild his career. The reformation of the famous group was the most promoted reunion of the year in 1996. Still, the group's motives were more commercial than sentimental. "No one should believe we got back together for the hell of it," revealed Michael Bivins. The singer told *Newsweek* in 1996: "I can see things clearing up for me. This is my year."

Selected Awards

Billboard's Year in Music Awards, 1) Top Pop Male Singles Artist, 2) Top Pop Male Album Artist, and 3) Top Black Artist, 1989.

SKC Boston Music Awards, 1) Act of the Year, 2) Rhythm and Blues Act of the Year, 3) Top Male Vocalist, and 4) Top Rock Single for "My Prerogative," 1989.

Soul Train Music Awards, Best Male Rhythm and Blues/Urban Contemporary Album of the Year, for *Don't Be Cruel,* 1989.

American Music Awards, 1) Favorite Male Pop/Rock Artist and 2) Favorite Soul/Rhythm and Blues Album, 1990.

Grammy Awards, Best Male Rhythm and Blues Vocal Performance, for "Every Little Step," 1990.

Rolling Stone Critics' Awards, Best Rhythm and Blues Artist, 1990.

Rolling Stone Readers' Picks Awards, 1) Best New Male Singer, and 2) Best Rhythm and Blues Artist, 1990.

SKC Boston Music Awards, 1) Outstanding Male Vocalist, and 2) Outstanding Rhythm and Blues Act, 1990.

Coca-Cola Atlanta Music Awards, Outstanding Male Vocalist, 1992.

American Music Awards, Favorite Male Soul/Rhythm and Blues Artist, 1993.

Boston Music Awards, 1) Act of the Year, 2) Outstanding Rhythm and Blues Vocalist, and 3) Outstanding Rhythm and Blues Album for *Bobby,* 1993.

Selected Discography

King of Stage (MCA), 1987.

Don't Be Cruel (MCA), 1988.

Dance! ... Ya Know It! (MCA), 1990.

Bobby (MCA), 1992.

Remixes in the Key of B (MCA), 1993.

Further Reading

Castro, Peter, "Mr. Misunderstood," *People Weekly,* September 16, 1996, p. 32.

Cunningham, Kim, "Gotta Dance," *People Weekly,* April 22, 1996, p. 149.

"Disappointingly Small Step," *Time,* September 21, 1992, p. 69.

Samuels, Allison, and Karen Schoemer, "From Boyz to Men," *Newsweek,* September 9, 1996, p. 66.

Contact Information

MCA Records
70 Universal City Plaza
Universal City, CA 91608

TEVIN CAMPBELL

American rhythm and blues singer

Born November 19, 1978, in Waxahachie, Texas (near Dallas)

"Singing is still the important thing to me. I love singing. I wouldn't be putting myself through all this if I didn't."

With three popular R & B albums on the shelf before he turned eighteen, Tevin Campbell has been compared to R & B child singing sensations Stevie Wonder and Michael Jackson. Demonstrating a passion for singing by the age of four, Campbell began by singing gospel, first as a choir member, and then as a soloist at Jacob's Chapel in Waxahachie, Texas, a small town just south of Dallas. Apart from his favorite singer, Aretha Franklin, his greatest influence as a child was probably his mother, Rhonda Byrd. Then a postal worker, she was known to the Texas congregation as "little Aretha."

Born in Texas in 1978, Campbell moved with his mother to the Los Angeles, California, area as a child. In 1988 a friend of Campbell's mother arranged for the budding young singer to audition for jazz flutist Bobbie Humphrey by singing over the phone to her in New York. Humphrey took an immediate interest in Campbell and submitted an audio and videotape to Warner Bros., which led to a meeting with Benny Medina, the label's senior vice president and general sales manager of black music.

First break came with producer Quincy Jones

Campbell's first big break came when Quincy Jones was in the process of assembling an all-star cast for his *Back on the Block* album. By the ripe old age of twelve, Campbell was assigned to Jones's label, Qwest, and spotlighted on two tracks of the 1990 platinum-selling, Grammy-winning album. One of those songs, "Tomorrow (Better You, Better Me)," made it to number one on *Billboard's* Hot R & B Singles chart.

Later in 1990, Campbell was featured in the musical film, *Listen Up: The Lives of Quincy Jones,* and performed on "Listen Up," a song paying tribute to Jones. Within a year, Campbell was whisked away to Paisley Park Studios in Minneapolis, Minnesota, to record "Round and Round" for **Prince's** (see entry) movie *Graffiti Bridge,* in which he also snagged a role. "Round and Round" was considered by many critics to be the best single from the soundtrack; it earned Campbell a Grammy nomination for best male R & B vocalist.

Can you spell T.E.V.I.N.?

Campbell had hoped that Prince would take charge of his first solo outing, but co-executive producers Jones and Medina had other ideas. As Jones told Dennis Hunt of the *Los Angeles Times,* "Tevin needed to work with some different producers, to explore several directions and maximize his potential." His debut album, *T.E.V.I.N.,* features songs written by Al B. Sure! and Kyle West; Marilyn and Alan Bergman; Narada Michael Walden; and several tracks cowritten by

Singer found time for special projects

Following the release of T.E.V.I.N., Campbell found time to contribute to three special projects: Handel's Messiah, a Grammy Award-winning album produced by Mervyn Warren of Take 6; a Special Olympics Christmas album, featuring Campbell's rendition of "Oh Holy Night"; and Barcelona Gold, the 1992 Olympics album, which includes Campbell's "One Song."

Campbell. The only Prince-influenced song on the release is the soul-mix edit of "Round and Round," which may explain why the album captures less of the much-anticipated funk attitude Campbell displayed in *Graffiti Bridge.*

Campbell's thirteen-track solo album was warmly received upon its release in November 1991, and the single "Tell Me What You Want Me to Do" became Campbell's second number one R & B hit, reaching number six on the pop chart. Connie Johnson of the *Los Angeles Times* gave it three out of four stars and declared the single "positively stunning." Phyl Garland of *Stereo Review* called it "one of the best debut vocal albums I have heard in many, many years.... [Campbell] sings with an authority of attack, certainty of tone, and maturity of interpretation that immediately command respect. There is a passion in his work that marks the true artist."

"I had no idea we would create a household name with Tevin before the album came out," Benny Medina told Janine McAdams of *Billboard* magazine. "This album was three years in the making, but Tevin has proven he's one of the blessed ones. When you take someone this talented and expose him to great talents like Quincy and Prince, he can only grow."

Campbell showed he was ready

The singer's second solo effort, the 1993 release *I'm Ready,* was also produced by Jones and Medina. "I wanted to make a more mature-sounding album to reflect my current state of mind," the then fifteen-year-old Campbell explained to J. R. Reynolds in *Billboard* magazine. "*I'm Ready* says a lot about who I am as a person because of the things I've been through during the last four years or so. I hope people will see that I'm not the same young kid that I was on my first album."

Part of Campbell's emotional development during this time stemmed from his difficult first meeting with his father, who lived "somewhere in Arkansas." Campbell related the encounter to Christian Wright in a *Vibe* interview: "I wanted to meet him. It's not that I wanted to bond with him or have some sort of relationship, 'cause my mother raised all three of us on her own. I just wanted to meet him 'cause I had never met my father."

When *I'm Ready* made its debut at Number Four on the Top R & B Albums chart, Campbell left no doubt he was capable of tackling almost any style of song. A diverse mix of ballads, soul, dance tracks, and a smattering of rap are included on the release, with Prince's influence

evident on about a quarter of the tracks. "Can We Talk," "I'm Ready," and "Always in My Heart" all reached the top ten on *Billboard*'s R & B chart, with "Can We Talk" topping the chart for three weeks.

After three years, Campbell came back to the world

After the success of *I'm Ready,* Campbell made a wise decision—he decided to put his career on hold and pay more attention to growing up. Removing himself from the spotlight, he spent about three years discovering himself and what growing up was all about. When Campbell was ready to return to his recording career in 1996, he recorded his third album, *Back to the World.* The album featured a dozen new songs, a variety of producers, and new tracks written and produced by Campbell himself. Like his previous albums, this one showed a more mature Campbell and a more polished singer.

Selected Awards

"Round and Round," Grammy Award Nomination, Best Male R & B Vocalist, 1992.

Selected Discography

T.E.V.I.N. (Warner Brothers/ Qwest), 1991.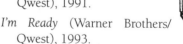

I'm Ready (Warner Brothers/ Qwest), 1993.

Back to the World (Warner Brothers/Qwest), 1996.

Further Reading

Billboard, November 16, 1991.

Garland, Phyl, "T.E.V.I.N.," *Stereo Review,* June 1992.

 Parents Aren't Supposed to Like It

Levitt, Shelley, "Sizzling Campbell," *People Weekly,* January 27, 1992, p. 77.

Los Angeles Times, December 15, 1991.

Malkin, Nina, "17 Questions: Tevin Campbell," *Seventeen,* June 1994, p. 79.

"Tevin Campbell Attracting Teens and Adults with Hit Album 'I'm Ready,'" *Jet,* March 14, 1994, p. 14.

"Tevin Campbell Comes 'Back to the World' with New Album," *Jet,* July 8, 1996, p. 61.

"Tevin Campbell: 19 and Ready," *Ebony,* December 1994, p. 24.

Vibe, November 1993; March 1994.

Contact Information

Warner Brothers Records
3300 Warner Blvd.
Burbank, CA 91505-4694

Web Site

http://www.wbr.com/tevin/

En Vogue

American rhythm and blues group

Formed in
San Francisco, California, in 1988

"You have to, first and foremost, respect each other's individuality. When you learn to respect those differences, you can move forward." –Terry Ellis

En Vogue—Cindy Herron, Dawn Robinson, Terry Ellis, and Maxine Jones—are making a statement in what has long been considered a man's industry. As the spokespersons of New Jill Swing, they have redefined "girl groups" forever. The girl group phenomenon started in the 1950s and 1960s. Original girl groups were comprised of well-mannered, noncontroversial, good—but not great—singers. While these socially acceptable ladies created very nice public relations for the media of the day, the groups actually were notorious for their infighting, cattiness, and fierce solo ambitions. En Vogue's New Jill Swing changed all that.

Funky divas

By definition, New Jill Swing requires that each member of a girl group have a powerful voice and behave boldly—from singing sexy songs to wearing revealing clothing to establishing herself as a successful solo artist. In short, each must have the sound and image of a funky diva.

Together En Vogue have a remarkable four-octave range

Group success

This was the plan when En Vogue signed with noted producers Denzil Foster and Thomas McElroy. The producers intended to recreate The Supremes, a great group of the 1960s that faded when their lead singer, Diana Ross, opted for a solo career. Foster and McElroy wanted each member of the group to pursue individual stardom as well as the group's success. The exceptional talents and drive of Cindy Herron, Dawn Robinson, Terry Ellis, and Maxine Jones positioned them well for group and individual success. Together, En Vogue had a remarkable four-octave range; individually, each member had a huge potential for success.

En Vogue sold more than four million records in just a few years. Their first album, released in 1991, was certified platinum. The group's next album, *Funky Divas,* sold more than three million copies and dominated the charts, reaching the number one spot on the rhythm-and-blues album charts and number eight on *Billboard*'s Top 200. Two single releases—"My Lovin' (You're Never Gonna Get It)" and "Giving Him Something He Can Feel"—both achieved number one status on the rhythm-and-blues singles charts. En Vogue's albums and singles also received numerous

But in the meantime, I'm also working on other avenues for expanding my horizons in the business. The challenge is to grow and learn."

Following the 1993 release of *Runaway Love,* En Vogue took an extended break that lasted until they recorded their 1997 album, *EV3.* While Terry Ellis released a solo album, *Southern Gal,* in 1995, Cindy Herron and Maxine Jones started families. In December 1996 En Vogue released the single, "Don't Let Go (Love)," for the soundtrack of the "girls-in-the-hood" film, *Set it Off.* In April 1997 Dawn Robinson announced that she was leaving the group. The 1997 album, *EV3,* featured the group performing as a trio.

The independent work of En Vogue members seemed to rejuvenate and refresh them for new work with the group. Their forays into acting, solo albums, and production challenged them in new and different ways, but at no time threatened their commitment to En Vogue—the girl group that changed the way the public would view all future girl groups.

awards, including prestigious Grammy and American Music Awards.

Individual achievements

As planned, En Vogue's members attained individual success as well. Both Cindy Herron and Maxine Jones effectively pursued acting careers, but Terry Ellis was the first to issue a solo album. Her earlier success with En Vogue made her a "proven commodity" at record stores. As *Billboard* explained, the album gave Ellis "the chance she deserves to prove her chops as an individual stylist worthy of widespread approval." For her part, Ellis looked at the album as an opportunity to fulfill some personal goals, yet she remained committed to En Vogue.

Dawn Robinson also issued a solo album—and established her own production company, Break A Dawn. She explained similar sentiments to those of Ellis in *Billboard:* "It's important to know that I can be successful in other aspects of the business as well as with En Vogue. As long as En Vogue works I'll be there.

Selected Awards

Soul Train Music Awards, Best Rhythm and Blues/Urban Contemporary Single by Group or Duo, 1991.

MTV Video Music Awards, Best Choreography in a Video Award, for "My Lovin' (You're Never Gonna Get It)," 1992.

American Music Awards, Favorite Album, Soul or Rhythm and Blues, for *Funky Divas,* 1993.

Rolling Stone Critics' Picks, Best Rhythm and Blues Group Award, 1993.

Bay Area Music Awards, 1) Outstanding Urban/Contemporary Album or EP, for *Funky Divas,* and 2) Outstanding Female Vocalist, 1993.

Grammy Award nominations for Best Rock Duo or Group and for Best Short Video, 1993.

MTV Video Music Awards, 1) Best Rhythm and Blues Video, 2) Best Dance Video, and 3) Best Choreography in a Video, all for "Free Your Mind," 1993.

Soul Train Music Awards, 1) Best Rhythm and Blues/Soul Album for *Funky Divas,* and 2) Sammy Davis, Jr., Award for Entertainer of the Year, 1993.

MVPA Awards, Best Urban/Rhythm and Blues Song Award, for "Whatta Man" (with Salt-n-Pepa), 1994.

American Music Awards, Best Soul or Rhythm and Blues Band, Duo or Group, 1994.

MTV Video Music Awards, 1) Best Dance Video, 2) Best Rhythm and Blues Video, and 3) Best Choreography, all for "Whatta Man" (with Salt-n-Pepa), 1994.

NAACP Image Awards, Outstanding Duo or Group Award, 1994.

Grammy Award nomination, Best Rhythm and Blues Performance by Duo or Group with Vocals, for "Whatta Man" (with Salt-n-Pepa), 1995.

Selected Discography

Born to Sing (Atlantic), 1991.

Remix to Sing (East West), 1991.

Funky Divas (East West), 1992.

Runaway Love (East West), 1993.

"Don't Let Go (Love)" (East West), 1996.

EV3, (East West), 1997.

Further Reading

Chaprell, Kevin, "What's Happening to Female Groups," *Ebony,* March 1996, p. 46.

"En Vogue for Real," *Seventeen,* December 1992, p. 88.

Reynolds, J. R., "IAAAM '94 Focuses on Opportunity, Creativity, and a Wonder-ful Performer," *Billboard,* June 18, 1994, p. 21.

Reynolds, J. R., "En Vogue's Ellis Steps Out with East West Solo Debut," *Billboard,* October 12, 1995, p. 13.

Ritz, David, "Viva Divas," *Rolling Stone,* July 8, 1993, p. 64.

"Still-Fab Four," *People Weekly,* April 14, 1997, p. 27.

Contact Information

Atco/EastWest Records
75 Rockefeller Plaza
New York, NY 10019

Web Site

www.execpc.com\~mwildt\envogue.html

Prince

(THE ARTIST FORMERLY KNOWN AS PRINCE)

Funk, R & B, soul singer, guitarist, producer, actor, executive

Born Prince Rogers Nelson in Minneapolis, Minnesota, on June 7, 1958

"When I'm reading a review of my work, this is what I'm listening to (a lack of understanding). They're (critics) always a year late." –Prince

To his devoted fans, he's Prince, "His Royal Badness," "The Artist Formerly Known As Prince," or simply, "The Artist"— who rewrote 1980s and 1990s music-making rules single-handedly. To those who dismiss his name changes and his penchant for junking entire albums, he's "The Artist Formerly Known As Talented," as radio "shock jock" Howard Stern chose to label him.

Love Prince or not, it's hard to dismiss him, even after his contract-clearing *Chaos and Disorder* (1996) album sold only 100,000 copies. The next year, Prince sold out his first arena show in Chicago in over a decade, at $75 per ticket—and that was during a slow concert season when the Chicago Bulls won a fifth basketball title in 1997.

It's all part of his penchant for spontaneiety. Freed of a twenty-year deal with Warner Brothers, Prince planned to release what and when he wishes on his own NPG (New Power Generation) label. Such devil-may-care attitudes reaped megahits like "When Doves Cry," which benefited when Prince took out the bass lines.

"Prince is a very mercurial guy," said sax player Eric Leeds in *Rolling Stone*. "He could change his mind tomorrow."

Home-life seemed complicated

Born Prince Rogers Nelson in Minneapolis, Minnesota, on June 7, 1958, he established himself at a young age as a creative prodigy bent on doing things his way. His jazz pianist father named the boy after his band, The Prince Rogers Trio; mother Mattie worked as a public school teacher. Prince learned guitar fundamentals from his father, but found no peace at home—from which he ran away at age twelve, citing problems with his stepfather. Eventually, he lived at friend Andre Anderson's (later Andre Cymone) house, using their basement jams to master two dozen instruments. It was the start of his famed nonstop creativity.

"Why do people have to know who I am?"

By age sixteen, Prince had already quit high school, where he'd met future bassist Mark Brown (later known as Brown Mark), Terry Lewis, and vocalist Morris Day (both later of the Time). His first sessions occurred in 1976, when Prince was invited to play guitar by Brooklyn artist Pepe Willie at a Minneapolis studio. Sound engineer Chris Moon became his first manager, funding part of the studio time in exchange for a portion of the proceeds from anything released from the sessions. By 1978, Prince had signed a long-term contract with Warner Bros. He wrote, sang, and played virtually everything on his 1978 debut album, *For You.*

A suggestive single, "Soft & Wet," established Prince in the R & B (rhythm and blues) market by selling 350,000 copies, though mainstream radio avoided it. His second, self-titled 1979 album improved that track record, quickly selling 500,000 copies (and scoring a number twenty-two chart position) before going platinum (one million copies sold) in 1980. Its "I Wanna Be Your Lover" single made number eleven in January 1980. Those albums soon seemed outdated, however, as Prince cut the next, *Dirty Mind* (1980), which scored with R & B audiences but failed to reach the pop market.

'1999' became Prince's time

From the start, Prince cultivated a sense of mystery about himself and his background. This baffled mainstream audiences, who had yet to hear of him, even as Prince demanded in 1979: "Why do people have to know who I am?"

The consequences of people not knowing who he was could be brutal. In June 1980, Prince visited Britain—only to cancel after one night, due to poor attendance. In 1981, he got booed off by a Los Angeles crowd wishing to see the headlining Rolling Stones. That year, two singles from *Controversy* did well on the R & B charts, but again missed the pop charts.

Critics had trouble interviewing Prince, finding him "struck dumb by very simple questions," but those critics had a big surprise coming — the *1999* album. Released in 1982 and supported by a six-month tour—which included Prince and The Revolution, the Time, and the all-girl Vanity 6—the album reached the Top Ten by mid-1983. It made Prince the planet's biggest, baddest crossover artist (able to reach both mainstream and R & B audiences), showcased a hot band in The Revolution, and established suggestive lyrical content as a selling point on party singles like "Little Red Corvette" and the title track.

By 1984, Prince would even surpass those expectations with a $7 million film, *Purple Rain*, essentially a thinly-disguised autobiography. As "The Kid," Prince pouted and strutted past arch-rival Morris Day; despite a cast of mostly non-actors, *Purple Rain* made $60 million in just over two months at the box office.

Accompanying album outdid competition

The accompanying *Purple Rain* album, also credited to Prince and & The Revolution, began a twenty-four-week, number-one chart run; by 1994, it would sell nearly 11 million copies. The leadoff single, "When Doves Cry," made references to a troubled childhood ("Maybe I'm just too demanding / Maybe I'm just like my father") on its march to number one, followed by "Let's Go Crazy" at number two, and the anthemic title track at number eight.

Suddenly, Prince could no wrong. He won three American Music Awards and two Grammy Awards in 1985, the start of many trophies in his career. He also spun off numerous side projects and pushed Minneapolis onto the musical map. "That [tour] was the closest thing to the Beatles that I've ever experienced," keyboardist Matt Fink told *Mojo* about touring with Prince. "It was just insanity."

Following the chart-topping *Around the World in a Day* (1985), Prince announced his "retirement" from live performances, (He returned in mid-1986 with an extravagant tour for *Parade—Music from Under the Cherry Moon.*) *Around the World in a Day* had a more psychedelic bent than *Purple Rain*'s funk/rock mixture. Singles from the album included "Raspberry Beret" and "Pop Life."

That same year, Prince was among several artists, including heavy metal band Twisted Sister, to weather attacks from the Parents Music Resource Center (PMRC)—whose spokesman, Tipper Gore, wife of future Vice President Al Gore, questioned the lyric content of tracks like "Darling Nikki." Such lyrics, said Ms. Gore, were unfit for younger listeners, while rockers like Frank Zappa defended them on free speech grounds.

Record sales began slumping

In 1986, Prince again tried his hand at film, pushing *Under the Cherry Moon*'s original director into an "advisory" role and filming it in black and white. Critics called the results messy and disjointed, though Prince's *Parade—Music from Under the Cherry Moon* album—which found him reclaiming his old funk turf—still went platinum.

By the year's end, Prince had dismissed The Revolution—including loyal standbys Wendy and Lisa—in favor of his old one-man-band methods. An urban-themed double album, *Sign O' the Times,* reached number six on the U.S. chart in 1987, but its accompanying concert movie flopped. Having cancelled the American and British legs of a proposed world tour, Prince hoped the concert movie would fill in for audiences there.

To sax player Eric Leeds, "That was the biggest mistake he ever made.... He told us [that] the concert movie would fill in for the [cancelled American] tour ... but nobody went to see it."

Years later, Prince told *Rolling Stone* that *Sign O' the Times* had orignally been a triple album, until Warner Bros. objected: "'You'll overwhelm the market,' I was told. 'You can't do that.' Prince seemed to further stumble in 1988, when he abruptly pulled *The Black Album,* a collection of erotic funk and rap songs, from record stores. Critics called it a pre-release scam for *Lovesexy* (1988), which still went gold (500,000 copies sold) before the year's end. It was supported by European and American tours, Prince's first U.S. tour since 1984.

Rebounded with New Power Generation

By the end of the decade, Prince's star no longer beamed at its mid-1980s peak. His records still sold strongly, but critics found his ambition too much to stomach, especially when another film— *Graffiti Bridge* (1990)—flopped (although its soundtrack went gold). But he still had major successes. Prince experienced multi-platinum success with the *Batman* soundtrack album (1989), which spent six weeks at number one; he even performed songs like the number eighteen U.S. single, "Partyman," on NBC-TV's "Saturday Night Live." In 1991, he premiered the New Power Generation, considered his best band since The Revolution; its debut, *Diamonds and Pearls* (1991), restored him to multi-platinum status with two million copies sold. Singles from the album included the chart-topping "Cream" and the title track.

In 1992, NPG powered Prince's next album, known as *The Love Symbol Album* because its title was an unpronounceable symbol (allegedly symbolizing the union of male and female characteristics). Strong dance tracks such as "My Name Is Prince" and the rap-flavored "Sexy M/F" helped the album reach a number five chart position.

In April 1993, Prince startled his fans by announcing he would "retire" from recording to pursue multi-media ventures. Then, on his thirty-fifth birthday, he announced he was changing his name to the unpronounceable symbol used on his current album. Thereafter, he became known as The Artist Formerly Known As Prince (TAFKA), or simply as "The Artist." Associates like ex-Paisley Park manager Alan Leeds scoffed at Prince's retirement, suggesting he was tiring of his problems with Warner Bros. "There's only three things for sure in life," he told *Rolling Stone.* "We're all born, we all die, and Prince will make another record one of these days."

Wrestled freedom from Warner Bros.

By 1994, Prince's dissatisfaction was no secret; he began playing gigs with "slave" written on his cheek, citing a desire to release music faster than his contract permitted. By February, Paisley Park was closed; in March, a single, "The Most Beautiful Girl in the World," sold a million copies on the independent Bellmark label, after Warner Bros. wouldn't release it.

"If they rule the artist, is it really art?" Prince asked *Forbes* in 1996. "When you stop a man from dreaming, he becomes a slave. I had 'slave' on my face. Is that the end of the story?" Suddenly, Prince had changed his media-cool posture to include in-store appearances and interview blitzes to air his discontent.

At the same time, a flood of albums appeared to satisfy the contract. Hence, Prince's consent to release the previously recorded *The Black Album*. The poorly received *Come,* on the other hand, appeared without his approval in 1994. Fans also snapped up the career compilations, *The Hits I, The Hits II,,* and *The Hits/B-Sides,* sending them to platinum, while *The Gold Experience* (1995) did equally well, reaching number six—even if critics questioned the New Power Generation's presence on the tracks.

To *Rolling Stone's* Carol Cooper, *The Gold Experience* was "his most effortlessly eclectic set since 1987's *Sign O' the Times.*" Nobody said the same for *Chaos and Disorder,* a searing exploration of Prince's rock guitar abilities; assembled to satisfy the terms of his contract with Warner Brothers, it sold just 100,000 copies.

Gambled on triple-CD set

On November 19, 1996, Prince again played live at his studio complex for an "Emancipation Day" event—his official leave from Warner Bros. to issue records on his own NPG label. That same year, he married longtime stage dancer Mayte Jannell Garcia in a private Minneapolis ceremony. The couple had a son, reportedly named "Boy Gregory," who died just one week later, on October 23, 1996, of a rare bone condition. When assistants questioned the circumstances, about which Prince made no public comment, a grand jury investigated the matter—but ruled out any improper activity.

The baby's heartbeat was a prominent feature in "Sex in the Summer," one of thirty-six songs on a sprawling triple-CD set, *Emancipation,* which slid onto racks in fall 1996. Under his new distribution deal with EMI, Prince no longer commanded the $10 million advances he'd gotten before, but he stood to make far greater money. Listed at an imposing $36-40 price, critics considered the project a gamble—especially with slumping industry sales. *The Detroit News's* Jon Bream spoke for many when he called *Emancipation* "bold and often brilliant, sometimes riveting and sometimes indulgent, occasionally odd and occasionally ordinary." If nothing else, added Bream, it showed Prince to be "one of us—not a reclusive weirdo."

Judging by recent comments, Prince has no problems with that status. After selling 100 million records over twenty years, he sees himself as a multi-media enterpreneur. As an "evolved" family man, he's no longer worried about his image. "I had the knowledge and power all the time but did not know how to use it," he told *Ebony*. "But then I saw it instantaneously. I wasted time out of fear and ego. Other things kept me in a negative space. I now feel at peace."

Selected Awards

Favorite Single, Soul/R & B; Favorite Album, Soul/R & B; Favorite Album, Pop/Rock, American Music Awards, 1985.

BRIT Awards for 1) Best International Artist, and 2) Best Film Soundtrack for *Purple Rain,* 1985.

"Purple Rain," Grammy Award for Best Group Rock Vocal Performance; "I Feel for You," Grammy Award for Best R & B Song, 1985.

Purple Rain Soundtrack, Academy Award for Best Original Film Score, 1985.

"Raspberry Beret," MTV Video Music Award for Best Choreography,, 1986.

"U Got the Look," MTV Video Music Awards for 1) Best Male Video, and 2) Best Stage Performance, 1988.

Batman, Best Soundtrack, BRIT Awards. 1990.

Special Award of Achievement, American Music Awards, 1990.

Honored with "Prince Day," Minneapolis, Minnesota, 1990.

Best Songwriter, *Rolling Stone* Readers' Picks, 1991.

Best International Artist, BRIT Awards, 1992.

"Cream," MTV Video Music Award for Best Dance Video, 1992.

Best International Solo Artist, BRIT Awards, 1993.

Outstanding Contribution to the Music Industry, World Music Awards, 1994.

Best International Male Artist, BRIT Awards, 1995 and 1996.

Selected Discography

For You (Warner Brothers), 1978.

Prince (Warner Brothers), 1979.

Dirty Mind (Warner Brothers), 1980.

Controversy (Warner Brothers), 1981.

1999 (Warner Brothers), 1982.

Purple Rain (Warner Brothers), 1984.

Around the World in a Day (Warner Brothers/Paisley Park), 1985.

Parade—Music from "Under the Cherry Moon," (Warner Brothers/Paisley Park), 1986.

Sign O' the Times (Warner Brothers/Paisley Park), 1987.

Lovesexy (Warner Brothers/Paisley Park), 1988.

Batman (Warner Brothers/Paisley Park), 1989. Movie soundtrack.

Graffiti Bridge (Warner Brothers/Paisley Park), 1990. Movie soundtrack.

Diamonds and Pearls (Warner Brothers/Paisley Park), 1991.

love symbol (Warner Brothers/Paisley Park), 1992.

The Hits/The B-Sides (Warner Brothers/Paisley Park), 1993.

The Hits I (Warner Brothers/Paisley Park), 1993.

The Hits II (Warner Brothers/Paisley Park), 1993.

Come (Warner Brothers), 1994.

The Black Album (Warner Brothers), 1994.

The Gold Experience (Warner Brothers), 1995.

Chaos and Disorder (Warner Brothers), 1996.

Emancipation (NPG/Bellmark), 1996. Three-CD set.

Crystal Ball (NPG), 1997.

Films and soundtracks

Purple Rain, 1984.

Under the Cherry Moon, 1986.

Sign O' the Times, 1987. Concert movie.

Graffiti Bridge, 1990.

Other Soundtrack Albums

Girl 6 Soundtrack, 1996.

Further Reading

Bream, Jon, *"Emancipation,"* album review, *Detroit News,* November 23, 1996, p. 37D.

Cooper, Carol, "Two Princes," (*The Gold Experience* album review, *Rolling Stone,* November 2, 1995, p. 66.

DeCurtis, Anthony, "Free At Last: The Artist Formerly Known as Prince," *Rolling Stone,* November 28, 1996, p.61.

Farley, Christopher John, "The Artist Formerly Known as Hot," *Time,* November 25, 1996, p. 100.

Goldberg, Michael, "Prince Retires—Maybe: He Says He's Quitting Studio Work, but Don't Hold Your Breath," *Rolling Stone,* June 10, 1993.

Hill, Dave, *Prince: A Pop Life,* Crown, 1989.

Jacobson, Mark, "The Artist, Formerly Known (as Prince)," *Esquire,* March 1997, p. 39.

Levine, Joshua, "Prince Speaks: The Pop Singer Who Used To Go by the Name of Prince Tells of His Plans for Life after Warner Bros.," *Forbes,* September 23, 1996, p. 180.

Light, Alan, "Superbad!: The Elusive Prince Returns Triumphant," *Rolling Stone,* April 29, 1993, p. 15.

Norment, Lynn, "The Artist Formerly Known as Prince Has a New Wife, New Baby and a New Attitude," *Ebony,* January 1997, p. 128.

Sinclair, Tom, "Prince's Saddest Song: Singer May Be Keeping the Death of his Newborn Son Quiet," *Entertainment Weekly,* December 20, 1996, p. 7.

Weingarten, Mark, et al., "Prince: A Special Investigation," *Mojo,* February 1997, p. 38.

Contact Information

NPG
7801 Audobon Road
Chanhassen, MN 55317-8201

Web Site

http://wbr.com/goldexperience/

TLC

American rhythm and blues,
hip-hop trio

Formed 1991 in Atlanta, Georgia

With two multi-platinum albums and a string of top ten R & B hits, TLC scorched the airwaves in the first half of the 1990s with their unique blend of rap, rhythm and blues, and pop. That particular blend, known in some circles as New Jill Swing (New Jack Swing if performed by men), altered the traditional R & B girl group format made popular in the 1960s by such groups as the Supremes and Martha and the Vandellas.

Combining New Jill Swing with hard-hitting messages about love and sex, TLC spoke directly to young women about self-assertiveness and self-protection. And they weren't afraid to act as role models for their teenage listeners. With songs that redefined women's roles in relationships and in the world, TLC were confirmed in 1995 by the Recording Industry Association of America (RIAA) as the all-time biggest-selling all-female recording act in the United States.

Unfortunately, the group's career almost went up in flames when one of the members, Lisa "Left Eye" Lopes, was charged

"You don't have to wear tight slinky outfits to make it. We stand up for the (girl groups) who always wanted to dress like this, but couldn't. We didn't show a stitch of our skin and we made it." –Tionne "T-Boz" Watkins of TLC

with setting fire to the Atlanta, Georgia, mansion of her boyfriend, football star Andre Rison, in 1994. In 1995 the group dropped its manager, Pebbles (Perri M. Reid), who then filed a $10 million lawsuit against TLC's label, LaFace Records. Further troubles plagued TLC in 1996, when the group declared bankruptcy.

TLC formed in Atlanta, Georgia, in 1991

TLC took its name from the first letters of the nicknames of its three members: Tionne "T-Boz" Watkins (born April 26, 1970, in Des Moines, Iowa), Lisa "Left Eye" Lopes (born May 27, 1971, in Philadelphia, Pennsylvania), and Rozonda "Chilli" Thomas (born February 27, 1971, in Atlanta, Georgia). All three had difficult backgrounds, either being raised by their single-parent mothers (Watkins and Thomas) or an abusive father (Lopes).

Watkins and Lopes were performing in Atlanta as a teen-duo called Second Nature, when they were discovered by R & B performer Pebbles. Pebbles had good connections in the R & B music industry. She was married to one of the top R & B producers, Antonio "L.A." Reid, who together with Kenneth **"Babyface"** Edmonds (see entry) co-founded Atlanta's LaFace Records. Pebbles signed them to a contract with her management company, Pebbitone, and completed the trio when she signed Thomas. Thomas, who had some experience singing in talent contests, was at the time working as a

dancer with Damian Dame, an act signed to LaFace Records.

The three worked well together as a trio. Chilli, with her dance experience, choreographed TLC's live performances and videos, while adding a new vocal dimension. Left Eye, with her rebellious, outrageous rhymes, was the rapper, and T-Boz sang.

Debut album generated instant excitement

When *Ooooooohhh ... On the TLC Tip* hit record stores in 1992, its blend of rap, rhythm and blues, and pop put TLC and LaFace Records on the map. Three singles from the album reached the top ten on both the pop and R & B charts, proving TLC had a wide appeal. The first was the rap-based "Ain't 2 Proud 2 Beg," co-written by Left Eye and producer Dallas Austin, which sampled five songs by different artists, including soul/funk singer James Brown and the classic blues-rock band AWB (Average White Band). That was followed by "Baby-Baby-Baby," a song co-written by L.A. Reid, Babyface, and Daryl Simmons. It stayed at number two on the pop chart for six weeks and was the group's first number one R & B hit. "What about Your Friends," released in the fall of 1992, was certified gold by November.

Writing in *Rolling Stone,* Alan Light called the album "a New Jill Swing gem." He praised TLC's "independent, street-level feminism." On the album, TLC delivered safe-sex messages with a sense of humor and openess that was disarming.

A busy two years before next album

Unexpectedly, it took more than two years for TLC to release its second album, *Crazysexycool,* toward the end of 1994. Part of the delay was due to the group's busy schedule. They exposed audiences to their hyperactive live act while on tour with rap artist **Hammer** (see entry) in 1992 and soul singer **Bobby Brown** (see entry) in 1993. They also appeared in the movie, *House Party 3,* and recorded "Get It Up" (written by **Prince** [see entry]) for the soundtrack to the Janet Jackson film, *Poetic Justice.*

Then, on June 9, 1994, Left Eye set fire to her boyfriend Andre Rison's $2 million mansion in Atlanta. Pleading guilty to arson charges later in the year, Left Eye was given a $10,000 fine and five years probation. Another lawsuit stemming from the fire was later filed against Left Eye by insurance giant Lloyd's of London, which had insured the home for $1.3 million and sought about half a million dollars from the rapper.

TLC emerge Crazysexycool

"Crazysexycool is a word we created to describe what's in every woman," Lopes told Joan Morgan in *Vibe.* The album of that name found the artists more involved in their own recording; Lopes, who had always written her own raps, contributed the songs "Waterfalls" and "Kick Your Game" and joined in the actual production of the record.

"My challenge," said L.A. Reid, who acted as creative director for *Crazysexy-cool,* according to *Vibe's* Morgan, "was to give their fans good music but allow TLC to grow in a way that would keep them around. I want them to be larger than just hiphop. I want them to be thought of as true creative forces."

Critics agreed that *Crazysexycool* was better than TLC's first album. Writing for *People Weekly,* Jeremy Helligar declared that the "sharp funk and libidinous R & B of *Crazysexycool* easily outgrooves its predecessor's sloganeering bubblegum hiphop." *Billboard's* J.R. Reynolds reported that the "musical evolution of TLC is marked by stronger voices, closer harmonies, and tighter raps." *Time's* Christopher John Farley found "the vocals ... stronger and the melodies more piquant than ... on the first album."

Crazysexycool went on to sell more than nine million copies by 1996, making it the biggest-selling U.S. album ever by an all-female act. The album spawned four top ten R & B hits. The first, "Creep," sampled Slick Rick's "Hey Young World" and became TLC's second number one R & B hit, staying atop the chart for an amazing nine weeks. "Red Light Special" followed in the spring of 1995, "Waterfalls" in the summer, and "Diggin' on You" toward the end of the year.

"Waterfalls" won four MTV Video Music Awards in 1995, while "Creep" won TLC a *Billboard* Music Award and a Grammy. *Crazysexycool* also won a Grammy and was named Favorite Album at the second annual Blockbuster Entertainment Awards in March 1996.

Bankruptcy hearings disrupted career

1995 was a banner year for TLC, but they spent much of 1996 in court dealing with financial problems. Toward the end of 1995 the three members of TLC declared bankruptcy. LaFace and Pebbitone protested that TLC was simply trying to pressure them into renegotiating the group's contract. By December, a settlement was reached, but a confidentiality clause prohibited comment on the financial details or other specifics.

No strangers to adversity, TLC have a lot to put behind them if they are to get their highly successful career back on track. At the end of their bankruptcy hearings, TLC released a statement saying they were "glad to be done with all of the legal maneuvering and happy to be back to just being recording artists."

Selected Awards

Ooooooohhh ... On the TLC Tip certified triple platinum (sales of three million copies), 1995.

"Waterfalls," MTV Video Music Awards for 1) Best Video, 2) Best Group Video, 3) Best R & B Video, and 4) People's Choice of the Year, 1995.

Billboard Music Awards for 1) Top Artist of the Year, 2) Top R & B Single for "Creep," and 3) Top R & B Artist, 1995.

Crazysexycool certified multi-platinum for U.S. sales of nine million copies, 1996.

Grammy Awards for 1) Best R & B Vocal Performance, Duo or Group, for "Creep," and 2) Best R & B Album for *Crazysexycool,* 1996.

Crazysexycool, Blockbuster Entertainment Award for Favorite Album, 1996.

Selected Discography

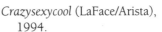

Ooooooohhh ... On the TLC Tip (LaFace/Arista), 1992.

Crazysexycool (LaFace/Arista), 1994.

Further Reading

Burkstrand, Beth, "TLC Settles Suit, Setting Aside a Troubling Use of Bankruptcy," *New York Times,* November 11, 1996, p. D2.

Chambers, Veronica, "TLC: Hot and Bothered," *Essence,* February 1993, p. 48.

Cooper, Carol, "Burn, Baby, Burn: The Women of TLC Stay Cool under Fire," *Rolling Stone,* August 24, 1995, p. 27.

Farley, Christopher John, "TLC: CrazySexyCool," *Time,* December 19, 1994, p. 77.

Light, Alan, "TLC," *Rolling Stone,* May 28, 1992, p. 22.

Morgan, Joan, "TLC," *Vibe,* November 1994.

Plummer, William, "In the Heat of the Night," *People Weekly,* June 27, 1994, p. 36.

Samuels, Anita M., and Diana B. Henriques, "Going Broke and Cutting Loose," *New York Times,* February 5, 1996, p. D1.

Thompson, Malissa, "Crazysexycool," *Seventeen,* May 1996, p. 166.

Contact Information

LaFace Records
3350 Peachtree Rd., NE, Suite 1500
Atlanta, GA 30326-1040

Web Sites

http://geocities.com/SunsetStrip/Palms/2154/tlc.html

http://aristarec.com/tlc/

ROCK AND ROLL

When rock and roll first became popular in mainstream circles in the 1950s, it seemed like its biggest threat was going to be authority figures. Parents, teachers, and religious leaders didn't like it, thinking the music's wild rhythms and crude lyrics would certainly lead kids down the wrong roads.

Blues to rock

Rock and roll has its roots in rhythm and blues, which combined in different ways with forms of boogie-woogie, jazz, country, gospel, and folk music. The term rock and roll came from the Mississippi Delta and electric blues cultures, and was used to attract a mass multiracial audience to rhythm and blues. The majority of R & B performers in the early 1950s, however, made no distinction between rhythm and blues and rock and roll. One R & B artist who made a particularly successful transition to rock and roll was New Orleans-born pianist Antoine "Fats" Domino. Although he had produced a great amount of strong R & B material before his career in rock and roll, Domino did not hit the charts

Chuck Berry

until 1955 with "Ain't That A Shame," followed by the classics "Blueberry Hill" and "I'm Walking."

Another R & B pianist/singer to enter the rock and roll field was Little Richard Penniman, a former gospel singer whose career in pop music began in 1956 with the hit "Tutti Frutti." In the next few years he produced a string of hits, icluding "Long Tall Sally," "Rip It Up," and "Good Golly Miss Molly."

In 1955, as Fats Domino's New Orleans style R & B tunes climbed the charts, a young guitarist from St. Louis named Chuck Berry achieved nationwide fame with a country-influenced song named "Maybelline," which reached number five on the charts. Backed by bluesman Muddy Waters's rhythm section, "Maybelline" offered a unique form of R & B combining white hillbilly, or rockabilly, with jump blues. Berry revolutionized R & B by featuring a guitar as a lead, rather than a rhythm instrument. Modeled after his blues-guitar mentor T-Bone Walker, Berry's double string guitar bends and syncopated up-stroke rhythm created a driving backdrop for his colorfully poetic tales of teenage life. A highly creative musician, Berry incorporated the sounds of urban blues, country, calypso, Latin, and even Hawaiian music into his unique brand of R & B. His classic "Johnny B. Goode," recorded in 1958, became a standard in almost every rock and roll band's repertoire.

Bill Haley hit the charts with "Rock Around the Clock" in the 1950s. Then Elvis Presley, remembered as the Father of Rock 'n' roll, came out with his smash hit "Heartbreak Hotel," and soon followed with "Don't Be Cruel," "Hound Dog," and "Blue Sued Shoes." Presley's sound had evolved from his roots in the Deep South and combined elements of country and western, rhythm and blues, and gospel. His smoldering good looks and captivating smile, coupled with the pelvic "bump-and-grind" rhythm, projected an exciting sexuality that was unprecedented in the music world.

Among many other big developments that helped shape rock and roll were the 1960s British invasion, when bands like the Beatles reinvented American rhythm and blues, and Motown, which brought soul to a wider audience.

State of flux is the norm

Rock and roll, at its core, is about rebellion, fighting the status quo, or the way things are. So rock and roll always has to change and reinvent itself to stay dangerous or current or at least different enough to bother a parent or two. One side effect of rock and roll constantly reinventing itself is that there are new branches of rock and roll forming all the time. Music like heavy metal, rap, and folk rock are all different mutations of rock and roll. *The All Music Guide to Rock,* for example, lists over forty different sub-categories of rock, including psychedelic rock, bubblegum, British punk, and American alternative.

These sub-categories ebb and flow in popularity. Some, like punk, don't make a big wave at the time, but turn out to be very influential to later bands. Others, like

Parents Aren't Supposed to Like It

psychedelic rock, are very popular for a short period of time, then fall out of favor. A category like bubblegum will stick around for years and occasionally a song in that style will score a hit (like Hanson's "MMMBop"), but it never becomes the main force in music. And an offshoot like funk can mingle with rock (Lenny Kravitz's "It Ain't Over 'Til It's Over") or evolve so much that it becomes something completely new-sounding (George Clinton's "Atomic Dog").

Despite many changes and offshoots of the form, plain old rock and roll remains a popular standard. **Bruce Springsteen** (see entry) has been playing innovative varieties of his working man's rock and roll for over two decades, and is beloved by a huge and devoted following. Similarly **Melissa Etheridge** carried her leanings toward political issues and blues roots to a peak of old-fashioned rock and roll that drives her fans wild. Bands like **Hootie and the Blowfish, Blues Traveler,** and **Counting Crows** (see entries) are exploring tried and true rock formulas for a new generation. The Counting Crows, for example, have often been compared to Van Morrison; the Rolling Stones were once considered to be stealing their music from Chuck Berry. Chuck Berry was developing sounds from rhythm and blues artists that came before him.

Bruce Springsteen

Current bands influenced by 1960s and 1970s rock

The Black Crowes is unabashedly derived from classic rock. Singer Chris Robinson even looks like he's from the the past, with his long hair and flared pants. The band dresses like Rod Stewart, sounds like the Stones or the Faces, and they got famous singing a cover of Otis Redding's "Hard To Handle." Despite

Melissa Etheridge in concert

Adam Duritz sounds a lot like rock veteran Van Morrison—so much so that the band filled in for Morrison at a Rock & Roll Hall of Fame ceremony. Besides the Morrison connection, they have other strains of both new and old rock running throughout their music. Duritz' angst-ridden (some say whiny) lyrics may have been influenced by the tortured lyrics of grunge.

Lenny Kravitz (see entry) is another artist with an obvious love for classic rock. In fact, he has been criticized for recreating the old sounds too faithfully. Kravitz isn't doing covers of old songs, but it sounds like he could be. A listener doesn't have to try hard to hear echoes of Jimi Hendrix, Led Zeppelin, and Curtis Mayfield in Kravitz's tunes.

New groups influenced by the Grateful Dead

Blues Traveler takes their cues from the extended jamming style of the classic 1960s and 1970s sound of the Grateful Dead. The band also borrowed from the Dead their technique of constant touring to slowly gain a devoted group of fans. Lead singer John Popper's frequent use of his harmonica and the band's song structures are taken from the blues. Blues Traveler is often lumped in with other Dead-influenced bands like Widespread Panic and **Phish** (see entry).

Phish doesn't sound much like the Grateful Dead (except for a bluegrass influence here and there), but draw comparisons because of a similarity in attitude—the jam-filled concerts and the constant touring style. Otherwise, Phish's influ-

their heavy roots in old time rock, the Black Crowes have a sound that is current and popular with many fans of alternative rock.

The Counting Crows also make music that sounds like classic rock. Singer

ences are obvious from their concerts, where they'll do anything from singing "Freebird" in barbershop quartet style to re-creating entire albums note for note.

The Spin Doctors (see entry) also rose from the neo-Dead scene. They dress like hippies and enjoy playing long blues jams. The twist the Spin Doctors added to the formula was combining their music with pop hooks and shortening their jams into quick, hummable songs.

New sounds from old sounds

Back when Live (see entry) formed in Pennsylvania in 1985, the most popular bands were R.E.M. and U2, and the influences are clearly detectable in the bands music. The Gin Blossoms (see entry) have a sound that borrows from the folk-rock guitar of the 1970's-era band the Byrds and 1980's college rockers R.E.M. The Gin Blossoms is considered a rootsy band, since it sticks with simple song structures, harmonies, and the basic guitar-bass-drums set-up.

Guided By Voices (see entry) throws all kinds of influences together and see what they come up with. For example, the band has mixed 1960s British Invasion sounds like early Pink Floyd and the Who with the short and fast song structure of later British punk bands and use the lo-fi recording process of garage bands. Atlanta-based band Collective Soul (see entry) scored a hit in 1994 by combining a 1970's F.M. radio sheen with a slightly alternative sound. Contrary to their name, there doesn't seem to be too much actual soul in their music.

The Dave Matthews Band (see entry) gets its mix of sounds from its mix of players. Singer/guitarist Dave Matthews lived in South Africa and North Carolina, so it's no surprise that the band adds Southern rock and world beats to their sound. The rest of the band members come from a jazz background which gives the music a jazzy feel, like Sting's music.

The traditional Hispanic sounds of Los Lobos is combined with elements of country, blues, folk, and rock. the subdudes (see entry) play roots music with a twist, using a percussionist instead of a drummer. They go way back in history for their influences, coming up with a mix of New Orleans funk and rhythm and blues.

Country influence

Son Volt and Wilco (see entries) were formed when the two main figures of the group Uncle Tupelo, Jay Farrar and Jeff Tweedy, decided to split. Uncle Tupelo had started a revival of roots country music, music that was different from the image-conscious music coming from the country mainstream. Son Volt and Wilco picked up where Uncle Tupelo left off. Farrar's Son Volt has drifted toward the slower, more acoustic side of country, and Tweedy's Wilco plays a more upbeat, rocking variety.

Hootie and the Blowfish's (see entry) countrified sound became really popular, really fast. Maybe that was because every few years, rock and roll fans seem to want to hear some new country rock. But the band also borrows from other popular kinds of rock. The Hootie formula is a combo of folk rock, blues rock, Southern rock and pop.

Rock and roll is, like most music, a hybrid form (one that is formed from a combination of musical genres) that embraces and unites many traditions, while constantly breaking trends and bucking established conventions. In the same vein, rock and roll has long been accepted as a musical convention in almost all mainstream circles, and yet as new rock offshoots arrive, they form the waves that rock the boat and shake up the music world.

THE BLACK CROWES

American rock and roll band

Formed 1988 in Atlanta, Georgia

Often dismissed as a mere retro outfit mired in 1970s rock and blues, the Black Crowes was one of the few bands of the late 1980s and 1990s who shunned the fad of angst rock and gave their audience something to dance to. Its sound owes a lot to forerunners like the Rolling Stones, and its live jams are similar to classic rock bands like the Grateful Dead and the Allman Brothers Band. Although lead singer Chris Robinson sometimes seems like a modern-day version of Rod Stewart when he fronted the Faces, the Black Crowes' ability to build on what came before them and their own musical foundations adds a freshness to the mix. From their multimillion selling 1990 debut, *Shake Your Money Maker*, to their more recent *Three Snakes and One Charm*, the Crowes grow more ambitious with each recording. Despite almost consistent friction between Chris and guitarist Rich Robinson, the brothers that lead the group, the band continues to fly.

"The Crowes carry an Olympic-size torch for the sort of no-frills, feel-good, fundamental rock that most bands have forgotten how to make." –Parke Puterbaugh, *Stereo Review*

Chris and Rich Robinson performing

The Black Crowes carry on rock tradition

Rock 'n' soul debut on Def American

After signing to Rick Rubin's Def American label, the band released its debut, *Shake Your Money Maker,* in early 1990. With a hit version of soul singer Otis Redding's "Hard to Handle" and soulful originals like "Jealous Again" and "She Talks to Angels," the album sold millions. Soon the band was performing live before tens of thousands; at the same time they were being criticized for lack of originality. Rich Robinson complained to Neely, "There's no new music ever, period. It's all an interpretation of music that's come before. I interpret Keith Richards in the same way that Keith Richards interpreted Muddy Waters and Chuck Berry. If anyone's going to accuse us of ripping off the Stones, they'd better listen to a couple of Chuck Berry records."

> "There's no new music ever, period. It's all an interpretation of music that's come before. I interpret Keith Richards in the same way that Keith Richards interpreted Muddy Waters and Chuck Berry."

Early days in Atlanta

The Robinson brothers grew up in Atlanta and discovered blues and roots music from the diverse record collection of their musician father, Stan. "I couldn't tie my shoe until I was nine," Chris admitted to *Rolling Stone*'s Kim Neely in 1991, "but I knew how to work the stereo." In 1984 eighteen-year-old Chris and Rich, then fifteen, formed a semi-punk band called Mr. Crowes Garden. By 1988 the group included drummer Steve Gorman, bassist Johnny Colt, and guitarist Jeff Cease. Now called the Black Crowes, the band settled into their sound of swaggering blues and R & B (rhythm and blues) stomps.

Guitar-powered rock and roll

The band followed up with another multimillion seller, *The Southern Harmony and Musical Companion,* in 1992. Parke Puterbaugh of *Stereo Review* declared the album "strikes a blow for that endangered species, the old-fashioned, nontrendy, guitar-powered rock-and-roll band.... No mere Seventies-rock revivalists, the Black Crowes are a band of substance and solidity that sound like they're here to stay."

With guitarist Marc Ford replacing Cease and the swelling Hammond organ of Eddie Harsch now in place, the Crowes seemed stronger than ever. The band continued with the psychedelic-influenced *Amorica* in 1994. A good deal of the press about the recording centered on the controversial cover—a close-up photo of an American flag bikini bottom.

Fourth album a charm

The band continued to tour without a break and went back into the studio for 1996's *Three Snakes and One Charm*. "The honky-tonk gospel of 'Good Friday' and the rhythmic strum of 'How Much for Your Wings?' recaptured the knock-'em-dead sonics that made *Southern Harmony* such a fine musical companion," wrote Jeremy Helligar in his review for *People Weekly*. Puterbaugh of *Stereo Review* agreed, saying the band "synthesizes [combines] the best aspects of their first two releases ... into what may well be their finest effort to date," adding, "the Crowes carry an Olympic-size torch for the sort of no-frills, feel-good, fundamental rock that most bands have forgotten how to make."

Selected Discography

Shake Your Money Maker (Def American), 1990.

The Southern Harmony and Musical Companion (Def American), 1992.

Amorica (American), 1994.

Three Snakes and One Charm (American), 1996.

Further Reading

Dunn, Jancee, "Chris Robinson of the Black Crowes," *Rolling Stone,* October 31, 1996, p. 36.

Helligar, Jeremy, "Three Snakes and One Charm," *People Weekly,* July 29, 1996, p. 21.

Hochman, Steve, "The Black Crowes," *Rolling Stone,* November 17, 1994, p. 75.

Rotondi, James, "Crowing Pains," *Guitar Player,* January 1995, p. 104.

Russell, Rusty, "As the Black Crowes Fly," *Guitar Player,* November 1996, p. 67.

Stereo Review, September 1992, p.73; October 1996, p. 102.

Contact Information

American Recordings
3500 W. Olive Ave., Ste. 1550
Burbank, CA 91505

Web Sites

http://www.tallest.com

http://www.rockweb.com/rwi/listeners/black-crowes/

http://www.american.recording.com/

BLUES TRAVELER

American rock and roll band

Formed in New York City in 1987

Blues Traveler started out like so many young rock bands; they played area high schools. Partly because of their heavy touring schedule and their merry band of traveling fans—so called "Fellow Travelers"—they were often compared to the legendary classic rock band Grateful Dead. Without the air play and media attention that so often supports a band, Blues Traveler has maintained a steady and loyal following since the late 1980s. In fact, the band insists that they perform better onstage than in the studio. As lead singer and harmonica player John Popper pointed out in *Billboard*, "We've always been predominantly a live band. Our studio albums are nice tries, but the live shows just totally blow them away." Their music is, as Steve Dougherty in *People Weekly* wrote, "a laid-back brand of blues-based rock and roll more appropriate to the acid-washed '60's than the grunged-out '90's."

From high school band to rock and roll

Blues Traveler came together when John Popper recruited fellow Princeton High (Princeton, New Jersey) musician, drummer

John Popper

Brendan Hill. Hill is originally from London, England, while Popper had lived in Stamford, Connecticut, until he was fifteen. Guitarist and Princeton High lacrosse player, Chan Kinchla, joined the band in 1985. The final Princeton High classmate to join the band was bassist Bobby Sheehan, who came on board in 1987. At the time they simply called themselves the Blues Band.

> ## "We view blues not as a style of music, but as a level of honesty you play with. It's ... Zeppelin listening to Muddy Waters (blues musician), and us listening to Zep."

After graduating from Princeton High the four set out to make it big in New York City. Popper, Hill, and Sheehan enrolled in New York's New School to briefly study jazz. They were college students by day and a club-playing band by night. They soon changed their name to Blues Traveler after a character in the film *Ghostbusters*.

The good, the band, and the ugly

Bill Graham, a well-known concert promoter and band manager, became their manager, and with his connections they signed with A&M Records in 1989. Chan Kinchla told *People Weekly*'s Steve Dougherty, "We kicked New York's ass, some record company had to sign us, no matter how ugly we are." Performing from sixteen to twenty shows a month, the band had a steady following. In 1990 they released their first album, the self-titled *Blues Traveler*. Popper explained it this way to Mike Flaherty of *Entertainment Weekly*, "We view blues not as a style of music, but as a level of honesty you play with. It's ... Zeppelin [rock band Led Zeppelin] listening to Muddy Waters [blues musician], and us listening to Zep." Popper's vocals and strong harmonica playing gave the band's music a focus.

The band's second album, *Travelers & Thieves*, came out a year later in 1991. Heavy touring followed, but the band was derailed when John Popper was involved in a serious motorcycle accident in 1992. Despite wheelchair confinement, Popper and group were back on the road in two months. "The doctor said I shouldn't do it," Popper related to Dougherty, "But it was a mandate from the crowd." It was around this time that Popper founded H.O.R.D.E. (Horizons of Rock Developing Everywhere), an annual touring festival oriented toward blues and roots rock.

Can't keep a good band down

With Popper temporarily laid up, the band went into the studio and finished recording *Save His Soul*, which was released in 1993. It wasn't until 1995, however, that the band began receiving critical and commercial notice. With the release of *Four*, the band became MTV darlings. Their video "Run-Around" was among the top five on the music channel's video countdown. Oddly, the video features a group of camera-friendly lip-synchers, while Blues Traveler is only partially hidden behind a curtain. Drum-

The H.O.R.D.E. festival

Around the time of his motorcycle accident in 1992, John Popper decided to organize a summer touring festival that would feature new bands that played in a blues or classic rock style. Called H.O.R.D.E. (Horizons of Rock Developing Everywhere), the first year's tour was headlined by the Blues Traveler and consisted of eight dates, with attendance averaging about 7,500 people per show.

By 1995 the H.O.R.D.E. tour had grown to 23 dates, with crowds averaging about 15,000. Among the bands that have performed on the tour are the **Spin Doctors** (see entry), Big Head Todd and the Monsters, **Black Crowes** (see entry), reggae singer Ziggy Marley, **Wilco** (see entry), **Sheryl Crow** (see entry), and **Melissa Etheridge** (see entry).

With the Blues Traveler withdrawing from the 1997 H.O.R.D.E. tour (except for a few dates), the lineup included **Beck** (see entry), **Neil Young** (see entry), Big Head Todd and the Monsters, **Primus** (see entry), **Morphine** (see entry), and others. In 1997, however, crowds were diminishing at the annual festival.

mer Brendan Hill explained to *People Weekly*'s Dougherty, "Some bands get noticed because they have a certain look. We wanted to make a statement that the music matters." "Run-Around" went on to earn Blues Traveler its first Grammy.

New release

In 1996 the band released *Live from the Fall,* a two-disc collection of previously released selections, plus two previously unreleased tracks and covers of "Imagine," by John Lennon and "Low Rider," by War. A&M promoted the double album by saying the collection captures the Blues Traveler doing what they "do best: play hard, play long and play live." Other reviews haven't been so generous. David Browne in *Entertainment Weekly* gave it a D rating, noting that "Popper sounds uncannily like a blues singer on helium (read, Donald Duck)."

No matter, their fans (primarily college age) still love them. When not touring with H.O.R.D.E. (although the band announced they would not be playing the 1997 tour), Blues Traveler can be found in Alaska and other points on the road. Shrugging off their neo-hippie label, Popper (born in 1967) said in the *People Weekly* article, "We don't know what was going on in the '60s," and adds, "We're making music that people our age like. Do we seem like hippies? I'm packin' heat for cripes sake!"

Selected Awards

Blues Traveler, certified gold, 1995.

Four, certified double platinum, 1995.

Grammy, Best Rock Performance By a Duo or Group with Vocal, for "Run-Around," 1996.

Selected Discography

Blues Traveler (A&M Records), 1990.

Travelers & Thieves (A&M Records), 1991.

Save His Soul (A&M Records), 1993.

Four (A&M Records), 1994.

Live from the Fall (A&M Records), 1996.

Straight on Till Morning (A & M Records), 1997.

Further Reading

"Blues Traveler," A&M Records Press Release Biography, July 1996.

Browne, David, "Live from the Fall," *Entertainment Weekly,* July 12, 1996, p. 57.

Dougherty, Steve, and Michael Small, "Fellow Travelers," *People Weekly,* September 11, 1995, p. 91.

Flaherty, Mike, "H.O.R.D.E. Is Their Shepard," *Entertainment Weekly,* August 25, 1995, p. 20.

Gardner, Elysa, Review, *Rolling Stone,* August 22, 1996, p. 96.

Smith, Ethan, "Popper's Fresh Go," *Entertainment Weekly,* April 12, 1996, p. 71.

Contact Information

A & M Records, Inc.
1416 North La Brea Avenue
Hollywood, CA 90028

Web Site

http://www.bluestraveler.com/

Collective Soul

American alternative pop/rock band

Formed in Stockbridge, Georgia, in 1990;
disbanded 1992; re-formed 1993

"When I start feeling down, I feel like I'm being selfish, because there are so many people out there who wish they could be doing what we're doing." –Ed Roland, songwriter, vocals, guitar

The old saying, "If at first you don't succeed, try, try again," would best describe the story behind the band Collective Soul. After being rejected year after year by the major record companies, success suddenly seemed to jump right into the hands of the band. Ironically, the group had to break up before they would get their big break. Of course hard work, talent, and luck had something to do with the group's transition from virtual unknowns to platinum-record stars, but Collective Soul stands as another example for aspiring artists who struggle to share their talent with a broader audience while furthering their career dreams.

Close, but no call

In the late 1980s, after receiving classical music training at Berklee College of Music in Boston, Ed Roland (Collective Soul's founder, guitarist, and vocalist) decided to form a music group called Marching Two Step back in his hometown of Stockbridge, Georgia. The band sent demo tapes out to the record companies and played the local circuit around Atlanta. Always rejected by the labels they

Ed Roland

contacted, the band never achieved the kind of recognition Roland was seeking.

In 1990 Roland caught guitarist Ross Childress playing in another band. Roland was so inspired by his style and skill that he asked him to join Roland's band. When Childress agreed, the band's name was changed to Collective Soul (a concept written about in the Ayn Rand novel *The Fountainhead*). Thus began a string of close calls with getting a major label recording contract. Although Collective Soul solicited dozens of record companies with their demos (and even had opportunities to perform live showcases before record executives), they still found themselves without the label support they needed to take their music careers to the next level. Frustration and disappointment soon set in, forcing Roland to dissolve the group by the end of 1992. Roland then decided to try a different career approach to music.

Band shines on the radio

After spending years trying to get a recording contract for his band, Ed Roland decided he would instead put his efforts into writing songs for other established artists. With the help of his former Collective Soul bandmates—Ross Childress on lead guitar, Will Turpin on bass, and Shane Evans on drums—Roland spent the early part of 1993 working in his manager's basement studio recording a new batch of material for the songwriting demo he was planning to send out, hoping to obtain a publishing contract.

Almost as a lark, Roland decided during his mailings to music publishers that he would send a copy of his demo to a local college radio station, Georgia State University's, WRAS-FM. The station immediately added the song "Shine" from the demo to their regular airplay rotation. "Shine" was an instant hit at the station and was soon being picked up by other college radio stations throughout the South. With the growing popularity of Roland's new single, offers came in for the band to perform some benefit shows. Roland immediately put Collective Soul back together, adding his kid brother Dean on rhythm guitar to the group.

Opportunity finally knocks

With all the attention Collective Soul was receiving, it wasn't long before Atlantic Records found out about them and offered the group the recording contract that had eluded Roland for so long. After signing the band, the label felt the momentum behind the song "Shine" was so big at the time, they couldn't afford to wait to have the band re-record all the songs before releasing the album.

In early 1994, after receiving the band's consent, Atlantic decided to release Roland's demo, minus one song, as Collective Soul's debut CD, *Hints, Allegations and Things Left Unsaid*. Referred to by industry insiders as the bridge between classic 1970s rock and 1990s alternative grunge, *Hints* made up for any perceived production imperfections (remember that the album was only supposed to be a songwriter's demo) with its refreshingly new-sounding songs that also carried a familiar twist to them.

Within a few short months of its release, the smooth and upbeat single "Shine" went to #1 on the charts. Almost overnight Collective Soul found themselves with a platinum album (over 1,000,000 units sold), playing at the Woodstock II festival, touring with rock legends Aerosmith, and winning a coveted Billboard "Song of the Year" award.

Things keep getting better

After touring to support their debut album, Collective Soul quickly returned to the recording studio to produce their second album. It was their first real effort recording together as a band. In the spring of 1995 the self-titled album, *Collective Soul,* was released to very good reviews by the critics. The album's first single, "Gel," was also featured on the soundtrack for the *Jerky Boys* movie.

The album's next single, "December," became a huge hit for the band. A strong and moody song, "December" was a stylistic departure from the band's first big hit, "Shine," but it allowed the group to show people their "other side." With other notably diverse tracks such as "Where the River Flows" and "The World I Know," *Collective Soul* silenced critics who felt the band was incapable of bettering their debut release. The group would not easily give up its success, which took so long to obtain.

Disciplined breakdown

Collective Soul waited about two years before releasing their third album, *Disciplined Breakdown,* to lukewarm reviews. After noting that ten of the CD's twelve songs concerned romantic love, *People Weekly*'s Ken Baker complimented singer-songwriter Ed Roland's emotive voice and lyrics, which he described as "the intense poetry of testosterone-infused American rock and roll." Unfortunately, the critic also found the music "uninspired," a judgment with which other reviewers seemed to agree. It remained to be seen how the fans would vote with their wallets and how the album would fare on the charts.

Selected Awards

Billboard Song of the Year, for "Shine," 1994

Hints, Allegations and Things Left Unsaid, certified platinum.

Selected Discography

Hints, Allegations and Things Left Unsaid (Atlantic Records), 1994.

Collective Soul (Atlantic Records), 1995.

Disciplined Breakdown (Atlantic Records), 1997.

Further Reading

Evans, Paul, "Collective Soul," *Rolling Stone,* June 15, 1995, p. 83.

Farinella, David John, "Disciplined Breakdown," *Guitar Player,* June, 1997, p. 23.

Gill, Chris, "Collective Soul: Georgia's Three-Guitar Army?," *Guitar Player,* August, 1995, p. 33.

Graff, Gary, "Georgia Band Collective Soul Scores an Instant Hit with 'Shine,'" *Knight-Ridder/Tribune News Service,* June 27, 1994.

Parents Aren't Supposed to Like It

Contact Information

Atlantic Records
1290 Avenue of the Americas
New York, NY 10104

Web Sites

http://www.atlantic-records.com/Collective_
Soul/

http://www.csoul.com/

COUNTING CROWS

American rock and roll band

Formed 1991 in San Francisco, California

"Things are disastrous for a lot of people in my songs. They don't have the communication skills to get what they want and they end up hurting other people—and getting hurt—when they try." –Adam Duritz

In 1996, the pressure was on for Counting Crows. The band's folksy, roots-based debut record *August and Everything After,* had been a huge hit. The record sold over six million copies in the United States and *Rolling Stone* named the band "the biggest new band in America." The band had become so popular so fast that there was Counting Crows backlash. Critics put the band down for everything from copying Van Morrison's style to "being whiny," according to the *Los Angeles Times.* "The Crows were seen as blunting the triumph of grunge," said *Rolling Stone.* People were predicting that the band's second record *Recovering the Satellites* would be a big bomb. But it wasn't. *Recovering the Satellites* debuted at number one on the Billboard 200 album chart.

The quick rise from Bay Area coffee house band

Singer and songwriter Adam Duritz (a video store clerk and college drop-out) and guitarist David Bryson were introduced by a San Francisco Bay Area musician, and the first time they got together, they wrote a song. The two started writing together regularly and playing as an acoustic duo at coffee houses and small clubs around Berkeley, California. They named themselves Counting Crows after an old English divination rhyme (a rhyme on interpreting signs to foretell the future).

Big breaks #1 and #2

Things happened fast for the band. A year after recruiting fellow bandmates, bassist Matt Malley, keyboardist Charles Gillingham, and drummer Steve Bowman, the band got their first big break—a performing slot at a BMI New Music Showcase in San Francisco. One month later, they had a record deal. Two months after that, they were opening for Bob Dylan.

"If you're a person who has difficulty relating to people and if you're not completely happy, then success doesn't fix that for you. You're just a more successful person that still has those hang-ups."

The band's second big break was filling in for Van Morrison at the Rock and Roll Hall of Fame induction ceremony. The band's performance and Duritz's soulful singing and his vocal similarity to Morrison generated excitement for the band's first record.

Instant fame

"I feel like we really got launched up into the sky at one point. I mean, much further than we expected, or even maybe wanted, at the time, to go," said the dred-

locked Duritz to the *Los Angeles Times*. *August and Everything After* arrived to almost instant acclaim, most of this due to the atypically upbeat single "Mr. Jones," which the *Los Angeles Times* called "an infectious tune about an aspiring rock star, complete with Van Morrison-esque 'sha la las.'" *Rolling Stone* gave the record four stars and called it "one of the best rock releases of the year." The band almost immediately became famous, appearing on *Saturday Night Live* and touring with the Cranberries and the Rolling Stones. For a while, Duritz even dated *Friends* star Jennifer Aniston.

Depression and writer's block

Duritz realized just how famous he had become when he returned to his house in Berkeley after a big tour. "Dan (Vickrey, the newest guitarist) and I were sitting in the living room and looking out the window and all of the sudden I hear these kids go, 'There he is! He's right there!' They were going to the drive-in and we were the movie," he said to the *Los Angeles Times*.

This massive success was hard on Duritz. "If you're a person who has difficulty relating to people and if you're not completely happy, then success doesn't fix that for you. You're just a more successful person that still has those hang-ups," said Duritz to *Time*.

Duritz wanted out. "I found I just didn't like playing music anymore. I didn't see it was making my life good; it was just making me a lot of money," he told the *San Francisco Sunday Examiner & Chroni-

cle. Duritz moved to Los Angeles and went to work at the Viper Room, Johnny Depp's club, to get away from the music scene and to overcome his writer's block.

New record, new hope

Duritz finally broke through with *Recovering the Satellites.* It's about Duritz's dark experiences and emotions after the success of *August and Everything After.* "You got a piece of me / but it's just a little piece of me," he sings in "Have You Seen Me Lately?" By the end of the album, Duritz gets less grumpy with songs of hope like "A Long December." Duritz's new girlfriend, Courtney Cox of *Friends,* is in the video.

The album has been well received and, ironically, brought the band more of the fame that Duritz is so ambivalent about. "(Fame) is like a dream where you're in school, and you're not wearing the right clothes. You're in your underwear or your pajamas, or you're naked ... I've been naked at school for three years now. I had to learn to adjust to that," said Duritz in the *Los Angeles Times.*

Selected Awards

August and Everything After certified six times platinum.

MTV Video Music Award, Best New Artist, for "Mr. Jones."

American Music Award, Favorite Artist, Alternative Music.

Selected Discography

Recovering the Satellites (DGC), 1996.

August and Everything After (DGC), 1993.

Further Reading

DeCurtis, Anthony, "Recovering the Satellites," *Rolling Stone,* November 28, 1996, p. 134.

Farley, Christopher John, "First Class Flyers," *Time,* October 20, 1996, p. 76.

Nichols, Natalie, "As the Crows Flew," *Los Angeles Times,* October 13, 1996, p. 7.

Uhelszki, Jaan, "How Success Spoiled Adam Duritz," *San Francisco Sunday Examiner & Chronicle,* p. 40.

Wild, David, "Birds Wire," *Rolling Stone,* June 30, 1994, p. 48.

Contact Information

DGC
9130 Sunset Blvd.
Los Angeles, CA 90069

Web Site

http://countingcrows.com

MELISSA ETHERIDGE

American singer and songwriter of rock music
Born on May 29, 1961, in Leavenworth, Kansas

At the Triangle Ball, a 1993 gay inaugural party for President Clinton, Melissa Etheridge amazed many by announcing her sexual preference. She had not really intended to make the announcement. "It just came out," she told *People Weekly*. Nevertheless, she revealed to the world what she had known since her teens—that Melissa Etheridge was a lesbian and that she was proud to be one. Then she waited for the reaction.

Since Etheridge's big announcement, she has received more exposure than other gays in the media, yet she has felt no negative effects on her career. In fact, her success as a singer and songwriter continued to grow. Months after her announcement, *Billboard* called Etheridge the "artist who has set the pace for female rockers of her generation."

Written from the heart

Etheridge left her hometown of Leavenworth, Kansas, on her twenty-first birthday to pursue a music career in Los Angeles. She

> "The sweetness is in having success with something you truly believe in." –Melissa Etheridge

earned a reputation for her passionate voice early on, but she felt she needed more to really be heard in the business. So Etheridge started writing to build stronger connections with her audience. She emerged as a blues songwriter in 1988, with a confessional, straight-from-the-heart style.

Etheridge wrote of yearning, passion, and desire—often taking a tortured view of love and relationships. The singer also wrote about causes dear to her heart, in effect becoming a spokesperson for contemporary issues she felt about strongly. The singer told *Billboard* in 1995: "In my own heart, I have feelings about causes that affect me. AIDS is definitely one of them, because I've lost many friends to it; women's issues; of course, gay rights and all that stuff, because it effects me personally. So I'm going to offer my time and energy to [those causes]."

One example of Etheridge's commitment to a cause is her song "All American Girl." The song warns against the dangers of unprotected sex, so it was selected for use in AIDS awareness public service announcements. While working on the announcements, Susan Lachter David of the National Institute on Drug Abuse noted: "Melissa speaks from the heart, and in her own words; [she] carries a message that sounds so real. It makes for a unique and special kind of communication."

Stardom

Frequently compared to Janis Joplin in her commitment to personal beliefs and to Bruce Springsteen because of her ability to connect with regular folks, Etheridge has nearly universal appeal. "Melissa Etheridge is one of the best examples of pop music that we have," noted Dave Robbins, a program director at a Columbus, Ohio, radio station. "I have no doubt," concurred chairman of Island Records Chris Blackwell, "that she will be the biggest female rock performer in the world."

Album aplomb

The 1994 album *Yes I Am* established Etheridge as a superstar in the United States. The album was certified as quadruple platinum for selling more than four million copies in the United States. It remained on the Billboard 200 for two years and resulted in two Top Ten singles, "I'm the Only One" and "Come to My Window." "Come to My Window" stayed on the record charts for forty-five weeks, breaking Rod Stewart's 1993 record of forty-four weeks for "Have I Told You Lately That I Love You." Etheridge's 1996 album, *Your Little Secret,* was equally successful and positioned her for international success, particularly in Germany, Holland, Australia, and Canada.

Despite the magnitude of her achievements, Etheridge believes that there is nothing magical about her success. Her honest approach to music and life is enough for her fans. She learned that "I can just do what I love and feel and hopefully that's what people want to hear."

Selected Awards

Grammy Awards, Best Female Rock Vocal Performance Award for "Ain't It Heavy," 1993.

Grammy Awards, Best Female Rock Vocal Performance Award for "Come to My Window," Best Rock Song nomination for "Come to My Window," Best Rock Song nomination for "I'm the Only One," 1995.

American Society of Composers, Authors, and Publishers (ASCAP) Pop Music Awards, Songwriter of the Year Award, 1996.

Selected Discography

Melissa Etheridge (Island), 1988.
Brave and Crazy (Island), 1989.
Never Enough (Island), 1992.
Yes I Am (Island), 1994.
Your Little Secret (Island), 1995.

Further Reading

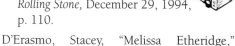

Cohen, Rich, "Melissa Etheridge: The Rolling Stone Interview," *Rolling Stone,* December 29, 1994, p. 110.

D'Erasmo, Stacey, "Melissa Etheridge," *Rolling Stone,* June 2, 1994, p. 20.

Flick, Larry, "Island Ready to Build on Etheridge's '94 Breakthrough," *Billboard,* January 7, 1995, p. 3.

Luck, Joyce, *Melissa Etheridge: Our Little Secret,* ECW Press, 1997.

Miller, Mark, "'We're a Family and We Have Rights,'" *Newsweek,* November 4, 1996, pp. 54-55.

Newman, Melinda, "Island Targeting Etheridge Abroad," *Billboard,* October 14, 1995, p. 1.

Nickson, Chris, *Melissa Etheridge: The Only One,* St. Martin's Griffin, 1997.

Russell, Deborah, "Etheridge Promotes AIDS Awareness," *Billboard,* April 8, 1995, p. 53.

Contact Information

Shock, Inc.
629 5th Ave.
Pelham, NY 10803

Web Site

www.polygram.com\metheridge

GIN BLOSSOMS

American rock and roll band

Formed in Tempe, Arizona, in 1987

"When I was nineteen, my mind was filled with thoughts of uniting the world, and peace and love and all that. And now if I can write a good song about an ex-girlfriend, then that's fine with me." –the Gin Blossoms' Robin Wilson

When the Gin Blossoms started work on *Congratulations I'm Sorry,* the follow-up to their 1992 hit record *New Miserable Experience,* they had more than the usual sophomore slump to worry about. Doug Hopkins, the ex-member who had written some of the record's biggest hits on *New Miserable Experience* like "Hey Jealousy" and "Found Out About You," had killed himself. Now the Gin Blossoms were on their own. Could they make it without Hopkins?

Arizona start

Guitarist Douglas Hopkins and bassist Bill Leen went to high school together in Tempe, Arizona. Two years after graduating they started a band. "I bought a bass and didn't know how to play it. Doug had a guitar that he couldn't play. So we started a band the next week," said Leen in *People.* One Christmas night they debuted a new band they had formed, the Gin Blossoms, with guitarist Jesse Valenzuela on vocals. In an eerie foreshadowing of

Hopkins's eventual alcohol abuse, they named the band after a skin condition caused by heavy drinking.

A few months later Robin Wilson, who was a skateboarding friend of Hopkins's, signed on as the singer. "When I was little, I would come home from school to lip sync to Kiss records, dreaming of being a rock star when I was nineteen," said Wilson in *Phoenix* magazine. Philip Rhodes, who had just gotten out of the Navy, joined soon after Wilson. The Gin Blossoms became a popular band around town and by 1990 had a record contract with A&M.

Hopkins gets worse

By the time the band went into the studio to record their debut in 1992, Hopkins's drinking was out of control. He couldn't function and at one point left the studio, telling the others to get someone else to do the guitar parts. He showed up drunk to gigs and fought with his band mates. The band kicked him out. "Even Doug admitted we couldn't have succeeded with him in the band," said Wilson to *People*. "He also felt we betrayed him."

"'I bought a bass and didn't know how to play it. Doug had a guitar that he couldn't play. So we started a band the next week."

Hopkins was especially upset over the deal the band offered him over valuable publishing rights. *Rolling Stone* reported that after the firing Hopkins said: "I understand why they fired me, but did they have to get so ... cold and ruthless about it?"

The band rises, Hopkins falls

Meanwhile, with new guitarist Scott Johnson on board, the band pressed on. They toured heavily for a year, often playing two shows a day, but the public ignored *New Miserable Experience*. They learned to deal with the strain of touring and being stuck in a tiny van together. "We get into these periods where we sort of ignore each other," said Wilson in *Phoenix* magazine.

Finally, after a year of constant touring and promotion, "Hey Jealousy" and "Found Out About You" became hits. *Stereo Review* called the record "gorgeous chiming folk-rock" and "a guitar-filled jangfest." The Gin Blossoms played prominent shows, including a slot at Farm Aid VII and a spot on the Late Show with David Letterman. Hopkins, who suffered from depression, became increasingly upset watching the band get famous without him, reported *People*. In 1993, he shot himself.

Moving on

One year after Hopkins' death and almost four years after *New Miserable Experience* was first released, the band put out *Congratulations I'm Sorry*. "Everything that's happened in the last four years has helped to make us a stronger band and stronger individuals," said Wilson in a record company press release that noticeably doesn't mention Hopkins' death. "*New Miserable Experience* breaking (onto the charts) forced us to either fall apart or get it together."

When *Congratulations I'm Sorry* came out, the Gin Blossoms surprised a lot of their critics who thought the band would fail without Hopkins writing the songs. The record hit number ten on the charts in its first week out. *Rolling Stone* gave the record a lukewarm review, saying the record's "hook-laden, wall-of-guitar power pop" felt "more like a sequel than its own unique entity."

Even though the band proved they could make it on their own, they know that they will always be indebted to Hopkins. "I feel fortunate to be the instrument through which Doug expressed himself," Wilson said in *Rolling Stone*. "I thought he and I would be the (Aerosmith's) Perry and Tyler of the '90s, but it wasn't to be."

Selected Awards

New Miserable Experience, double platinum.

Congratulations I'm Sorry, platinum.

Selected Discography

New Miserable Experience (A&M), 1992.

Congratulations I'm Sorry (A&M), 1996.

Further Reading

Baird, Robert, "Ex-Blossom Dies," *Rolling Stone,* February 10, 1994, p. 15.

Dougherty, Steve, "Haunted by Success," *People,* April 4, 1994, p. 53.

Manning, Kara, "Congratulations I'm Sorry," *Rolling Stone,* March 21, 1996, p. 99.

Newman, Melinda, "Gin Blossoms Cultivate Fan Base," *Billboard,* January 27, 1996.

Puterbaugh, Parke, "Gin Blossoms: New Miserable Experience," *Stereo Review,* October 1992, p. 83.

Contact Information

A&M Records
1416 N. La Brea Ave.
Hollywood, CA 90025

Web Site

http://www.amrecords.com/current/ginblossoms/index.html

Grant Lee Buffalo

American pop/rock band

Formed in Los Angeles, California, in 1991

There are definitely traditional elements to what we do, though we usually get off on twisting and uprooting those elements and putting them together in a different way," said Grant Lee Phillips, singer and guitarist for the band that sort of bears his name, Grant Lee Buffalo, in *Guitar Player*. His bandmate, bassist Paul Kimble offers a different perspective on what, exactly, Grant Lee Buffalo is trying to do with their music. "You have to be open to accidents and ideas that might strike you as strange. There is nothing more satisfying than having your train of thought derailed and led off into some new direction," he said in a press release for *Mighty Joe Moon*.

Following their music wherever it takes them hasn't added up to high record sales, but has gained the band critical acclaim and a solid group of fans. The *Los Angeles Times* called the music "ambiguous and haunting" and raved about Grant Lee Buffalo's blending of "roots-rock, folk-rock and classic-pop currents into a dreamlike canvas whose scale ranges from the intimate to the panoramic, the personal to the historical." "Call the outfit a smart

"I think a lot of these songs are kind of searching.... digging for some kind of meaning." – Grant Lee Phillips on *Mighty Joe Moon*

Grant Lee Phillips

rock band and that pretty much covers it," said Mercury News Online.

Church music in Stockton, punk bands in Los Angeles

Grant Lee Phillips learned about music on childhood trips to his grandparents' church. His grandfather and great-grandfather were preachers who played fiddle and his grandmother was a gospel singer. "It was Pentecostal, but musically, if you walked in, you'd think it was the Church of Jerry Lee Lewis," said Phillips in the *Los Angeles Times,* referring to one of the pioneers of rock and roll, known for rocking songs like "Great Balls of Fire."

After high school, Phillips moved to Los Angeles to go to film school but instead got more interested in the Hollywood music scene. "The idea of punk rock and independent music was really the light at the end of the tunnel. There were people making records on their own regional labels, regardless of whatever trash the industry was churning out," said Phillips in Mercury News Online. He worked as a house roofer in the day and at night would play in a band called Shiva Burlesque with future Buffalo drummer Joey Peters. According to *Rolling Stone,* one night Paul Kimble saw Shiva Burlesque playing and thought "Wow, I'm going to play with that guitar player and drummer someday." And that's just what happened.

The band is born

The new trio played together under names like Mouth of Rasputin, the Ma-

chine Elves, and Soft Wolf Tread, finally settling on Grant Lee Buffalo in 1991. They built up a steady following around Los Angeles and sent a demo of the song "Fuzzy" to Singles Only, the label run by Husker Du and Sugar veteran Bob Mould. The single led to a deal with the record company Slash and an album also called *Fuzzy.* "An intriguing if unfocused blend of evocative, hazy poetics and cutting commentary, framed in a sort of folk- and jazz-flavored bohemian swing sound," said the *Los Angeles Times.*

> **"We've always been into the idea that you don't come to a show to recite something, you come to share in something that's bigger than any one of us."**

Low record sales, good reception

Although *Fuzzy* didn't sell particularly well, it did introduce the band's music to bands like the Replacements and Pearl Jam, who both invited Grant Lee Buffalo to tour. Phillips was happy to notice that Pearl Jam, like his band, changed their show every night. "We've always been into the idea that you don't come to a show to recite something, you come to share in something that's bigger than any one of us," he said to *Rolling Stone.* Grant Lee Buffalo followed up this intense period of touring with a second record, *Mighty Joe Moon.* Again the record didn't sell very well, but this one caught the attention of R.E.M., who invited the band to open on their tour. When R.E.M. drummer Bill Berry suffered a non-fatal aneurysm on the tour, Peters took over the set that evening.

What now?

Grant Lee Buffalo's pattern of slow record sales but good critical acclaim has continued with their 1996 release, *Copperopolis*. "Phillips layers his rootsy bedrock with string-laden touches of Philly soul, ambitious vocal harmonies and dense, ultra-sustained washes of guitar feedback," said *Guitar Player*. The band has no plans to try and make their music somehow more commercial. For Phillips it's about the music, not record sales. As he said to *Rolling Stone*: "I'm aiming for the transcendent."

Selected Discography

Fuzzy (Slash), 1993.

Mighty Joe Moon (Slash/Reprise), 1994.

Copperopolis (Slash/Reprise), 1996.

Further Reading

Cromelin, Richard, "Where Grant Lee Buffalo Roams," *Los Angeles Times*, December 1, 1994, p. 10.

Cromelin, Richard, "Grant Lee Buffalo Stampedes Fans with Passion at Whisky," *Los Angeles Times*, June 10, 1994, p. 13.

DeRogatis, Jim, "Grant Lee Buffalo: Copperopolis," *Rolling Stone*, June 13, 1996, p. 78.

Powers, Ann, "Grant Lee Buffalo," *Rolling Stone*, August, 19, 1993, p. 24.

Zuniga, Todd, "Grant Lee Buffalo Pays Visit to Chicago," *DePaulia Online*.

Contact Information

Record Label:

Slash/Reprise
3300 Warner Blvd.
Burbank, CA 91505-4694

Fan Club:

11333 Moorpark St., #42,
North Hollywood, CA 91602

Web Sites

http://www.geocities.com/SunsetStrip/5923/index.html

http://www.RepriseRec.com/

GUIDED BY VOICES

American rock and roll band

Formed 1983 in Dayton, Ohio

Guided By Voices is known as the ultimate basement rock and roll band. Together since the early 1980s, they've recorded and released more than twenty-four records—most of them on a Radio Shack four-track. After finally getting the recognition they deserve, Guided By Voices was poised to enter the mainstream. "Basically," said singer/songwriter Bob Pollard, "Guided By Voices has always been me and this revolving cast of people from the time we started in '83." *Rolling Stone's* Michael Corcoran wrote that the band "have been tossing out colorful hooks since 1986 with the frequency and precision of fly-fishermen." While some may find their low-grade sound difficult in this age of digital electronics, it has made Guided By Voices very accessible, and their music "startlingly vivid."

Local beginnings

Guided By Voices started out as a heavy-metal bar band called Anacrusis. Lead singer Bob Pollard, drummer Kevin Fennell, and bassist Mitch Mitchell played local clubs in their hometown of

Northridge, a Dayton, Ohio, community. Kicked out of the club when they imitated new-wave band Devo, Pollard and Mitchell turned to their day gigs. For Pollard that meant teaching.

"We'd drop off five copies at stores and would go back five years later and all the records would still be there."

For five years not much happened. Fellow teacher Pete Jamison changed all that. "We played this softball tournament in Toledo," Pollard said in *Alternative Press.* "So we drove up there and we got to know each other ... he came over and I played him some stuff I recorded ... he freaked out and said, 'We gotta do something with this.'"

Basement band

Gathering together Mitchell and Fennell, Pollard took out a loan from the Dayton Public Schools Credit Union. With the help of his brother Jimmy and Pete Jamison, Pollard used the money for his very first recordings. They recruited guitarist Tobin Sprout and got to work. Using Sprout's four-track machine, they recorded *Forever Since Breakfast* and released it as an EP in 1986 on the local Dayton label I Wanna.

They followed with *Devil Between My Toes, Sandbox, Self-Inflicted Aerial Nostalgia,* and *Same Place the Fly Got Smashed* over the next five years.

When none of the recordings sold, Pollard admits they were ready to hang it up. "We'd drop off five copies at stores and would go back five years later and all

the records would still be there." He went on to say that even local labels were turning them down.

First big break

Luck works in mysterious ways. Cleveland, Ohio-based Scat Records president Robert Griffin was given a copy of *Propeller* (Rockathon, 1992) and gave Pollard a call. Pollard's response: "I don't really know if we're still around."

Still very much "around," they soon released *The Grand Hour* and *Vampire on Titus* in 1993, then *Bee Thousand* in 1994. The last two releases won them serious critical acclaim and started an underground buzz. Michael Azerrad, writing in *Rolling Stone,* called *Bee Thousand* "a tour de force by an old-fashioned American basement genius." Writing that the band was, "Influenced by classic English pop rock filtered through with sounds of Robyn Hitchcock, Cheap Trick, Daniel Johnston, and Pavement, GBV [Guided By Voices] produces a complex, [and] unnamable ... sound."

Other voices helped the buzz

Following these releases, other musicians (including members of the Breeders, Sonic Youth, and the Beastie Boys) began speaking out about Guided By Voices. The band also resumed touring. Their record label Scat brought in indie-label superstar, Matador Records, to widen distribution. In the fall of 1994, MTV began playing the band's first music video, "I Am a Scientist."

Their next release, *Alien Lanes* (Matador, 1995), solidified their standing with the critics. Matt Diehl, in *Rolling Stone,* wrote that "If anything, *Alien* outshines *Bee Thousand* in its startling consistency." Diehl went on to call the album " ... a magnum opus [masterpiece] of pure pop for now people."

Critical acclaim

Quitting their day jobs just before the *Alien Lanes* release, the band was able to focus solely on the music. While their earlier efforts were labeled brilliant, later work was, as Tom Sinclair wrote, coming "close to capturing the high-flying dynamics of the band's live sound."

GBV embarked on their first European tour in 1995, then followed with their first big tour in the States. This tour was cut short when drummer Kevin Fennell injured his back.

Guided By Voices released *Under the Bushes, Under the Stars* in 1996 on the Matador label. *Rolling Stone* reviewer Michael Corcoran wrote that "*Under the Bushes* searches for something new in the pop-rock ruins and finds that the quest is the thing." He noted that the "two minute tunes aren't fragments so much as full compositions that say plenty in a short period of time." In support of the album, GBV successfully toured Canada, Europe, and the United States in the spring of 1996.

Trying something different

Solo releases by guitarist Tobin Sprout and singer Bob Pollard fueled rumors that the band was splitting up. "A lot of people think we're broken up," Pollard told Robert Cherry, "but I don't think it's gonna be that big of a change except for the fact that it's going to sound a lot better."

Recorded with Cleveland band, Cobra Verde, backing lead singer Bob Pollard, GBV released *Mag Earwhig!* in the spring of 1997. According to *Rolling Stone* writer Ben Kim, "The difference [of recording with a new band] is immediately striking." The critic noted that where some songs once staggered, they now swagger. Like many of the band's past reviews, *Mag Earwhig!* received a solid four stars and a big thumbs-up.

What accounts for the GBV's continuing success is Pollard. Now in his late thirties, he takes chances and tries new approaches, but he never strays far from his smart rock conventions. While GBV hasn't always enjoyed mainstream approval, critics and other musicians have regularly respected them for knocking out a body of work that is grounded in rock and roll and uniquely their own. Matt Diehl of *Rolling Stone* explained the band's appeal: "GBV's individual outlook and infectious enthusiasm make old ingredients seem new, mixing them into a brilliant collection of songs whose importance feels predestined."

Selected Discography

Forever Since Breakfast (I Wanna), 1986.

Devil Between My Toes (E), 1987.

Sandbox (Halo), 1988.

Self-Inflicted Aerial Nostalgia (Halo), 1989.

Same Place the Fly Got Smashed (Engine #9), 1990.

Propeller (Rockathon), 1992.

The Grand Hour (Scat), 1993.

Vampire on Titus (Scat), 1993.

Bee Thousand (Scat), 1994.

Box (Scat), 1995.

Alien Lanes (Matador), 1995.

Under the Bushes, Under the Stars (Matador), 1996.

Mag Earwhig! (Matador), 1997.

Further Reading

Azerrad, Michael, "Bee Thousand," 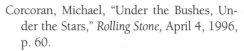 *Rolling Stone,* August 11, 1994, p. 66.

Corcoran, Michael, "Under the Bushes, Under the Stars," *Rolling Stone,* April 4, 1996, p. 60.

Diehl, Matt, "Recording Voices Carry," *Rolling Stone,* March 23, 1995, p. 119.

Kim, Ben, "Mag Earwhig!," *Rolling Stone,* June 12, 1997, p. 112.

Petkovic, John, "24 Hours with Guided By Voices," *Alternative Press,* September, 1996, p. 51.

Web Page

http://www.gbv.com/

HOOTIE AND THE BLOWFISH

American rock and roll band

Formed in Columbia, South Carolina, in 1986

"I refuse to let popularity keep me from going to the mall."–Jim "Soni" Sonefeld, drums

With a "what you see is what you get" attitude, the members of Hootie and the Blowfish hang on to their "regular guy" image with a passion. It's something they don't want to lose, regardless of how famous they become. Their hugely successful debut album sold more than most other artists sell in their entire careers—and more than any one album by Pearl Jam, U2, the Rolling Stones, and even the Beatles. "Hootie" entered American music history with their sincere and emotional blend of melodic southern folk rock. Meanwhile, they've kept a humble perspective in the light of sudden super stardom.

There's no business like show business

Formed on the campus of the University of South Carolina, Hootie and the Blowfish (a name derived from two unique-looking friends of lead singer and guitarist Darius Rucker) played fraternity parties and local "beer joints" while building a loyal following of enthusiastic college-aged fans. After graduating from college in 1989, Rucker, along with his bandmates Mark Bryan (guitar), Dean Felber

Darius Rucker

(bass), and new drummer Jim "Soni" Sonefeld, incorporated their own company, Fishco Inc. They began rigorously touring and marketing themselves across the southeastern United States. While averaging about 250 shows a year from 1990 to 1993, Hootie successfully recorded and released their own two independent releases, *Hootie and the Blowfish* (1990) and *Time* (1991), which they sold at shows and at local record stores.

When a short-lived record contract with California-based indie label J.R.S. Records didn't work out, Hootie released a third independent record, *Kootchypop* (1993), this time enlisting the assistance of R.E.M. producer Don Dixon. With the help of a distribution deal from the music wholesale company Rock Bottom, the six-song EP *Kootchypop* quickly sold 50,000 copies regionally, resulting in major record companies taking an interest in the group.

Records weren't the only thing the band was selling. Rucker later confirmed that the band had already sold over a quarter million dollars worth of hats, t-shirts, and other Hootie merchandise before making it big.

Straight to the top

On Halloween of 1993, Atlantic Records signed Hootie and the Blowfish and prepared to record and release their major label debut album, *Cracked Rear View* (1994). With a steady climb over the next ten months to the top of the charts, *Cracked Rear View* featured Rucker's powerful and soulful voice on straightforward melodic rock songs, such as "Hold My Hand," "Only Wanna Be with You," and "Hannah Jane." The album would eventually become the number two top-selling debut album of all time, with more than fourteen million copies sold. (Only Boston's self titled debut album has sold more, at fifteen million copies.) Hootie, who was in heavy rotation on VH-1, MTV, and radio stations across the United States, suddenly found itself as much more than a mere college bar band, they had become a musical phenomenon.

Taking the good with the bad

The group became frequent guests on national television. During one of the band's nearly half dozen appearances on CBS-TV's *Late Show with David Letterman,* Letterman held up a copy of *Cracked Rear View* and proclaimed, "If you don't buy this album, there's something wrong with you." Despite the band's smashing success, not everyone cared for the group. Some music critics compared the band to a minstrel show, and one called Rucker the "reigning crybaby" of rock in early 1996. Even with the bit of negative industry backlash that Hootie received, it went on to win two awards at the 38th Annual Grammy Awards in 1996, including Best New Artist.

Right place, right time?

Some have speculated that it was Hootie's timing that made their album sell so well. After the shotgun suicide of Kurt Cobain (singer from the band **Nirvana**) just three months before the release of

Hootie and the Blowfish, a bunch of regular guys

Cracked Rear View, Americans began developing a growing disinterest in the whole grunge movement (a popular music fad started in the late 1980s in Seattle, Washington, and typified by loud biting guitars and cynical, angry, and depressing lyrics). Audiences were ripe for a friendlier, more comforting music message, and Hootie, with their "regular guy" image (beer-drinking buddies who like to play golf in their spare time) and sensitive unpretentious tunes were just the answer.

Don't give a Hootie anymore

As with any band that has a huge smash record, Hootie prepared for a sales letdown on their next effort. The group knew that no matter how well their second album sold, it wouldn't come close to outselling the first album, and would therefore be considered a failure by the critical music industry standards. In spite of concerns by industry insiders that the band had been overexposed, and that poor timing of the second release might risk their public appeal, Atlantic Records released *Fairweather Johnson* in April of 1996.

The album made its debut at No. 1 on the charts and stayed there only two weeks. It contained slightly moodier lyrics than Hootie's first album, but the album was still lightened by the group's upbeat

Parents Aren't Supposed to Like It

musical style and Rucker's expressive baritone voice (although muddier and somewhat more difficult to hear in the mix).

Fairweather Johnson proved to be the big sales letdown everyone had expected. It received very mixed reviews from the critics. As easily as the band seemed to have gone to the top, it seemed just as hard for the group to be able to shake the infamous "sophomore jinx." Since *Fairweather Johnson*'s release, Hootie has slipped farther and farther away from the public spotlight they once dominated. Critics wait to see if the band's third album will be able to take them back to the top of the charts again, or if Hootie will join the ever-growing list of "flash-in-the-pan" music artists.

Selected Awards

South Carolina Music and Entertainment Association, South Carolina Artist of the Year, 1994.

23rd Annual American Music Awards, Favorite New Artist Award.

Grammy Award, Best New Artist, 1996.

Grammy Award for Best Pop Vocal Performance by a Duo or Group, for "Let Her Cry," 1996.

Selected Discography

Kootchypop (Fishco Inc./Rock Bottom), 1993.

Cracked Rear View (Atlantic), 1994.

Fairweather Johnson (Atlantic), 1996.

Further Reading

Farley, Christopher John, "Can 13 Million Hootie Fans Really Be Wrong?," *Time,* April 29, 1996, p. 74.

Farley, Christopher John, "Southern Exposure," *Time,* February 27, 1995, p. 75.

Jacobson, Mark, "Why Hate Hootie?," *Esquire,* August 1996, p. 32.

McCollum, Brian, "Pop's Top-selling Band Hopes To Avoid Sophomore Slump with New Album," *Knight-Ridder/Tribune News Service,* April 11, 1996.

Willman, Chris, "Hootie Ya Love?," *Entertainment Weekly,* May 3, 1996, p. 18.

Contact Information

Atlantic Records
1290 Avenue of the Americas
New York, NY 10104

Web Site

http://www.atlantic.records.com/hootie

Live

American rock and roll band

Formed in 1984 in York, Pennsylvania

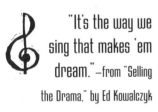

"It's the way we sing that makes 'em dream." –from "Selling the Drama," by Ed Kowalczyk

Serious, hardworking, a great live show, and a message with something to really hold onto has made Live both popular and successful. Described as a band with a "straightforward spin" on 1980s classic rock, Live continues to turn out a deeply personal, "speaker rattling sound." And while critics may be divided on the band's musical merit, Live will continue to push for success. "In about ten years," lead singer Ed Kowalczyk says, "there's gonna be this island of bands ... that are standing all together and have weathered all the trends ... And I really honest to God believe we'll probably be there on that island."

Small town boys

Live started out in York, Pennsylvania, as a group of four thirteen-year-olds called Public Affection. Schoolmates Patrick Dahlheimer (bass), Chad Gracey (drums), Ed Kowalczyk (vocals), and Chad Taylor (guitar) formed to play in their eighth-grade talent show. With their music teacher urging them on, they decided to keep playing. Upon graduation from William Penn Senior High

Ed Kowalczyk

School in 1989, they were faced with a big decision: Go to college or keep playing. "That was the serious turning point," guitarist Chad Taylor told *Musician,* "deciding not to go to college."

Focused and committed, they were determined to move ahead. As Public Affection they released their first album, *Death of a Dictionary,* in 1989. Released independently, the album grabbed the attention of Talking Heads keyboardist Jerry Harrison, who named them "up-and-coming rock rookies" in *Rolling Stone.* Radioactive Records took notice and signed them on in 1991.

Four songs and a name

Changing their name to Live, they began working with Harrison on their first EP for Radioactive, *Four Songs.* Harrison told *Musician* that the band was "out of the mainstream" and as a result were "less derivative, more indigenous." He went on to explain that the band wasn't "looking over their shoulders at what some other band was doing." Nevertheless, critics have compared them to Irish rock band **U2** (see entry) for their sincerity, and alternative pop/rock band **R.E.M.** (see entry) for lead singer Ed Kowalczyk's vocals.

"We've tried to make *Throwing Copper* more than your average trip down angst lane."

In 1992, Live released their first full length album, *Mental Jewelry.* The single, "Operation Spirit" was a success, leading to their first big tour with rock band

Blind Melon and experimental new wave band Public Image Ltd., among others, on the "MTV 120 Minutes" tour. Embraced by MTV, the album caused media types to begin gushing with praise. Don McLeese wrote in *Rolling Stone,* "It's hard to imagine a more serious band than ... Live, whose moral earnestness makes early U2 sound frat-band frivolous."

Throwing Copper

The praise continued with the release of their next album in 1994, *Throwing Copper.* Elysa Gardner wrote in *Spin* that the new album was filled "with spiritual imagery and social commentary." Two singles ("Selling the Drama" and "I Alive") from *Throwing Copper* went into heavy rotation on MTV and increased Live's popularity.

"We've tried to make *Throwing Copper* more than your average trip down angst lane," Kowalczyk explained in the band's Radioactive Records bio. And the band felt the new album marked real growth. "We like to say that the soundscape of Live has totally transformed," Kowalczyk added. The critics agreed. Neil Strauss in the *New York Times* wrote, "The difference between Live and many of its slacker contemporaries is that Live treats songs reverentially, as if they are truly inspired by a higher force."

The fans love 'em

Fans agreed too. Less than two years after its release, *Throwing Copper* had sold more than five million copies. In 1995 the band picked up *Billboard*'s Rock Artist of the Year award. They were also named Artist of the Year in *Rolling Stone*'s 1996 Readers Picks. Live followed the release of *Throwing Copper* with "endless touring, five radio and video smashes and a judiciously timed appearance on MTV Unplugged," wrote Jason Cohen in *Rolling Stone.*

Live "is more about searching than raging," continued Cohen, from the same article. "Lyricist Kowalczyk is unafraid of sentiment, favoring Big Subjects like love, religion and ... the circle of life —as in birth, death and rebirth." Chad Taylor told Cohen, "We're earnest people."

Secret Samadhi

Live released their third album, *Secret Samadhi* in the spring of 1997. The title track, "Lakini's Juice" received plenty of play, but critics panned the album. Jeremy Helligar wrote in *People Weekly* that "Live has the same overstatement problem U2 had in its ... '80s days: too much bluster and not enough subtlety." Jim Farber, reviewing the video for *Entertainment Weekly,* complained that the "cheerless tone fits the band's scolding image."

Rolling Stone's Cohen wrote that Live were not critical favorites, but the band wasn't intimidated. "Man, we were never credible," explained bassist Patrick Dahlheimer. "Just because some critic doesn't think we're cool doesn't faze us," Kowalczyk added. What Live cares about are the people who come to see them play, the fans who buy their records, and the 12,000 who daily visit their official web site. "They know," said Kowalczyk, "they can feel the passion of the songs."

Selected Awards

Throwing Copper certified quintuple platinum (five million copies sold), 1995.

Mental Jewelry certified gold, 1995.

Rock Artists of the Year, *Billboard,* 1995.

Artist of the Year, *Rolling Stone*'s Readers' Picks, 1996.

Selected Discography

Death of a Dictionary (independent release), 1989, as by Public Affection.

Four Songs (Radioactive), 1991, EP.

Mental Jewelry (Radioactive), 1992.

Throwing Copper (Radioactive), 1994.

Secret Samadhi (Radioactive), 1997.

Further Reading

Cohen, Jason, "Live, Hootie, Live, Hootie," *Rolling Stone,* January 25, 1996, p. 34.

Considine, J.D., "Secret Samadhi," *Entertainment Weekly,* March 7, 1997, p. 64.

Farber, Jim, "Lakini's Juice," *Entertainment Weekly,* March 28, 1997, p. 66.

Gardner, Elysa, *Spin,* 1995.

Hellegar, Jeremy, "Secret Samadhi," *People Weekly,* April 4, 1997, p. 26.

Musician, April 1992.

Rolling Stone, April 18, 1991; April 16, 1992; May 14, 1992; August 11, 1994.

Strauss, Neil, *New York Times,* June 9, 1994.

Contact Information

Radioactive Records
70 Universal City Plaza, 3rd Floor
Universal City, CA 91608

Web Page

http://www.radioactive.com

LOS LOBOS

American rock and roll band

Formed 1974 in Los Angeles, California

D uring their twenty-five years together, Los Lobos has emerged as one of the most respected and original bands around. Combining rock, folk, blues, R & B, country, and Tex-Mex with traditional Mexican music, they've continually tried new sounds and confounded anyone who tries to classify them.

"It became a mission, almost a crusade ... bringing music together to bring people together." –Los Lobos' Louie Pérez.

Primero

David Hidalgo, Conrad Lozano, Louie Pérez, and Cesar Rosas formed Los Lobos (Spanish for "The Wolves") in 1974. They were high school friends from East Los Angeles. "We were friends before we were ever a band. I think that's one of the reasons we've been around as long as we have," said Pérez, drummer and multi-instrumentalist, in a record company biography.

Singer/guitarist Hidalgo has been playing guitar and listening to rock music since he was eleven. He learned the drums and played in a Christian rock band in the early 1970s. Guitarist Rosas moved to Los Angeles from Sonora, Mexico, when he was seven.

He taught himself guitar in high school. Bassist Lozano was a musician who had been playing in another Los Angeles band, Tierra. Pérez, who learned guitar at twelve, joined the band as a guitarist (he later switched to drums when the band decided they needed a drummer.)

It wasn't like the band set out to be the adventurous, unique outfit they are today. Originally they were a garage band. "After awhile, trying to match licks with [guitarist Eric] Clapton got a little old and we started listening to the music we'd grown up with," said Pérez in a press release for *The Neighborhood*. "We pulled out all those records we used to beg our parents not to play around our friends and found an incredible wealth of music. These guys were doing amazing things with their instruments and we started trying to pick up on it."

They played at weddings and parties, before getting their first real gig at a Mexican restaurant. "It wasn't even a real Mexican restaurant—one of those tourist joints," said Rosas in *Guitar World*. "We were working there because we had come to a point where we had to either make more money from music or find other jobs."

> "After awhile, trying to match licks with [guitarist Eric] Clapton got a little old and we started listening to the music we'd grown up with. We pulled out all those records we used to beg our parents not to play around our friends and found an incredible wealth of music."

The band started getting more equipment and experimenting with an electric sound trying to get closer to a Tex-Mex sound. Then they realized how close the songs sounded to the rock and roll format. "We brought our bigger amps and we started playing real loud. Soon after that, we got fired," said Pérez in a record company bio. But the band had discovered its sound.

Coming into their own

They raised money from their friends and recorded an album *Just Another Band from L.A.,* for the New Vista label. They sold the record at their shows, which were becoming increasingly popular around Los Angeles. It was an active time on the L.A. music scene, when a lot of bands were fans of roots rock. At one show, Los Lobos opened for rockabilly group the Blasters and made friends with the band. The Blasters' saxophone player, Steve Berlin, was especially impressed by Los Lobos and eventually signed on as their sax player. The Blasters also helped Los Lobos get a deal with their record label, Slash.

In 1983 the band put out their major label debut, the EP *...And a Time To Dance*. The record earned the band their first of many Grammy Awards, this time for the song "Anselma." And maybe even better, after the EP sold 50,000 copies the band had enough money to buy a second-hand van for touring.

With a little more money to work with, the band recorded *How Will the Wolf Survive?* which mixed traditional Mexican songs, rock and roll, and blues. The record caught the attention of Paul Simon, who asked the band to sing on his *Graceland* record, and **Elvis Costello** (see entry), who had them sing on *King Of America*. The band worked on their own music, too, and came up with the more pop-oriented *By the Light of the Moon*.

La Bamba

Anyone who hadn't already heard of Los Lobos certainly did in 1987. That's when the band's version of Ritchie Valens' "La Bamba," from the movie of the same name, became a number one hit. But instead of following the record up with a commercial release, Los Lobos tried something different entirely—a recording of traditional Mexican songs called *La Pistola Y El Corazon*, Spanish for "the pistol and the heart." "We talked about doing something like this since the day we signed a deal with the company, to take this music and record it properly," said Hidalgo in *Guitar World*. The *All Music Guide to Rock* gave the record four out of five stars, saying it "isn't a history lesson, but a celebration of their heritage and its joyous music, which means that it's just as exciting and entertaining as their rock and roll records."

Los Lobos took two years off and returned with *The Neighborhood*. It was recorded informally. "We didn't want to run the songs into the ground. When you think about something too much, things tend to lose some spirit and heart. So we would just roll tape and go with our instincts," said Pérez, in a press release for the record. *Rolling Stone* called the record, along with *How Will the Wolf Survive?* and

Rock pioneer Ritchie Valens

As anyone who has seen the 1987 movie, La Bamba, knows, Ritchie Valens was a hero to the Mexican-American community in Southern California. Raised by Mexican-Indian parents, Valens recorded his first single "Come On, Let's Go/Framed" in early 1958 for Del-Fi. It was good enough to win him an appearance on Dick Clark's American Bandstand television show. Toward the end of 1958, he recorded a second single, the love ballad "Donna." For the B-side, he updated a Mexican wedding song and sang it in Spanish, calling it "La Bamba." Before the two-sided hit could climb the charts, Valens was killed in a tragic airplane accident on February 3, 1959, that also claimed the lives of rockers Buddy Holly and the "Big Bopper" (Jiles Perry Richardson).

By the Light of the Moon "masterpieces." In retrospect, Hidalgo views the record differently. "It's not a bad record, but the business side of that record took us out for a while. It came out while we were on the road, and it didn't get any push. Nobody even heard about it, and we came back from the road in debt," said Hidalgo in *Guitar Player*.

Yet another masterpiece

In 1992 the band came out with what many critics and fans think is their best record, *Kiko*. On the record, they mixed their roots music with a glossy, atmospheric production. The record made "album of the year" in newspapers across the country, including the *Los Angeles Times* and the *Chicago Tribune*. An inventive video for the song "Kiko and the Lavender Moon," didn't get much airtime on MTV, although it did win an MTV award.

The band celebrated twenty years together by releasing a two-CD compilation, *Just Another Band from East L.A ... A Collection*, including material from live shows, out-takes, and material from their early indie records. Before regrouping for their next big release, the members of Los Lobos worked on various side projects. They put out the children's record *Papa's Dream* and worked on songs for the movies *Desperado* and *Feeling Minnesota*. Hidalgo and Pérez teamed up for the Latin Playboys, an avant-garde roots band.

On to *Colossal Head*

The band recorded *Colossal Head* quickly, trying to catch the first sparks of inspiration. "We were working really fast," said Pérez in a press release for *Colossal Head*. "We couldn't second guess ourselves. I would be writing something in the studio lounge, and it was like 'Are you ready to record that yet?' But I really think that the first thought is usually the best thought."

Unfortunately, many critics didn't agree. *Entertainment Weekly* gave the record a "B-", saying they "waste too much time groaning leaden beat-generation platitudes." *Rolling Stone* was even harsher, giving the record two out of five stars and saying the band was "still searching for the right balance between experimentation and craftsmanship, and between concepts and passion."

The band would agree with *Rolling Stone* on one thing: they are "still searching" and will continue to do just that, like they have throughout their long career. "Hey, it's got to be different!" said Cesar Rosas in press materials for *Colossal Head*. "Who would want to make the same record over and over again? That would be so boring!"

Selected Awards

Grammy, Best Mexican/American Performance, "Anselma," 1984.

Golden Eagle Award, Best Film Soundtrack, "La Bamba," 1988.

Grammy, Best Rock Performance By A Duo or Group, *La Pistola Y El Corazon*, 1988.

MTV Music Video Awards, Breakthrough Video, "Kiko and the Lavender Moon," 1993.

Grammy, Best Pop Instrumental, "Mariachi Suite," 1995.

Selected Discography

How Will the Wolf Survive? (Slash/Warner Bros.), 1984.

By the Light of the Moon (Slash/Warner Bros.), 1987.

The Neighborhood (Slash/Warner Bros.), 1990.

Kiko (Slash/Warner Bros.), 1992.

Just Another Band from East L.A.: A Collection, (Slash/Warner Bros.), 1993.

Colossal Head (Slash/Warner Bros.), 1996.

Further Reading

Andrews, Jon, "Colossal Head," *Downbeat*, June 1996, p. 58.

Eddy, Chuck, "Colossal Head," *Entertainment Weekly*, March 22, 1996, p. 75.

Forte, Dan, "Los Lobos," *Guitar Player*, July 1995, p. 38.

Himes, Geoffrey, "Colossal Head," *Rolling Stone*, April 18, 1996, p. 70.

Hochman, Steve, "Los Lobos," *Rolling Stone*, October 1, 1992, p. 34.

Thompson, Art, and Ellis, Andy, "Flex Mex: New Twists from Los Lobos," *Guitar Player*, October, 1996, p. 68.

Contact Information

Slash
3300 Warner Blvd.
Burbank, CA 91505

Web Site

http://www.wbr.com/loslobos/

Dave Matthews Band

American rock and roll band

Formed in Charlottesville, North Carolina, in 1991

"Hey, how y'all doin'? We're the Dave Matthews Band, and we're from somewhere in Virginia" – Dave Matthews onstage at the 1996 H.O.R.D.E. festival

The Dave Matthews Band has been constantly compared to the Grateful Dead throughout their career. It's for two reasons. First, it's their loose, jazzy music filled with what *People Weekly* magazine calls "Dead inspired jams." Second, like the Grateful Dead, the band has quietly gathered a large group of fiercely loyal fans. "It's been a very natural, very low-key progression. I don't feel like we've had this drastic, overnight success. It's basically been a matter of word-of-mouth—people liking what they've seen and bringing some friends with them the next time around," said Dave Matthews in a press release for the 1994 release of *Under the Table and Dreaming*.

South African roots

Matthews grew up in New York and South Africa. His dad died from cancer when Matthews was ten. In South Africa, he was "an indifferent high school student whose antics earned him the lash," according to *Rolling Stone*. He was more interested in playing the guitar and listening to music than in studying. "He listened

Dave Matthews

584

The Dave Matthews Band winning a Grammy Award in 1997

very purposefully. He knew every word to every single Beatles album," said his sister Jane in *Rolling Stone*. Matthews also became interested in the sound of drums in South Africa. "That's my obsession, percussion. Plus, I've always loved to dance. The spins of African rhythms, Latin rhythms—they send me into throes of ecstasy," said Matthews to *Guitar Player*.

Back to the States

Matthews moved to Virginia in 1986 and took a job as a bartender at Miller's, a musicians' hangout. Eventually Matthews asked some of his regular customers to form a band with him. *Rolling Stone* asked Matthews if creating a multi-racial band was a way to make up for the segregation he experienced and hated in South Africa. "I approached Carter [Beauford, drums], LeRoi [Moore, sax] and Boyd [Tinsley, violin] because they were the most fantastic musicians I'd ever seen. But if the way our band looks onstage—two white guys and three black guys all playing together—sends out some kind of positive racial message, that's a bonus," Matthews answered.

The grass roots uprising

The Dave Matthews Band took an unusual route to success. They built up a grass roots following by constant touring, almost 200 days a year. They played everywhere—frat houses, beach clubs, and anywhere else that would pay. Their technique worked. Fans made bootleg tapes of shows and told their friends about the band. The band's first indie record, *Remember Two Things,* sold over 300,000 copies, outstanding for a release on an independent label.

The breakthrough

The Dave Matthews Band's breakthrough year came in 1995 with an opening spot on the Grateful Dead tour, appearances on the *Tonight Show,* and playing dates on the H.O.R.D.E. tour. They released *Under the Table and Dreaming,* which was called "unpeggable and totally addictive" by *Details* and "loose folk fusion" by *People Weekly.* It went triple platinum, selling more than three million copies in the United States.

"That's my obsession, percussion. Plus, I've always loved to dance. The spins of African rhythms, Latin rhythms—they send me into throes of ecstasy."

The band recorded the follow up, *Crash,* live in the studio, sitting in a circle, to try and capture the energy of their live shows. "Facing each other, we could communicate better—the joy when someone hit something cool or the embarrassment when someone hit a bum note. Everything inside that room instantly became more alive, just like it is onstage," said Matthews to *Guitar Player.*

The success of *Crash* assured The Dave Matthews Band mainstream popularity which, predictably, also meant some backlash from the critics. Though one *Rolling Stone* reviewer complimented their mix of "jazz, fusion, funk and rock with rhythmic, lilting folk music," another *Rolling Stone* reviewer called Matthews's vocals "too much like Sting's at times" and the lyrics "banal."

But, criticism hasn't hurt the band's career one bit. And Matthews says he doesn't read reviews anyway, unless they're really bad. "A guy from New York *Newsday* gave us the best insult," he said to *Rolling Stone.* "He said our success was somewhere between America's tolerance for Barney and France's love for Jerry Lewis. I was like 'At least we're up there.'"

Selected Awards

Under The Table and Dreaming certified triple platinum.

Grammy, Best Rock Vocal, "So Much To Say," 1997.

Selected Discography

Remember Two Things (Bama Rags), 1993.

Under The Table and Dreaming (RCA), 1994.

Crash (RCA), 1996.

Further Reading

Abrahams, Andrew, "Crash," *People Weekly,* May 8, 1996, p. 25.

Jim Bessman, "Dave Matthews Back with a Bang," *Billboard,* March 23, 1996, p. 12.

Colapinto, John, "The Raging Optimism and Multiple Personalities of Dave Matthews," *Rolling Stone,* December 12, 1996, p. 52.

DeRogatis, Jim, "Crash," *Rolling Stone,* May 16, 1996, p. 54.

Parents Aren't Supposed to Like It

Mettler, Mike, "Profile: Dave Matthews," *Guitar Player*, August, 1996, p. 29.

Contact Information

RCA
1540 Broadway
New York, NY 10036

Web Site

http://www2.rlcom.net/dmbandnew/
  index.html

PHiSH

American rock and roll band

Formed 1983 in Burlington, Vermont

Phish from left to right: Page McConnell, Trey Anastasio, Jon Fishman, Mike Gordon

To the uninitiated, Phish may seem like just another band following the trail blazed by the legendary classic rock band, the Grateful Dead. While there are similarities—legions of fans (Phishheads) following them from show to show, the audience taping concerts, and extended live jams—Phish is a band with a character all its own. Like the Dead, however, Phish incorporates many different genres into their own music. "We play bluegrass, Latin, rock, funk, classical, jazz, calypso and hard-core," bassist Mike Gordon told Charles Hirshberg of *Life*. "Oh yeah," he added, "we've got a Broadway sound, too."

Early Phish

The first incarnation of Phish formed on the University of Vermont's Redstone Campus in 1983. There, guitarists Trey Anastasio and Jeff Holdsworth met and decided to form a band. The two recruited drummer Jeff Fishman and bassist Gordon and played their first concert at an ROTC formal dance, only to be drowned out by a tape of Michael Jackson's *Thriller.*

Undaunted, the band continued on and began playing regular shows at a bar in Burlington called Nectar's. Soon, they developed a local following that would travel to other cities in Vermont to hear them play and then to towns as far away as Boston. In 1985 keyboardist Page Mc-Connell joined the band. Holdsworth left the next year, leaving Phish the quartet it has been since.

For the next five years Phish toured almost constantly, seeing its audience steadily increase with each passing year. Part of the reason for the band's growing audience was its sheer musicianship and energetic performances. Other reasons were the eccentricities of the band's performances, such as Fishman wearing goggles and a muumuu or sometimes appearing nude, and Anastasio and Gordon performing while jumping on mini-trampolines.

Fans also enjoyed the adventurous nature of the shows; the band would spontaneously build around an improvisational riff that would take them from jazz-rock into bluegrass to hard rock to barbershop quartet to an extended jam that might go on for a half-hour. "We want to have a spontaneous adventure," Anastasio told Joannie M. Schrof of *U.S News & World Report,* explaining why the band doesn't know what it will play until it's onstage. "You can't plan an adventure, or it ceases to be one."

Phishheads and Phish Food

After two self-made releases, 1988's *Junta* and 1990's *Lawn Boy,* Phish had reached such a cult status that major labels could no longer ignore them. In 1991 the band signed to Elektra, who agreed to rerelease the two self-made albums as well as the album Phish had recorded prior to signing called *A Picture of Nectar.* None of the albums sold particularly well, but the concerts were almost always completely sold out.

The band continued to record an album a year, including 1993's *Rift,* 1994's *Hoist,* and *A Live One* in 1995; but it was their concerts and the growing legions of fans who followed them around the country—Phishheads—that attracted the most attention. In 1996 the band put on a two-day concert at an abandoned Air Force base in Plattsburgh, New York. Dubbed the Clifford Ball, it featured three sets of music from Phish each day, plus an assortment of other arts and entertainment. With an estimated 135,000 people in attendance, it was the largest concert in North America that year.

Phish's 1996 release, *Billy Breathes,* was the band's most popular. It debuted at number seven on the *Billboard* album chart, their highest charting ever. Steven Cook of *People Weekly* credited the album's success to producer Steve Lillywhite, who "manages to harness some of [Phish's] live energy and create[s] a lilting, album-long groove that rocks like a comfortable hammock." The band began 1997 by introducing a new flavor from that other Vermont mainstay, Ben & Jerry's. Called Phish Food, it's made up of chocolate ice cream, marshmallow nougat, caramel swirl, and fish-shaped fudge.

Selected Discography:

Junta (self-released), 1988; (Elektra), 1992.

Lawn Boy (Absolute a Go Go), 1990; (Elektra), 1992.

A Picture of Nectar (Elektra), 1992.

Rift (Elektra), 1993.

Hoist (Elektra), 1994.

A Live One (Elektra), 1995.

Billy Breathes (Elektra), 1996.

Further Reading

Budnick, Dean, *The Phishing Manual: A Compendium to the Music of Phish,* Hyperion Books, 1996.

Gordinier, Jeff, "High Tide," *Entertainment Weekly,* November 1, 1996, p. 30.

Lubell, David, "Phish and Friends Devour the Big Apple," *Relix,* February 1997, p. 22.

Lubell, David, "Phish Close Out the Year in Style," *Relix,* April 1997, p. 48.

Puterbaugh, Parke, "Phresh Phish," *Rolling Stone,* February 20, 1997, p. 42.

Resnicoff, Matt, "Swimming Against the Tide," *Guitar Player,* May 1996, p. 72.

Richmond, Peter, "Phishstock Nation," *GQ: Gentleman's Quarterly,* January 1997, p. 110.

Schrof, Joannie M., "Vermont's Hot Band Phishes for Musical Nirvana," *U.S. News and World Report,* December 25, 1995, p. 99.

Contact Information

Elektra Records
75 Rockefeller Plaza
New York, NY 10019

Web Site

http://www.phish.net, http://www.phish.com

son volt

American rock and roll band

Formed on the Mississippi River in 1994

It's impossible to talk about Son Volt without mentioning the band Uncle Tupelo. Uncle Tupelo was an influential late 1980s-early 1990s band that almost single-handedly invented a kind of music that combined country music with punk-style guitars. When the band broke up in 1994, it turned into two bands, Jay Farrar's Son Volt and Jeff Tweedy's **Wilco** (see entry). Instead of being the end of one good band, like many expected, the break-up turned out to be the beginning of two good bands with two different sounds. The difference? According to the *New York Times,* Wilco has more of a late 1960s Rolling Stones kind of sound, while "Son Volt has revived the consonant, fuzzy strumming of the Byrds' folk-rock."

With their critically acclaimed debut *Trace* followed up by *Straightaways,* the quiet and shy Farrar has established Son Volt as an important band known for making forlorn roots music. According to *Rolling Stone Online,* Farrar "could sing 'Sugar Sugar' [a very light and upbeat 1960s pop song] and make it sound tragic."

> "We're not a country band. I don't think anyone could line-dance through one of our shows." —Son Volt's Jay Farrar in *Interview.*

Jay Farrar

Mississippi River boy

Jay Farrar grew up in Belleville, Illinois, a quiet town near the Mississippi River. His father worked on a dredge boat on the river and collected cars. During his childhood Farrar's family only went on one vacation, which may have something to do with why Farrar's Son Volt albums are so concerned with travel and the open road.

Farrar picked up the guitar at twelve. He played in a few high school garage bands, then at fifteen hooked up with Jeff Tweedy and future Son Volt drummer Mike Hiedorn in a rock band, the Primitives. That was the band that turned into Uncle Tupelo. Eight years later they put out their first record, *No Depression*. Three records and much acclaim later, the band broke up. "It just sort of ran out of gas," said Farrar to *Newsweek*.

A Son Volt is born

Farrar put Uncle Tupelo behind him and formed Son Volt. In *Interview*, Farrar said the breakup was "depressing at first being alienated from all those guys, but it was liberating to be playing in this new lineup, because you never knew what was going to come out." The new line-up had Hiedorn and brothers Jim (bass) and Dave Boquist (guitar, banjo, fiddle, lap steel).

When the band started rehearsing for *Trace*, Farrar lived in New Orleans, and the rest of the band lived in St. Louis and Minneapolis. So Farrar was often on the road driving up and down the Mississippi. "I did a lot of driving," he said in the *Philadelphia Inquirer*. "It got

to be an inspiration. But I wouldn't pull over or anything, I'd keep going and hope I remember whatever I'd been thinking. A lot of the lyrics came that way." The paper described the music on *Trace* as "curtly strummed acoustic guitars kissed by lamenting violins, electric guitar solos that unwind against prickly banjo and mandolin backdrops." *Entertainment Weekly* gave the record an "A," praising the record's "equal parts twang and thrash." The *Village Voice* called Farrar a "weary-voiced, warm-hearted gentleman."

Too laid-back?

To follow up the success of the laid-back *Trace*, Farrar came up with a record even more slowed down, *Straightaways*. Although critical response to *Trace* was almost all completely positive, on the slower *Straightaways*, the reviews were more mixed. "Farrar comes perilously close to repeating himself after only two albums with Son Volt," griped MTV Online. Many of the bad reviews came from critics who wanted to hear a more rocking Son Volt. "Son Volt sounds asleep at the wheel," carped *Entertainment Weekly*. "A little more jolt in the volt, please," suggested *Stereo Review*.

Will Son Volt take the criticisms to heart and get "more jolt in the volt"? Even Farrar doesn't know. "Spontaneity is nice with this band because you never know what's going to happen next," he said in a press release. "There are no limits."

Selected Discography

Trace (Warner Bros.), 1995.

Straightaways (Warner Bros.), 1997.

Further Reading

Browne, David, "Straightways," *Entertainment Weekly*, April 25, 1997, p. 67.

Gordiner, Jeff, "Trace," *Entertainment Weekly*, November 10, 1995, p. 66.

Moon, Tom, "Echoes from the Highway in Son Volt's Debut Album," *Philadelphia Inquirer*, September 24, 1995, p. G1.

Nash, Alanna, "Trace," *Stereo Review*, April 1996, p. 85.

Schoemer, Karen, "The Midnight Rambler," *Newsweek*, October 2, 1995, p. 84.

Contact Information

Warner Bros. Records
3300 Warner Blvd.
Burbank, CA 91505

Web Site

http://www.wbr.com/sonvolt/cmp/

Spin Doctors

American rock and roll band

Formed in New York City, 1988

"I just want to carry the banner along for a little while—not by myself but with all these other great musicians. Just take this music down the street our little way and then give it up to some younger person." –

Chris Barron

In 1993 the airwaves were saturated with a trio of catchy, funky, lite tunes by the Spin Doctors. Described as hippie blues jammers, the Spin Doctors offered what *Newsweek* called a "sunny, sweet, view of life" in contrast to "the noise and negation" other young bands were offering at the time. Their debut album, *Pocket Full of Kryptonite*, initially received little attention. But when deejays began spinning "Little Miss Can't Be Wrong," the album soared. The Spin Doctors are not concerned with image, with slick productions, or hitching onto a stylized type of music. As lead singer Chris Barron told *Rolling Stone* in 1994, "Look we play songs. We've got stuff that you'll hear on the radio and stuff you'll never hear on the radio. We're at our fan's service."

From college to band

Three of the four original band members met at New York's New School for Social Research in the late 1980s. Lead singer Chris Barron (born 1968, Hawaii) went to high school in New Jersey and spent some of his youth in Australia. Original guitarist

From right: Mark White, Chris Barron, Aaron Comess (top), Anthony Krizan

Eric Schenkman (born 1963, Massachusetts) grew up in Toronto, Canada. He left the band in 1994. And drummer Aaron Comess (born 1968, Arizona) grew up in Dallas. In 1989 the Spin Doctors emerged as a band. Bassist Mark White (born 1962, New York) joined the group a short while later.

"Look we play songs. We've got stuff that you'll hear on the radio and stuff you'll never hear on the radio. We're at our fan's service."

Playing original tunes in New York City clubs, the band quickly formed a dedicated following. They never played the same set twice and worked to return rock and roll to its original pre-synthesizer roots. As Barron told *Rolling Stone* in 1992, "Everything sounded like fake drummers and synthesized bull—. We wanted to bake some pumpernickel, as opposed to all that pre-sliced stuff."

We'll do it our way

Soon, record companies became interested, despite the Spin Doctor's reluctance to play their more approachable songs. They signed with Epic Records in 1990, then released *Pocket Full of Kryptonite* in late 1991. Epic originally projected sales of the album at around 50,000 units. Most of Epic's attention at the time was focused on Pearl Jam's debut release, and the Spin Doctors were affected. They traveled to shows in London by subway and in the States by van. "A lot of the time we hid from Epic how hard this stuff was," Barron recalled in *Rolling Stone,* "We

put up a front because we wanted to be their ... band. But the Van was death."

Driving "Little Miss"

The van finally paid off. A Vermont radio station began playing "Little Miss Can't Be Wrong," and went so far as to criticize Epic for ignoring the band. They followed with a good natured, goofy video of the single, and by 1992, it was one of MTV's most requested plays. *Pocket Full of Kryptonite* eventually sold six million copies. Naturally, The Spin Doctors made appearances on David Letterman and Jay Leno's late-night television shows, and they were nominated for Grammy and MTV Music awards.

Basically unaffected by their level of success, band members kept their sense of humility and humor. Bassist Mark White told *Vox* interviewer Max Bell, "I wouldn't know anything except that we're exploiting the kids. I'm just a useless, talentless, no-good musician." Barron also joked in the same interview, "My position isn't necessary. We are lucky clowns."

Following *Kryptonite,* The Spin Doctors released *Turn It Upside Down* in June 1994. The critics were divided on its musical success. *Stereo Review* wrote, "Barron's ... stoned-cutup wordplay and the band's colorless automatic funk quickly wear thin over the course of an album." Jeff Giles for *Newsweek,* however, called it "a worthy successor to the band's splendid debut album."

On the road again

More touring followed. The summer of 1994—they played the second Woodstock in August—was spent in Europe and the United States. Near the end of the year they were opening for the Rolling Stones. They also appeared with Roger Daltry at Carnegie Hall, and for Chris Barron the experience was memorable. On meeting older rock musicians in general, Barron said in *Rolling Stone,* "It gives me a sense of being part of a living rock & roll. It makes me say anybody who thinks rock & roll is dead can go shove it."

Guitarist Eric Schenkman left the group in 1994 because of creative differences. They recruited Anthony Krizan and began working on their next release *You've Got To Believe in Something.* Coming out in the spring of 1996, the album, their third full-length effort, received a mild critical response. Tony Sherman of *Entertainment Weekly,* wrote that it has "A handful of fair-to-good tunes," while a review in *People Weekly* called it "musical and lyrical mediocrity."

The Spin Doctors were also featured on the sound track for the movie *Space Jam.* But here again, they struck out. David Browne, in his review for *Entertainment Weekly,* called their version of KC and the Sunshine Band's, "That's the Way (I Like It)," "clubfooted."

Constant touring and live shows filled with improvisational, get-down jamming were what made the Spin Doctors successful. Excessive only when it comes to playing—they did a four-hour gig in New York's Skyscraper Park in the summer of 1996, the band lacked the serious high-mindedness of U2 or the sideshow exploits of the Rolling Stones. They have yet to match the success they achieved with *Kryptonite,* But it seems the band is happy simply playing their music, their way.

Selected Discography

Up for Grabs (Epic), 1990 (live EP).

Pocket Full of Kryptonite (Epic), 1991.

Turn It Upside Down (Epic), 1994.

You've Got To Believe in Something (Epic), 1996.

Further Reading

Bell, Max, *Vox,* July 1994.

Castro, Peter, "You've Got To Believe In Something," *People Weekly,* May 20, 1996, p. 26.

Foege, Alec, "Spin Doctors," *Rolling Stone,* November 17, 1994, p. 135.

Giles, Jeff, "A Pocket Full of Funky Pop," *Newsweek,* July 4, 1994, p. 72.

Mundy, Chris, "Prescription Refilled," *Rolling Stone,* June 16, 1994, p. 18.

"Music From and Inspired by the Motion Picture," *Entertainment Weekly,* November 15, 1996, p. 68.

Rolling Stone, May 1992.

Scherman, Tony, "You've Got To Believe in Something," *Entertainment Weekly,* May 17, 1996, p. 61.

Stereo Review, October 1994.

Contact Information

Spin Doctors
PO Box 1027
Cooper Station
New York, NY 10276

Web Site

http://www.levity.com/spindoctors/
index.html

Parents Aren't Supposed to Like It

Bruce Springsteen

Influential American rock musician

Born September 23, 1949, in Freehold, New Jersey

Rock and roll traces its roots back to the blues and folk music. These music forms were simple to learn and allowed people to create music without formal training. Often times, folk songs told stories of people and situations that listeners could relate to. Following in the footsteps of folk-based singer/songwriters like Woody Guthrie and Bob Dylan came Bruce Springsteen, a young man from New Jersey who combined image-filled songs with gritty rhythm and blues (R & B)-influenced live performances to climb to the top of the rock world and become known as "The Boss."

Greetings from Asbury Park

Bruce Springsteen is the son of Douglas Springsteen, a bus driver, and Adele, a secretary. When he was fourteen, he bought his first guitar from a pawn shop for eighteen dollars. He taught himself to play by learning songs off the radio. He started writing his own songs and joined the band that his sister's boyfriend was in, the Castilles. They recorded demos of two of Springsteen's

"People deserve truth, they deserve honesty ... and the best music is there to provide you with something to face the world with."

—Bruce Springsteen

songs in 1966 and gigged constantly around the area, playing high school dances, parties, and clubs. Their success convinced the young guitarist to stay in New Jersey even when the rest of his family moved to California during his senior year in high school.

When the band broke up, Springsteen lived with various friends while finishing school. After graduation, he moved to Asbury Park, New Jersey, where he formed Earth, a power trio inspired by Cream. After they broke up, he had a series of bands: Child, Steel Mill, Dr. Zoom and the Sonic Boom, and The Bruce Springsteen Band among them. Some of these bands only lasted a few shows, but he kept at it, meeting other musicians in the scene that would lead him to stardom.

The wild, the innocent, and the E Street shuffle

In 1972 Springsteen signed a long-term management agreement with an aspiring producer/manager named Mike Appel. In keeping with a long tradition of naive musicians making questionable decisions, he signed the contract on the hood of a car in an unlit parking lot. While Appel fulfilled his end of the bargain by arranging an audition and subsequent record deal with CBS/Columbia Records, the contract would later cause major problems at a crucial point of Springsteen's career.

After signing a ten-year, ten-album record deal, Springsteen defied the label's vision of him as a solo folk performer and reformed his band. His first album,

Greetings from Asbury Park, NJ was recorded in three weeks and released in January 1973. Despite being made a priority by the label, sales were very weak, though one song, "Blinded by the Light," would become a hit for Manfred Mann's Earth Band in 1977.

His sophomore album, *The Wild, the Innocent and the E Street Shuffle,* was released in November of the same year. "E Street" in the title refers to the street that the mother of a band member lived on. Springsteen's backing band took the name of "The E Street Band." After some shuffling of members, the band's lineup settled into a group that would stay with him until 1989: Clarence Clemmons, saxophone, vocals; Garry Tallent, bass; Danny Ferderici, keyboards; Max Weinberg, drums; Roy Bittan, keyboards and "Miami" Steve Van Zandt, guitar, vocals. While critics took note of the album, sales were still slow.

"Rock and Roll's Future...Is Bruce Springsteen"

In early 1974, an influential rock critic named Jon Landau saw Springsteen perform in Cambridge, Massachusetts. After catching him a couple of times he wrote in the Boston-based *Real Paper:* "I saw rock and roll's future and it's name is Bruce Springsteen.... On a night when I needed to feel young, he made me hear music like I was hearing it for the first time." A long-term friendship developed between Springsteen and Landau, who went on to co-produce future Springsteen albums, including the landmark *Born to Run* in 1975.

Parents Aren't Supposed to Like It

"Baby we were born to run"

For his third album, Springsteen desired to make a record that would combine the songwriting style of Bob Dylan, the vocal style of Roy Orbison, and the production style of Phil Spector. The resulting album was *Born to Run,* released in 1975. With it's anthemic title track and songs like "Thunder Road," the album combined themes of despairing youth with hope for redemption by breaking out of the limits that life imposes. "Baby, this town rips the bones from your back / It's a death trap, it's a suicide rap / We've got to get out while we're young / 'Cause tramps like us, baby we were born to run" is just one lyrical image from this breakthrough album. Even though the imagery was a little grim, in 1980 a New Jersey state assemblyman proposed that "Born To Run" be named the state song.

A massive promotional campaign built around a misquoted version of Landau's review culminated in Springsteen being featured simultaneously on the covers of *Time* and *Newsweek.* This led to charges of hype that even upset Springsteen. He believed that it trivialized his music and made him appear to be an invention of the record company's publicity department. In a *Chicago Tribune* interview, he said: "After that *Time* and *Newsweek* thing ... All I could see ahead for me was 'Celebrity Bowling.'" But it became apparent to skeptics that, if anything, Springsteen had exceeded the claims of the advance publicity. His first national tour, following the release of

Darkness on the Edge of Town

Instead of being able to capitalize on his success, Springsteen's recording career was brought to a standstill in 1976 by difficulties with his manager, Mike Appel. After discovering that Appel was making four times as much as he was from every record sold, Springsteen asked Landau to help review his contract. Appel responded by tying him up with legal hassles and injunctions that prevented him from recording until May 1977, when Landau took over as Springsteen's manager.

In the meantime, Springsteen filled his time by touring and cementing his live reputation with legendary shows that would last up to three hours. He also gave songs to other artists: "Fire" went to New York rockabilly performer Robert Gordon (and was later remade by the Pointer Sisters). He also co-wrote "Because the Night" for Patti Smith, which was later a hit for 10,000 Maniacs in 1993. When Darkness on the Edge of Town was finally released in mid-1978, it reflected the bitterness and disillusionment Springsteen felt during that period. The songs on it were marked by a more adult, somber tone than his earlier compositions, and this starkness was matched by a stripped-down production style.

Born to Run in 1975, was a sellout wherever it went.

The River and Nebraska

It took nearly two years to complete Springsteen's next album, *The River,* released in late 1980. During this time he appeared on stage only twice. One of those performances was filmed and appears in the film, *No Nukes*.

The double-album sold well due to the anticipation that had built up. The inclusion of shorter, brighter songs like "Cadillac Ranch," along with his typical darker-themed ones, also helped album sales. "Hungry Heart" was Springsteen's first top ten hit, even though its lyrics about leaving an (imaginary) wife and kids behind could be considered inappropriate for such an upbeat tune. He embarked on another world tour of marathon-length shows.

When it came time to write the follow-up to *The River*, Springsteen sat down with his acoustic guitar to create demos of the new songs. Recording on a simple four-track tape recorder, he created what became *Nebraska*. Because he felt that the songs wouldn't benefit from a full-band, big-studio treatment, he decided to release what was actually a glorified demo tape. Even though no singles were released and the songs and performance were raw and rough, it reached #3 on the charts.

Born in the U.S.A

Springsteen spent 1983 writing and recording over 100 songs that were eventually whittled down to his biggest selling album, *Born in the U.S.A.* Its first single, "Dancing in the Dark," was accompanied by Springsteen's first video. The album eventually produced seven top-ten singles (tying Michael Jackson's *Thriller*) and sold over fifteen million copies. It was Columbia's largest-selling album ever and is one of the top-selling albums in history.

With it's patriotic-sounding title and rousing cry of "Born in the U.S.A.," many people, from politicians to car companies, tried to attach themselves to Springsteen. (Lee Iacocca, then-chairman of Chrysler Corporation, reportedly offered $12 million to license "Born in the U.S.A." for a series of commercials.) Springsteen rejected all attempts to co-opt his music for others' gain. The irony of the album's lyrics was obscured by the anthemic music and performance. The lyrics, particularly as voiced by the title song's Vietnam vet to "Dancing in the Dark's" cry of "I want to change my clothes / My hair, my face," reflect alienation and injustice in the lives of Americans.

In 1984 Steve Van Zandt amicably left the E Street Band, just before Springsteen embarked on another world-hopping tour for *Born in the U.S.A.* He was replaced by journeyman guitarist Nils Lofgrin. New Jersey native Patty Scialfa also joined the band as a backing vocalist. In May 1985, Springsteen married model/actress Julianne Phillips while on tour. The tour ended in October 1985. A year later, Springsteen released the personally-compiled, career-spanning *Live 1975-1985*, a five-album/three-CD box set.

Changes

In October 1987, after a year-and-a half of marriage, Springsteen released *Tunnel of Love,* a relatively subdued examination of love and relationships. The first single, "Brilliant Disguise," contained

Parents Aren't Supposed to Like It

the lyrics, "Now you play the loving woman / I'll play the faithful man / But just don't look too close / Into the palm of my hand," that foreshadowed trouble in Springsteen's marriage. While on tour in Europe during the summer of 1988, tabloids printed paparazzi photos of Springsteen in compromising situations with backup singer Scialfa. Phillips filed for divorce and the marriage ended in March 1989, after less than four years. Scialfa and Springsteen married in June 1991 and have three children.

Springsteen disbanded the E Street Band in late 1989. Only keyboardist Bittan would be held over for his new touring band, which he formed to support the simultaneously-released albums *Human Touch* and *Lucky Town*. The albums debuted at #2 and #3 respectively when released in March 1992 and were certified platinum (one million units sold) two months later.

Movie music

In 1993 Springsteen brought his music to Hollywood, writing and performing the song "Streets of Philadelphia" for the Academy Award-winning AIDS film, *Philadelphia,* starring Tom Hanks. The song won an Academy Award for Best Original Song, and Springsteen performed it at the awards ceremony. A year later, he performed the Oscar-nominated title song from *Dead Man Walking*. Another song recorded for the 1995 *Greatest Hits* album with a reunited (for the recording) E Street Band, "Secret Garden," was featured in the Tom Cruise film *Jerry Maguire*.

Back to his roots

In late 1995 Springsteen returned to the musical style of folk singer Woody Guthrie and released the solo folk album, *The Ghost of Tom Joad*. (Tom Joad was the lead character in John Steinbeck's novel, *The Grapes of Wrath,* which was made into a now-classic movie starring Henry Fonda.) The album, political and concerned with the plight of the poor and excluded, was almost a complete circle back to the style Springsteen evolved from, and it won a Grammy award for Best Contemporary Folk Record in 1997.

Selected Awards

Grammy Awards:

"Dancing in the Dark," Best Male Rock Vocal, Grammy Awards, 1985.

"Tunnel of Love," Best Solo Rock Vocal, Grammy Awards, 1988.

"Streets of Philadelphia," Song of the Year, Best Male Rock Vocal Performance, and Best Rock Song Written Specifically for Motion Picture or Television, Grammy Awards, 1995.

"The Ghost of Tom Joad," Best Contemporary Folk Album, Grammy Awards, 1997.

American Music Awards:

Favorite Pop/Rock Single, 1985.

Favorite Male Artist, Male Video Artist, Album (all in pop/rock categories), 1986.

MTV Music Awards:

Best Male Video for "I'm on Fire"; Best Stage Performance Video for "Dancing in the Dark," 1985.

Best Video from a Film for "Streets of Philadelphia," 1994.

BRIT Award, Best International Solo Artist, 1986.

"Streets of Philadelphia," Best Song, Golden Globe Award, 1994.

"Streets Of Philadelphia," Academy Award for Best Song from a Motion Picture, 1994.

Selected Discography

(All on Columbia)

Greetings from Asbury Park, NJ, 1973.

The Wild, the Innocent and the E Street Shuffle, 1973.

Born to Run, 1975.

Darkness on the Edge of Town, 1978.

The River, 1980.

Nebraska, 1982.

Born in the U.S.A., 1984.

Live 1975-1985, 1986.

Tunnel of Love, 1987.

Human Touch, 1992.

Lucky Town, 1992.

Greatest Hits, 1995.

The Ghost of Tom Joad, 1996.

Further Reading

Dawidoff, Nicholas, "The Pop Populist," *New York Times Magazine,* January 26, 1997, p. 26

Schrueb, Fred, "Bruce Springsteen Finds 'A Sense of Place'," *Rolling Stone,* February 6, 1997, p.18.

Wieder, Judy, "Bruce Springsteen: The Advocate Interview," *The Advocate,* April 2, 1996, p.46.

Books:

Cullen, Jim, *Born in the U.S.A.: Bruce Springsteen and the American Tradition,* HarperCollins, 1997.

Horn, Jeff, *Bruce Springsteen: Career of a Rock Legend,* Arrowood Press, 1996.

Humphries, Patrick, *Complete Guide to the Music of Bruce Springsteen,* Omnibus Press, 1996.

Marsh, Dave, *Glory Days,* Thunder's Mouth Press, 1996.

Rolling Stone Editors, *Bruce Springsteen: The Rolling Stone Files,* Hyperion, 1996.

Contact Information

Columbia Records
550 Madison Ave.
New York, NY 10022

Web Site

http://www.music.sony.com/Music/ArtistInfo/BruceSpringsteen.htm

tHe SUBDUDeS

American rock and roll band

Formed in New Orleans, Louisiana, in 1987; dissolved 1996

The subdudes successfully blended New Orleans-style rhythm and blues, gospel and soul, and acoustic folk. Like the influential rock group The Band some twenty years before, the subdudes were made up of multitalented instrumentalists and singers with a penchant for American storytelling. Formed in 1987 by singer/guitarist Tommy Malone, keyboardist/accordian player John Magnie, tambourine percussionist Steve Amadee, and bassist Johnny Ray Allen, the subdudes never achieved greater than cult status commercially, but their musicianship inspired a fierce loyalty from their fans. Although headquartered in Colorado, the band was forever linked with New Orleans, Louisiana, the city in which it was formed and where it gave its last performance in 1996.

Grew up together

Malone, Amedee, and Allen grew up together in Edgard, Louisiana, a sugarcane town forty miles north of New Orleans. Intrigued by the rich musical heritage of New Orleans, the trio head-

"the subdudes' timeless music will endure."–Scott Jordan, *Offbeat*

ed there in 1981 and met up with Magnie, a Colorado native who went there for the same reason. They quickly formed a band called the Continental Drifters, which played hard, electric rhythm and blues (R & B) before splintering off into their quieter approach one night at the legendary New Orleans club, Tipitina's.

Magnie had a weekly solo piano gig there and was joined by the rest of the group with acoustic instruments. They liked the quieter sound so much they decided to move in that direction, complete with Amadee's method of using a lone tambourine instead of a drum kit. Magnie persuaded the group to move to his hometown of Fort Collins, Colorado, in an effort to live more cheaply and develop their new sound away from the strict musical traditions of New Orleans. The next year they finished second in *Musician* magazine's Best Unsigned Band contest. The year after that, 1989, they were signed to Atlantic Records and released their first album, *the subdudes*.

The road to *Primitive Streak* and beyond

Their second album, 1991's *Lucky,* was recorded back in New Orleans. "Malone's, Allen's, and Magnie's original tunes mix R & B and country, and the best of their efforts sound familiar in the best sense of the word," Gil Asakawa observed in *Rolling Stone*. For the next three years the subdudes toured heavily, building up a fan base. They returned to the studio in 1994 to record *Annunciation* for their new label, High Street Records. *Annunciation* marked the first appearance of

guitarist Willie Williams, who became an unofficial subdude from that point on. Also during that time, Malone and Allen moved back to New Orleans, while Amadee and Magnie remained in Colorado.

Primitive Streak reached their biggest audience

Their biggest record in terms of audience turned out to be the subdude's last studio effort, *Primitive Streak,* released in 1996. In her review for *Stereo Review,* Alanna Nash exclaimed, "there's a celebratory feel to almost every track," while Micheal Tearson of *Audio* called it an "album of terrific Crescent City gumbo."

Following the release of *Primitive Streak,* the subdudes announced they were ending the band and set out on a farewell tour. The band ended where they began by giving their last performance at Tipitina's in November 1996. They recorded fifteen of the shows from the tour and released the highlights on a live album, *Live at Last.* Scott Jordan of New Orleans's *Offbeat* proclaimed, "the subdudes' timeless music will endure, and *Live At Last* is a moving musical scrapbook."

Selected Awards

Best Unsigned Band, *Musician,* 1988.

Selected Discography

the subdudes (Atlantic), 1989.
Lucky (EastWest/Atlantic), 1991.
Annunciation (High Street), 1994.
Primitive Streak (High Street), 1996.
Live at Last (High Street), 1997.

Further Reading

Billboard, February 26, 1994, p. 14; July 27, 1996, p. 86.

Los Angeles Times, May 15, 1996, p. F1.

Nash, Alanna, "Annunciation," *Stereo Review,* October 1994, p. 97.

Nash, Alanna, "Primitive Streak," *Stereo Review,* August 1996, p. 90.

Offbeat, May 1997, p. 158.

Rolling Stone, June 13, 1991, p. 16.

Tearson, Michael, "Primitive Streak," *Audio,* July 1996, p. 82.

Contact Information

subdudes
305 W. Magnolia, #217
Fort Collins, CO 80521

Web Site

http://www.windham.com

WiLCO

American rock and roll band

Formed in Chicago, Illinois, in 1994

Maybe one day there will be an article about Wilco that does-n't also mention **Son Volt** (see entry), but it's not going to happen anytime soon. Both bands sprung from the break-up of cult country/punk band Uncle Tupelo, and since then the two have been constantly compared. It hasn't helped that they've each released each of their two records at about the same times.

After the first records, Son Volt's *Trace* and Wilco's *A.M.*, it seemed like Son Volt was ahead with the critics. "I was the pop guy, the simplistic writer and Jay (Farrar, of Son Volt) was the po-etic genius and obviously the main guy in Uncle Tupelo," said Wilco singer and guitarist Jeff Tweedy in *Rolling Stone*. Now, with Son Volt's *Straightaways* getting lukewarm reviews and Wilco's *Being There* getting raves, Wilco seems to be ahead. For now at least.

Tweedy and Farrar

Jeff Tweedy grew up in Belleville, Illinois, a town he described as "blue-collar, boring, mundane" in *Rolling Stone*. When he was a kid, he went to family gatherings where relatives played guitars

Jeff Tweedy

606

Who is Uncle Tupelo?

Uncle Tupelo, the late 1980s/early 1990s band that sprouted both Son Volt and Wilco, was considered by many to be the best post-punk country band ever. The band started when Jay Farrar and Jeff Tweedy met in high school in Belleville, Illinois. On their four records—No Depression, Still Feel Gone, March 16-20 1992 and Anodyne—they combined folk ballads, gospel and country with punk rock guitars. The mix made country music sound fresh to a new generation of listeners.

But although Farrar and Tweedy had been friends for years, even sharing an apartment together for a short time, they were very different. "I'd be the one talking. Jay would be the one not talking. It was about as polar as that," said Tweedy in Rolling Stone. Right after their major label debut Anodyne, Farrar suddenly left the band. "I don't have any bad feeling toward Jay (although) I did—just because I couldn't believe that anybody would leave it. I was having such a good time." (Farrar, a shy man who doesn't talk much in interviews, hasn't said much publicly about Uncle Tupelo.)

Although Uncle Tupelo never sold that many records, to their fans they were heroes. The resulting No Depression scene (named after the band's 1990 debut) has spawned countless Internet groups devoted to Uncle Tupelo and similar bands and even its own magazine. Tweedy is perplexed about the whole thing. "It's curious as to how Uncle Tupelo became the legend," he said in Rolling Stone. "I'm a huge fan of music, not of the people behind it. It's like the idea of a band that has been romanticized."

and sang old songs. He was the youngest of four kids and learned about music playing his older siblings' records.

In English class at Belleville West High School, he met Jay Farrar. "It was a writing exercise where you have to stand up and say something about the person next to you," he remembered in *Rolling Stone*. "We didn't write about each other. But the people that wrote about us said, 'Jeff's favorite band is the Ramones'; 'Jay's favorite band is the Sex Pistols.'" The two punk rock fans made friends. Tweedy was "in awe" of Farrar's guitar skills. When the two were fifteen, they formed a band that eventually became Uncle Tupelo.

The Uncle Tupelo hoopla and beyond

Uncle Tupelo's country/punk sound was incredibly influential, starting a whole country/punk movement called No Depression. Although their four albums didn't sell well, the band had a fiercely dedicated cult following. But by the time of their last record, *Anodyne,* things inside the band weren't going well. It was basically "two songwriters sharing a band," according to Tweedy in *Rolling Stone.* One day after twelve years together, Farrar quit the band. "He finally decided he hated my guts," said Tweedy in *Rolling Stone.*

The break-up surprised Tweedy. "It was quite a shock," he said in a record company press release. "Even though Jay had his reasons for leaving, both personal and creative, we were really thrown for a loop. It took us awhile to find our footing again." Tweedy and the rest of Uncle Tupelo—John Stirratt (bass, guitar), Ken Coomer (drums) and Max Johnson (various string instruments)—took a month off, then reformed as Wilco.

"I was the pop guy, the simplistic writer and Jay was the poetic genius and obviously the main guy in Uncle Tupelo."

"It's exciting, and the attitude of everyone going in to it is to have fun and not let everything be as serious or melodramatic as Uncle Tupelo," said Tweedy about his new band in *Rolling Stone*.

Will comply

Wilco, named after the radio phrase "will comply," put out *A.M.* in 1995. The record was well-received by critics. "Wilco's no-frills recipe for heartfelt C&W rock is most satisfying," said *Rolling Stone*. *Entertainment Weekly* gave it a "B" and said Tweedy's "songwriting persona has the shaggy, winning air of a 30ish hippie struggling to grow up." Record buyers didn't go for the record, but the band followed it up with over 200 live dates and a spot on the H.O.R.D.E. tour. Then the band dropped out of sight for nine months while they worked on various side projects.

When they returned, they came back with something big, *Being There*, a two-CD set. Not only was the record long, a strange move for an unproven band, but it was a concept record. The idea was that the songs on the record were influenced by the songs that Wilco members loved. "I wanted our influences to be right on the surface in this one, because I don't hear many people doing that anymore. I really wanted it to be, 'Wilco quotes from their, or maybe your, record collection,'" said Tweedy in a press release for the record.

The concept worked. Critics heard classic rock bands such as Creedence Clearwater Revival, the Rolling Stones, The Band, the Kinks, and the Flaming Lips in the mix. Said *People*: "Wilco may be a whole new phenomenon in rock: an original band deluding itself that it's derivative." *Relix* said: "Like most great records, this one grows on you and gets better with each listen."

With the critical support and an exciting skydiving video for the first single "Outtasite (Outta Mind)" playing on MTV, the band is poised to come into its own. "We're doing better than ever, honestly," said a surprised Tweedy in *Rolling Stone*.

Selected Discography

A.M. (Reprise), 1995
Being There (Reprise), 1996

Further Reading

Fricke, David, "Wilco: Not Just a Country Rock Band," *Rolling Stone,* March 20, 1997.

Hendrickson, Matt, "Starting Over," *Rolling Stone,* May 4, 1995, p. 32.

Kenneally, Tim, "Jeff Tweedy: Wilco's Prolific Roots Radical," *Guitar Player,* November 1996, p. 63.

Kot, Greg, "Being There," *Rolling Stone,* November 14, 1996.

Pareles, Jon, "Bands Head Back to Country, in Their Own Ways," *New York Times,* October 30, 1995.

Smith, Roger Len, "Wilco Loves Being There," *Relix,* April 1997, p. 12.

Contact Information

Reprise Records
3300 Warner Blvd.
Burbank, CA 91505

Web site

http://www.RepriseRec.com/

Singers songwriters

What is a singer/songwriter? A person who writes their own songs and sings them. So technically, many modern musicians are singer/songwriters. The use of the category "singer/songwriter" has become more specific, to mean those masters of the song whose voices, lyrics, and music draw attention to the song itself rather than their overall sound. Probably the most distinguishing feature about singer/songwriters is that their audiences know them as singers individually, and not as part of a full band. With this said, it is clear that people in the singer/songwriter category almost always belong to other musical genres, since they write rock, alternative, folk, and other forms of songs. It is also worth noting that there are many singer/songwriters in other chapters of this book.

One of the earliest uses of the term singer/songwriter developed in the 1960s. Some songwriters, like Carole King, who had earned a living writing songs for other people, decided that they wanted to sing their own songs. Some of these songwriters, like Randy Newman, for example, didn't have traditionally good

Alanis Morissette

voices, but that didn't matter—it was the song and the words that were important.

At about the same time, Bob Dylan was coming onto the scene. Like the songwriters who had written songs for other people, Dylan's voice wasn't what people had traditionally considered to be a good singing voice. In Dylan's music, too, it was the song itself that counted—what he was singing.

The 1970s were a heyday for the singer/songwriter. Artists like Joni Mitchell, Paul Simon, and James Taylor helped define what a singer/songwriter was. They created their own musical identities through singing and writing their own material.

Back then, being a singer/songwriter usually meant having a folk or acoustic sound and playing music on simple instruments like a guitar and piano. Often the lyrics were highly political or very personal. A singer like Joni Mitchell was considered to have written confessional lyrics, since she sang about intimate and romantic topics. Though she rode the folk wave to notoriety with such 1960s anthems as "Big Yellow Taxi," "Both Sides Now" and "The Circle Game," Joni Mitchell soon emerged as one of pop's best songwriters and singers. Her most successful and best-loved records, the early 1970s collections *Court and Spark* and *Blue,* are personal but universal, filled with soulful, eclectic songs that have become classics. During the middle of the decade, Mitchell ventured into jazz and other challenging forms, producing influential work that was simply ahead of its time. She continued to produce vital recordings during the 1990s.

The stripped-down, unpretentiousness of the singer/songwriters' music fit perfectly with the 1970s positive attitude towards things that were simple and honest. Singer/songwriters like Joni Mitchell, Paul Simon, Cat Stevens, and James Taylor became huge-selling artists. Paul Simon's solo work recalled the finest work of pop songwriters not only in the rock era but in the so-called "Tin Pan Alley" period, when composers like the brothers Gershwin, Cole Porter, and Irving Berlin set clever, romantic lyrics to unforgettable melodies. Though he scored numerous hits during the 1970s, Simon hit a dry spell in the early part of the 1980s before teaming up with a group of African musicians for the best-selling *Graceland* album. A personal odyssey that resonated with rock history, the album also generated some controversy, since Simon violated an unofficial boycott of South Africa by other musicians due to the then-racist Apartheid system that governed the country. Simon worked with Brazilian musicians and styles on his follow-up "The Rhythm of the Saints."

Singers-songwriters of the 1990s

The alternative era ushered an eclectic batch of talented singer/songwriters into the spotlight. Among these were Matthew Sweet, **Michael Penn** (who scored a hit with "No Myth"; see entry), and Aimee Mann (who hit the charts with "That's Just What You Are"), and evocative composers like Freedy John-ston, Grant Lee Phillips (leader of the band **Grant Lee Buffalo**, see entry) and Victoria Williams, all of whom achieved a measure of recognition but generally struggled against the tide with their re-flective, soulful work. Williams' struggle with multiple sclerosis prompted a trib-ute album on which rock heavyweights like **Lou Reed**, **Pearl Jam**, and **Soul Asylum** (see entries) recorded her off-beat, warmly spiritual songs.

The late 1990s saw the emergence of several promising songwriters, such as smoldering teen hitmaker Fiona Apple and less commercially successful but ac-claimed artists like Ron Sexsmith, Kim Fox, Brendan Benson, Jason Falkner, Jon Brion, Eric Matthews, and Elliott Smith. But perhaps none was a bigger surprise than Ben Folds. The Chapel Hill, South Carolina-based pianist/singer/songwriter and his guitarless trio—misleadingly named Ben Folds Five—released a criti-cally admired 1995 debut album on an in-dependent label, then followed up with a sophisticated, symphonic major label re-lease, *Whatever and Ever Amen*. Folds' work recalled the soulful pop of Elton John, the melodic skill of Todd Rundgren, and the ambition of the Beatles.

Singer/songwriters known for their intensely personal music

Tori Amos (see entry) follows in the 1970s tradition of singer/songwriters by writing about intimate events in her life. The North Carolinian singer's songs are often stripped down, simply Amos and a piano. Of her songs, "Me and a Gun," is

Lenny Kravitz

perhaps the most well-known for its con-fessional lyrics. The song is about a rape, and it's autobiographical. For her honesty and openness about such private topics, Amos has been rewarded with a group of very dedicated and enthusiastic fans. **Bjork** (see entry) dove into her career by compiling private diaries and creating her unique, post-punk songs from them. **Alanis Morissette** (see entry) also be-came a star by telling personal stories. Co-writing with Glen Ballard about inti-mate subjects on her record *Jagged Little Pill*, Morissette struck a universal nerve with the hit single "You Oughta Know," which rages against a former boyfriend and lays bare her feelings of jealousy, hurt, and anger. Lenny Kravitz, who writes songs that are often called "retro," but delve into the roots of psychedelic, blues, soul, jazz, and rock and roll, also wrote his personal story into his songs when his media-ridden marriage to Lisa Bonet broke up.

Irish singer **Sinead O'Connor** (see entry) has been very willing to talk openly about difficult subjects. In interviews, she frequently gives her frank opinions on child abuse, the Catholic Church, and politics. This has gotten her into trouble in her regular life, but it's helped her music. On her first record, *The Lion and the Cobra*, O'Connor yells at a former lover and begs him to come back, all in the same song, "Just Like You Said It Would Be." Her bravery in being willing to show herself as weak, needy, angry, and hurt didn't make her look bad—it just made her music stronger.

Liz Phair's (see entry) debut, *Exile in Guyville*, was written as a response to the Rolling Stones' *Exile on Main Street*. Like the Stones, Phair takes what could be thought of as a macho approach. She sings brashly, she curses, and her record was like a tell-all book about her love life. In return, she made many music critics' top ten lists and helped expand a lot of people's attitudes about how women think.

Singer/songwriters as authors

Some singer/songwriters could be put into the category of "auteur," (French for author) because they take an artistic approach to their music, trying different styles and experimenting with new sounds. Artists don't get much more experimental than **David Bowie** (see entry). Through his long career, Bowie has tried practically everything, including dance/ pop, soul, psychedelia, minimalist mood music, noise rock, and straight-forward rock and roll. Sometimes when Bowie tries something new, he completely changes his look, or even his name. Like Bowie, **Neil Young** (see entry) has been a constant innovator. He's worked on all kinds of music including folk rock (*After the Gold Rush)*, grungy-sounding guitar rock (*Ragged Glory)*, country (*Old Ways)*, and rockabilly (*Everybody's Rockin')*.

Lou Reed (see entry) assured his place in rock history with his work in the influential and ground-breaking band The Velvet Underground, but he has been a daring artist in his solo career, too. He has made albums ranging from the pure noise of *Metal Machine Music* to the pop/rock of *Transformer*. Reed is also the kind of singer/songwriter who doesn't shy away from writing about extremely personal subjects. He often takes stories directly from his life—from the horrors of being addicted to drugs to the horrors of losing friends to disease. Like Bowie, Reed remains a vital and important artist because he continues to challenge himself as an artist. For example, on *Magic and Loss,* instead of trying to write music to appeal to teenagers, Reed writes about what it is like to be a middle-aged man facing the death of friends his own age.

Elvis Costello (see entry) has also had a long career because of his willingness to experiment. When he first came onto the scene in the 1980s, he was tagged as a nerd and an "angry young man." He wrote bitter songs that were short and catchy. But Costello moved beyond the stereotypes by making records that were completely different, like the almost country-sounding *King of America*.

k.d. lang (see entry) is a singer/songwriter whose music changes so much that it would be impossible to give her any other label. She first broke onto the scene in the 1980s as a country singer. Her approach to country music was revolutionary. Instead of the big hair and sweet dresses of earlier country singers, lang had short hair and said she was the reincarnation of country singer Patsy Cline. After making her own strange place in country music, she experimented with music styles ranging from pop ballads to big band songs.

Expanding on the "one singer plus guitar" approach

Bruce Springsteen (see entry) spent some time in the early 1970s as a folk singer, and it shows in the records he made later after he had a record deal and a rock and roll band. Like folk songs, Springsteen's songs often tell stories, such as the tales of young love on *Born To Run*. Through most of his career, instead of telling directly about his own life, Springsteen often sang about characters and their lives. The characters were frequently working-class people, and the songs told about their loves and relationships. Later in his career Springsteen dropped the characters and told stories about himself. On *Lucky Town,* for exam-

ple, Springsteen tells about his home life and dealing with fame.

Isn't it ironic, as Alanis Morissette would say, that singer/songwriter Joan Osborne's first big hit, "One of Us," was written by someone else? Just as ironic was that the song didn't sound that much like the rest of Osborne's work. But the song got Osborne the attention she needed to get people to listen to her record, *Relish.* Her own songs tend to be more gritty, bluesy, and soulful than the more pop-sounding "One of Us."

Sheryl Crow (see entry) started out as a background singer for people like Michael Jackson and Eric Clapton. She finally got a chance to test out her own songs on *Tuesday Night Music Club.* The songs passed the test, because the record was a huge hit in 1994. The light-hearted "All I Want to Do" told a story about a girl just wanting to have fun and helped make Crow a star.

Melissa Etheridge (see entry) is a singer/songwriter who expands upon the "one singer and a guitar" approach, but she has also made a name for herself by becoming a musical pioneer. Etheridge started out playing down-and-dirty, straightforward rock songs which—although other female artists like Janis Joplin had done this before—were still pretty uncommon.

It's clear that the artists here called singer/songwriters also fit into other musical categories (and many are to be found in other chapters of this book). Springsteen and Etheridge, for example, are singers-songwriters in the rock and roll category; Neil Young and Iggy Pop are singer-songwriters on the alternative scene. What these artist do have in common is that they write most or all of their music and that the song is of utmost importance to them.

TORI AMOS

American singer/songwriter and pianist

Born Myra Ellen Amos, August 22, 1963,
in Newton, North Carolina

With a devoted following usually reserved for male rock stars, Tori Amos is that rare performer with whom her audience both identifies and worships. Her ability to sing about God, love, betrayal, and rape—all wrapped around her swirling piano—has won the admiration of fans and critics alike. (There are more than 70 internet web sites devoted to her.) As a child prodigy she preferred to express herself creatively rather than drudge through the classics as they'd been played for centuries. Success brought her three multi-million selling albums, sold-out tours, her own record label, and the role as spokesperson for Rape, Abuse and Incest National Network (RAINN), a privately funded telephone hotline started by Amos in 1994 to help victims of sexual assault.

"I was more interested in free expression. I couldn't live with the piano in a regimented way. I just didn't want to do what was expected of me." –Tori Amos in her Atlantic Records biography

Child Prodigy

Born to a Methodist preacher and his wife in 1963, Myra Ellen Amos—she'd change her name to Tori at the age of seventeen—displayed a remarkable talent for piano early in life. She could play

Amos at the piano

Amos spent the rest of her teens playing piano in the bars of Baltimore and Washington, D.C. At the age of twenty-one she moved to Los Angeles where she fronted a hard-rock band called Y Kant Tori Read. The band's 1988 self-titled release on Atlantic was a critical and commercial failure. Undaunted, Amos returned to her piano bench and began to write personal, emotional songs that would make up her first solo album, *Little Earthquakes,* released in 1991. Most compelling on her debut was the song "Me and a Gun," which detailed the account of Amos's rape some years before. The album went on to sell more than two million copies worldwide.

In 1992 Amos released a five-song EP, *Crucify.* The disk included a remixed version of "Crucify" from the *Little Earthquakes* album, plus her piano/vocal version of Nirvana's hit, "Smells Like Teen Spirit," and covers of the Rolling Stones' "Angie," among other songs.

"I've done the girl with the piano thing."

Under the Pink, her full-length follow-up album to *Little Earthquakes,* was released in early 1994. Most of the songs were written and co-produced with her boyfriend, Eric Rosse, in Taos, New Mexico. With MTV favorites like "God" and "Cornflake Girl," *Under the Pink* also sold more than two million copies and debuted at number one in the United Kingdom.

Started RAINN

The same year, having been flooded with letters by other rape victims who'd

complete songs at the age of two-and-a-half and was composing her own musical scores by the age of four. At age five she was enrolled at the renowned Peabody Conservatory in Baltimore. "The whole idea was for me to be a concert pianist," she recalled in her Atlantic Records biography. "But I found that I was more interested in free expression. I couldn't live with the piano in a regimented [rigid] way. I just didn't want to do what was expected of me." Six years later Amos was expelled for failing to adhere to Peabody's standards of classical musicianship. A piece she had written for the school's examination board was considered too radical, and she refused to change it.

Parents Aren't Supposed to Like It

heard "Me and a Gun," Amos and the D.C. Rape Crisis Center in Washington came up with the idea of a national telephone hotline to assist victims of sexual assault. Amos convinced her record company, Atlantic, and their parent company, Warner Music Group, to provide the initial funding, and the Rape, Abuse and Incest National Network (RAINN) was born. "A lot of times you shut your whole heart off from your experience," she told Marianne Schnall of *In Style*. "You close the door and you wither and die. My hope is that the telephone line can be a bridge to the next step." By 1996 more than 600 rape crisis centers worked with RAINN, handling 50,000 calls a year.

In 1996 Amos released her most ambitious work, *Boys for Pele,* an eighteen-song account of the breakup of her six-year relationship with her producer, Eric Rosse. "This record goes to the depths of a relationship," Amos told *Providence Journal-Bulletin* writer Andy Smith. "The whole record is about that descent." Critics were quick to comment on Amos's jazzy piano playing, her whispering ballads, and the unusual use of a harpsichord on some tracks. Jeff Giles of *Newsweek* called the album "stark and thunderingly weird." The album is named after a Hawaiian volcano goddess who required ritual human sacrifices.

Asserting her independence, Amos also started her own record company, Igloo, in 1996. Although the label is closely identified with Amos, she told Justin Bergman of Gannett News Service that she hopes that in five years the label

Location, location, location

Tori Amos seems to gather inspiration from different places. She'll travel the globe in search of inspiration. In 1991, she moved to London, England. In 1993, she spent most of the year in Taos, New Mexico, where she wrote and co-produced her second album, Under the Pink. By 1994 she was a "permanent" resident of London again. Her 1996 album, Boys for Pele, was recorded largely in a rural church in Ireland.

has ten to fifteen acts making "interesting music" and that Igloo would be in a place that "won't be about me anymore."

Following her Dew Drop Inn world tour in support of *Boys for Pele,* Amos said she planned to take some time off and perhaps reinvent herself musically. "I've done the girl with the piano thing," she told Bergman. In the meantime, Amos continued to work for RAINN. In April 1997 she was honored by Speaker of the House Newt Gingrich and Senate Majority Leader Trent Lott for her work on behalf of sexual assault victims. Amos was further honored when RAINN day was designated as May 16, 1997, with MTV and radio stations across the country taking part by playing Amos's "Silent All These Years" from the *Little Earthquakes* album exactly at noon.

Selected Awards

Congressional Medal of Honor, 1997.

Grammy nomination for Best Alternative Music Performance, for *Boys for Pele,* 1997.

Selected Discography

Little Earthquakes (Atlantic), 1992.

Under the Pink (Atlantic), 1994.

Boys for Pele (Atlantic), 1996.

Further Reading

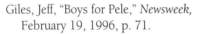

Gannett News Service, November 22, 1996.

Giles, Jeff, "Boys for Pele," *Newsweek,* February 19, 1996, p. 71.

Laskas, Jeanne Marie, "Tori Adore," *Entertainment Weekly,* July 12, 1996, p. 30.

McDonnell, Evelyn, "Boys for Pele," *Rolling Stone,* February 8, 1996, p. 48.

Mundy, Chris, "Tori Amos (interview)," *Rolling Stone,* November 17, 1994, p. 28.

Smith, Andy, "Tori Amos Knows She Evokes Strong Reactions in People," Knight-Ridder/Tribune News Service (originated from *Providence Journal-Bulletin),* August 28, 1996.

Toure, "Tori Amos," *Rolling Stone,* June 30, 1994, p. 66.

Contact Information

Atlantic Records
75 Rockefeller Plaza
New York, NY 10019

Web Sites

http://www.tori.com

http://www.aye.net/~mikewhy/toriamos.html

http://www.rainn.org

BJORK

Icelandic alternative pop/rock vocalist

Born November 21, 1965, in Reykjavik, Iceland

Bjork (pronounced as Bee-york) seems otherwordly. She believes in fairies and frequently is described as an Icelandic goddess or a sprite—wispy, vulnerable, and impish. However, in her case appearances can be deceptive. For instance, in 1996 Bjork attacked a reporter in Bangkok, throwing her down and hitting her head on the floor, for saying, "Welcome to Thailand," upon the singer's arrival at the airport. In reality, Bjork—a self-proclaimed anarchist who likes to attack society's established order—consciously adopted the impish public image to soften the force of her voice and creative genius. She felt that she would be less threatening to the established order that way. While Bjork's otherwordly mystique may have made her more acceptable to the mainstream, she remains—as Jeremy Helligar observed in *People Weekly*—an "acquired taste," and her music is far from conventional. Even Helligar admits, though, that Bjork's "quirky flavor is clearly catching on."

"If I have a philosophy, it's that I support the beautiful side of anarchy."

—Bjork

Bjork, a musical innovator who likes to experiment with the possibilities of sound

By age eleven, Bjork had recorded a best-selling pop album in Iceland, and she became a child pop star in her native land.

Group Work

Bjork continued her musical pursuits throughout her teen years. Influenced by the punk movement, she performed in clubs and composed music for experimental dance groups. Her most notable work during this time was done with punk and new wave groups such as Exodus in 1979, Jam 80 in 1980, and Tappi Tikarrass in 1981.

When she was eighteen, Bjork joined a punk rock and heavy metal band called Kukl that included her then-boyfriend Thor Eldon, a guitarist. Bjork married Eldon in 1986, and together they formed The Sugarcubes, an alternative band that signed with Elektra Records. Bjork and Eldon had a son, Sindri, whom they named after a mythical Norse blacksmith. Bjork's marriage lasted only three years. The band remained intact despite the divorce in 1989, for the group's arty, dance-oriented sound and style revolved around Bjork's thin, versatile voice. As its lead singer, Bjork became a cult idol before the band dissolved in 1992.

Going Solo

With the disbanding of The Sugarcubes, Bjork resolved to give greater voice to her own thoughts and songs. She embarked upon a private songwriting project based on her private diaries of the past ten years. The songs she wrote were all personal, designed to showcase her voice and ideas. "All the songs I wrote in my home after midnight," Bjork

Artistic beginnings

Born in Reykjavik, Iceland, in 1965 as Bjork Gudmundsdottir, Bjork was the only child of Gudmundur, an electricians' union chief, and Hildur, a homeopathic doctor and martial arts teacher. Bjork's parents divorced when she was one, and Bjork lived with her mother and stepfather Saevar Arnason in a commune for artists and musicians. The commune provided a musical and artistic childhood for Bjork. There she heard recordings by Janis Joplin and Jimi Hendrix that gave her goose bumps. Bjork's mother noticed her child's reaction to the recordings and started her on music lessons at age five.

revealed to Dev Sherlock in *Musician*. "And it's very kinda private and intimate." Some of the concepts in her diaries were unusual, but the compositions built upon them proved Bjork to be a capable songwriter. As Christopher John Farley explained in *Time*: "Everyone has odd thoughts now and again, but Bjork's are odder than most.... Bjork takes such things—ideas that ordinary brains and functioning industrial societies tend to filter out—and turns them into song."

In 1993 Bjork released her solo album, *Debut*. Mixing jazz with rave music, *Debut* featured mostly love songs that showcased Bjork's lust for life and special voice. Several of the tracks—"Human Behavior," "Venus As a Boy," "Big Time Sensuality," and "Violently Happy"—enjoyed success as singles. *Debut* peaked on *Billboard*'s chart at number sixty-one in September 1993 and ultimately sold more than two and a half million copies.

In June 1995, Bjork released another solo album, *Post,* which received critical acclaim for its musical surprises: the noises of "Headphones," the hypnotic techno "Modern Things," the Big Band swing, the string arrangements, and of course the voice. A *Billboard* reviewer called Bjork's songs "first rate," in particular "Army of Me," "Isobel," and "It's Oh So Quiet." More than anything, the songs were vehicles for Bjork's matured vocals. According to Farley, "Bjork has a throaty soprano capable of jagged growls and golden, pure vocal thrusts." Farley went on to praise the control Bjork had gained over her voice and her ability to display emotion in addition to her vocal talent.

The Sugarcubes

Most critics felt that The Sugarcubes' 1988 debut album, Life's Too Good, was their best. The album reflected the band's interest in punk and more experimental, arty musical forms. The debut single, "Birthday," featured Bjork's piercing vocals over a melodic rock guitar and vibrating bass lines. Two other singles followed, "Deus" and "Cold Sweat," that appeared on the first album. The band's second album, Here Today Tomorrow Next Week was not as well received as the first. After disappearing for a while, The Sugarcubes released Stick Around for Joy in 1992 before disbanding. The album displayed a growing interest in electronic and techno music.

Despite the commercial success of her solo efforts, Bjork continued to experiment with musical forms. In November 1995, she began working with Robin Rimbaud (also known as Scanner) and other electronic dance musicians on a show of experimental material. Later, in 1997, Bjork started on a remix album, which involved altering the sound of her previously recorded songs and rerecording them. She developed new versions of "Big Time Sentimentality," "Possibly Maybe," and other songs from *Post.* The album titled *Telegram* featured new vocals and collaborations with well-known, experimental, and electronic artists. *USA Today* called the album a "re-invention, not a lazy retooling." With *Telegram*, Bjork once again showed herself to be an innovator who, according to Christina Kelly

Legal battles and music

"Where there's a hit, there's a writ." This adage of the recording industry proved a hard lesson for Bjork in 1995. She was sued twice that year. The first suit involved Simon Lovejoy (real name Simon Fisher) who claimed to own the copyrights to Bjork's composition "Crying," a track on Debut, as well as several other songs from the album. The judge in the "Crying" case found that Lovejoy could not substantiate his claims and thus dismissed the case in June 1995.

Bjork settled her second legal battle that year in August when her British record company, One Little Indian, paid a 2,000-pound ($3,100) settlement plus 3,500 pounds ($5,250) in legal fees to Beechwood Music.

Beechwood Music claimed that the song "Possibly Maybe" contained at least ninety seconds of Scanner's song "Mass Observation." Bjork's managers initially negotiated with Scanner and his manager directly instead of with his record company. When this was brought to the company's attention, Beechwood accepted a settlement rather than proceeding with the suit in court.

The experiences left Bjork a little jaded. She told Jeremy Helligar of People Weekly: "When people think you're rich, they just try anything. If they washed your socks six years ago, they send you a bill for $100,000."

---

from Rolling Stone Online, "continues to push the post-rock envelope" by experimenting with the possibilities of sound.

With music playing such a big part of Bjork's life since her childhood, her plans for the future include more of the same: singing and composing for the rest of her days. "If I have any vision in my life," Bjork explained to John Savage in *Interview,* "I think I'll be singing until I die.... I could just as well move to a little island and live by the ocean and just be the village singer or whatever. Singing on Friday and Saturday nights, writing tunes for the rest of the week. That's my role."

Selected Awards

New Musical Express's BRAT Awards, Best Solo Artist and Object of Desire Awards, 1994.

BRIT Awards, International Female Solo Artist and International Newcomer Awards, 1994.

MTV Europe Music Awards, Best Female Performer Award, 1995.

Eye's Favorite Videos, for "It's Oh So Quiet" ranked number 1, 1995.

Grammy Awards, nomination for best music video (short form), 1996.

BRIT Awards, Best International Female Award, 1996.

International Dance Music Awards, Best Female Artist Award, 1996.

ASCAP Pop Music Awards, College Radio Award, 1996.

Selected Discography

Debut (Elektra), 1993.

Post (Elektra), 1995.

Telegram (Elektra), 1997.

Parents Aren't Supposed to Like It

Further Reading

Billboard, May 13, 1995.

Farley, Christopher John, "A Voice out of Reykjavik," *Time,* August 14, 1995, p. 68.

Helligar, Jeremy, "Out of the Shadows," *People Weekly,* September 25, 1995, p. 81.

Interview, June 1995.

Kelly, Christina, "Telegram," Rolling Stone Online.

Musician, May 1994.

Raphael, Amy, *GRRRLS: Viva Rock Divas,* St. Martin's Griffin, 1996.

Contact Information

Elektra Records
75 Rockefeller Plaza
New York, NY 10019

Web Sites

www.elektra.com\alternative_club\bjork\bjork.html

www.indian.co.uk/bjork/

Sheryl Crow

American singer and songwriter

Born February 11, 1965, in Kennett, Missouri

 "I have a philosophy that everything you write doesn't have to be good for everybody. There are going to be people that get irritated by some of the things I write— including my parents. And then there are going to be people that you draw in because of the pointedness of certain things."

–Sheryl Crow

Sheryl Crow chronicles modern middle America with a folksy, bluesy style of lyrics and easy, free-form music. Falling in love with music in her childhood home, Crow continued her musical pursuits through college, getting a music degree from the University of Missouri at Columbia. After going on the road as a back-up singer, she finally realized her musical dreams by making her first recording. Her success has resulted in a platinum album, a hit single, and three Grammy awards.

Musical beginnings

Sheryl Crow was born into a musical family. Her father, Wendell Crow, earned a living as an attorney, but he also played trumpet. Bernice Crow, Sheryl's mother, accompanied her husband on the piano, both of them playing big band/swing music. Not surprisingly, Sheryl Crow showed an early interest in music.

She began taking piano lessons at age six. After going to her first concert (reportedly a Peter Frampton concert) when she was thirteen, she began writing songs. Throughout high school she sang with various high school bands. Her musical education continued into college where she earned a fine arts degree in classical piano and voice in 1984 from the University of Missouri at Columbia.

From school to the road

After graduating, Crow spent two years teaching music at the elementary level in the public schools of St. Louis. She continued to sing in bands, and she sang with the city's African-American music choir. She also sang for a fast-food chain's television advertisement, "earning more money than she had in two years of schoolteaching." Becoming disillusioned and breaking up with her boyfriend, Crow decided to move to Los Angeles to pursue her musical goals. Arriving with little in the way of material possessions, Crow relied on her ambition and her talent.

That ambition gave her the guts to crash an audition for a position singing back-up on Michael Jackson's *Bad* tour. Winning the spot, she started touring with Jackson in 1984 for eighteen months. After the tour she returned to Los Angeles thinking that singing with such a high-profile pop star would result in more success. She related her feelings upon returning to California to the *Houston Chronicle,* "In many ways, the Jackson tour really [messed] me up, because landing a gig like that and not working up to it was a real crash course in the music industry. To have such a high profile and then be just nothing again was incredibly frustrating. I wound up pretty much crawling into bed and not getting up for seven or eight months."

Crow performing in Wisconsin, August 7, 1996

The struggle to record

During that seven or eight months, Crow looked for recording contracts. She was determined to record her own music; instead, she found her name linked to Michael Jackson. All recording offers came with the insistence that she record pop songs. Refusing such offers, Crow accepted work as a back-up singer for Don Henley (of the Eagles). Crow sang back-up on Henley's 1989 album, *The End of Innocence,* and toured with him. She sang backup on other major albums and tours as well, including tours with Rod Stewart, Joe Cocker, and George Harrison. As proof of her songwriting ability, she wrote songs that were covered by country singer Wynona Judd and classic rock guitarist Eric Clapton, among others.

"My life's very frenetic, and I'm rough around the edges, not at all a slick person."

With the support of Henley and Sting, Crow was eventually able to go solo. Former Police producer, Hugh Padham, heard and liked one of her demo tapes. After asking for and receiving a recommendation from Sting, who remembered working with Crow, Padham presented the tape to A&M records in 1992. A&M signed Crow after hearing the tape, and she and Padham began working on what should have been her first album.

After spending somewhere between a quarter and a half a million dollars on recording, Crow was unhappy with the results. She found Padham's production style too polished. As quoted in the *Houston Chronicle,* "My life's very frenetic, and I'm rough around the edges, not at all a slick person. And that album doesn't reflect that." Surprisingly, A&M agreed with her, and the album was never released. Crow was allowed to start again, this time with her friend Bill Bottrell, who produced and co-wrote Michael Jackson's number one hit of 1991-92, "Black or White."

Tuesday night music club

Crow, Bill Bottrell, drummer Brian MacLeod, and other musicians began meeting on Tuesday nights, forming a "music club" to trade ideas and jam musically. Out of these meetings came Crow's first album, the aptly named *Tuesday Night Music Club,* which was released in the fall of 1993. In addition to the music club regulars, the album includes Crow's father, whose trumpet accompanies his daughter's voice on the autobiographical song, "We Do What We Can," which Crow credits her father for inspiring.

The first single released from the album, "Leaving Las Vegas," was a minor hit, reaching number sixty on the *Billboard* charts. But it was her second single "All I Wanna Do" that blasted Crow to star status. Released in the summer of 1994, "All I Wanna Do" was inspired by a poem by New England poet Wyn Cooper. Crow added a refrain of her own and modified some of the other words in writing the song. After peaking at number two on *Billboard*'s charts, the single sold a million copies and was certified gold by November 1994.

Tuesday Night Music Club set off a whirlwind of activity for Crow, including a tour opening for Bob Dylan and playing at Woodstock II in the summer of 1994. Crow's first music award came when she was named VH-1's "Artist of the Month" for September 1994. At the Grammy Awards ceremony in February 1995, she took home three Grammys, including Record of the Year and Best Female Pop Vocal Performance for the song "All I Wanna Do," and Best New Artist.

This is Sheryl Crow, 1996

1996 brought Crow's second release, *Sheryl Crow*. The title reflected Crow's total artistic control of the album. Her record company, A&M, allowed her the freedom she'd ambitiously sought. For her second album she wrote the songs, produced the recording sessions, played a lot of the instruments (including organ and guitar), and sang about what she's seen, heard, and felt for the past few years. Her subject matter ranged from the crossdresser at her local coffee shop to the carnage in Bosnia.

Crow's second album resulted in a controversy with the department store chain, Walmart. One of the songs on the album contains a lyric about the chain selling guns to children. As a result, Walmart refused to carry the CD. Once

again, her record company (A&M) stood by Crow and refused to change anything on the album.

Selected Awards

Grammy Awards for 1) Record of the Year, for "All I Wanna Do"; 2) Best Pop Vocal Performance, Female, for "All I Wanna Do"; and 3) Best New Artist; 1995.

Selected Discography

Tuesday Night Music Club (A&M), 1993.

Sheryl Crow (A&M), 1996.

Further Reading

Fricke, David, "Sheryl Crow," *Rolling Stone,* December 26, 1996, p. 186.

Gold, Todd, "Sheryl Crow," *People Weekly,* September 23, 1996, p. 25.

Schoemer, Karen, "To Her Own Self Be True," *Newsweek,* September 16, 1996, p. 95.

Schruers, Fred, "Sheryl: She Only Wants To Be with You," *Rolling Stone,* November 14, 1996, p. 64.

Contact Information

A&M Records
1416 North La Brea Avenue
Hollywood, CA, 90028

Web Sites

http://www.amrecords.com/current/sheryl crow/index.html

http://www.pitt.edu/~rakst21/vsheryl/

http://www.asiaonline.net.hk/~paulhk/sheryl/derault.htm

Lenny Kravitz

American rock and roll singer/songwriter

Born Leonard Albert Kravitz, May 26, 1964, in Brooklyn, New York

"People would like to say that I'm romanticizing the past. But no, my ear knows what sounds better." –Lenny Kravitz in *Rolling Stone*

The first time the public heard about Lenny Kravitz was in 1987, when he was known mainly as the funky-looking boyfriend of "Cosby" kid Lisa Bonet. He said he was a musician, but many thought he was just a hanger-on. As *People Weekly* put it, "He hardly seemed like a candidate for rock-and-roll longevity." Once Kravitz started putting out records, he had new critics. Some thought that his flamboyant style of dress was a put-on. Some thought that his retro music was too idealistic. Others thought he sounded too much like Led Zeppelin or Jimi Hendrix or Curtis Mayfield. Others thought he was just acting too much like a hippie.

When his first album, *Let Love Rule,* came out in 1989, the *Los Angeles Times* wrote that it "overflows with enough exhumed peace and love to maybe make even Wavy Gravy choke. There are delusions of grandeur plenty in Kravitz's debut."

Kravitz has proven his critics wrong with a solid music career and several platinum records. As for that "rock-and-roll longevity?" Kravitz has had a remarkably long and successful career.

Not your usual childhood

"My style, my taste and everything is all kinds of styles just slammed together. That's how I've lived my entire life," said Kravitz to *Rolling Stone*. It all started in Kravitz's childhood. His father, Sy Kravitz, was a Jewish television producer. His mother was Roxie Roker, the African-American woman who played Helen Willis on the TV show *The Jeffersons*. Kravitz spent his early years in New York City, getting exposure to many different cultures. "I can switch on you like that. I can go from Bed-Stuy talk [tough street talk, originating in the Bedford-Stuyvesant area of New York City] to Beverly Hills [a very wealthy city in the Los Angeles area] in a second. That's the good thing about growing up the way I did. I can deal with whatever. I can live in a castle. I can live in the ghetto. It doesn't matter," he said in *Rolling Stone*.

Kravitz grew up in a household where people like jazzman Duke Ellington were family friends, and he heard the music of jazz greats Count Basie, Ella Fitzgerald, and Miles Davis. He says that when he was three or four, he started making music by banging kitchen utensils together, choosing certain sizes to get certain tones. "I really used to jam," he said in *Rolling Stone*. He wrote a "really cheesy" song in elementary school called "I Love You, Baby."

When his mother got the part on *The Jeffersons,* the family moved to Los Angeles. Kravitz got some acting gigs, includ-ing a spot on a Burger King commercial. He joined the prestigious California Boys Choir and went to Beverly Hills High (with classmates like Guns 'N Roses' Slash). When he was a sophomore in high school, he decided to leave home. "It wasn't that they didn't want me there. It was that I just decided that I needed to go out and do my thing. I didn't want to live under the rules that took place under that roof," he said in *Rolling Stone*.

On his own

Kravitz lived in friends' houses, recording studios, and cars. He earned money by doing odd jobs—working in a shoe store, a fish market, a restaurant. Finally, he told his parents that he wanted to be a musician instead of going to college. His father agreed to let Kravitz use his college fund toward studio time. Kravitz gave himself a new name, Romeo Blue, and cut an album's worth of songs. He now says those songs were horrible and pretentious. Still, they led to him getting a deal with Virgin Records under his real name.

In 1989 Kravitz married Lisa Bonet, whom he'd met in 1985 backstage at a New Edition concert. They were just friends at first, but then Kravitz's car broke down and he borrowed Bonet's. "If my car had been working during that time, I probably wouldn't be married to her. It started to be this thing—every day, wake up, take her to work, pick her up. We'd have dinner and then I guess it was one day we realized, like, we couldn't be apart or something," he said in *Spin*. After the couple's Las Vegas wedding, the media spotlight was on them. "I just married someone I loved and they just happened to be in the media and all of a sudden I was 'Lisa Bonet's husband.' But I was my own person," said Kravitz in *Ebony*.

Kravitz proved he was his own person by putting out his first record *Let Love Rule* that same year. On it, he wrote all the music, played most of the instruments, and used vintage equipment. "There were so many people in the industry saying, 'You can't make records like that anymore.' But I stuck to my thing ... and then everybody started going my way ... buying good guitars, old amps and real gear," he said in *Guitar Player*. *Let Love Rule* was a hit with its retro 1960s folk/soul/psychedelia sound. *Rolling Stone* called it "a hook-laden sound for sore ears." *Ebony* said, "(His critics) don't really know what to call him: rock artist, retro-60's hippie, Rastafarian, soulful White boy or a weird Black guy."

The breakup, mama said

After having a child, Zoe, Kravitz and Bonet broke up. Although he kept the reasons for the breakup private, he said in *Ebony*, "the whole media rigmarole didn't help. We were young as well. We were babies." Kravitz still had (and has) strong feelings for his wife. "That woman inspired me so much. It was a magical time that she and I shared. I just opened up artistically," he said in *Rolling Stone*. The breakup was very traumatic for him. "I was in a tremendous amount of pain when we broke up, tremendous.

For, like, six months, I only slept for two hours a day. The rest of the time I was just up, like a zombie. I was floored."

The experience and his hopes that they might reunite inspired many of the songs on his second record, *Mama Said*. "That's why I wrote that one ('It Ain't Over 'Til It's Over')," he said in *Ebony*. "I say as long as we're living and breathing, you never know. It might be in fifty years; you just don't know." The *All Music Guide to Rock* called the record "a sleek update of Philly soul, acid rock, psychedelia, hard rock and '60s pop." The record was a hit.

Kravitz comes into his own

Other artists wanted Kravitz's help in the studio. He worked with Mick Jagger, Aerosmith, Curtis Mayfield, and Al Green on their records. In 1993 he released his own record, combining soul and psychedelic rock on *Are You Gonna Go My Way*. Like his previous records, it was a hit. *Rolling Stone* called it "total ear candy." The *All Music Guide to Rock* called it "his most consistent and coherent album."

In 1995 Kravitz released *Circus,* a record he recorded by his house in New Orleans. It debuted on the charts at number one. *Rolling Stone* called the record a "studio-sharp mix of polished pop ballads and brittle dance rock." Kravitz followed up the record with lots of touring, including a spot on the 1996 H.O.R.D.E. tour and appearances on the "Late Show with David Letterman."

What's next? More of the same. "I want to do this till I'm old and little," he said in *Rolling Stone.* "I'd like to be like [blues legend] John Lee Hooker: all in my little suit, with my little gut hanging out, playing music, strumming my guitar. I know I want that."

Selected Awards

MTV Video Music Award for Best Male Video, for "Are You Gonna Go My Way?," 1993.

Mama Said, certified platinum, 1995.

Are You Gonna Go My Way? certified double platinum, 1995.

Let Love Rule, certified gold, 1995.

Circus certified gold, 1995.

Selected Discography

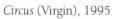

Let Love Rule (Virgin), 1989

Mama Said (Virgin), 1991

Are You Gonna Go My Way? (Virgin), 1993

Circus (Virgin), 1995

Further Reading

Helligar, Jeremy, "The Song Remains the Same," *People,* September 18, 1995, p. 31.

Norment, Lynn, "Lenny Kravitz: Brother with a Different Beat," *Ebony,* June 1994, p. 29.

Rotondi, James, "Castles Made of Sound: Lenny Kravitz's Rock and Roll," *Guitar Player,* July 1996, p. 42.

Strauss, Neil, "Lenny Kravitz," *Rolling Stone,* November 30, 1995, p. 49.

Wild, David, "Lenny Kravitz," *Rolling Stone,* May 17, 1994, p. 60.

Contact Information

Virgin Records
338 N. Foothill Rd.
Beverly Hills, CA 90210

Web Site

http://www.virginrecords/com/kravitz

K.D. Lang

Canadian singer and songwriter

Born Kathryn Dawn Lang on November 2, 1961, in Consort, Alberta, Canada

𝄞 "I've always been one for melding genres together, but I think that's because I'm really honestly interested in, and have been influenced by, such a broad spectrum of music that it can't help but come out that way."

A soulful singer whose cowpunk country roots put her on the musical map, k.d. lang defies the pigeon-holes of categorization by drawing on a multitude of musical tastes. For lang and for her avid fans, her mastery of singing and songwriting in a variety of modes is foremost, but the media has often focused on her vegetarianism and sexual orientation. "My music is the last thing people focus on," she told Andrea Orr of the Reuters News Service. "I think people think I'm very political. I'm not at all. I'm an artist in love with art and music."

Never one to purposely court controversy, the Canadian-born singer still finds herself saddled to stories that describe her as a shutout by Nashville, a militant vegetarian from cattle country, and the reigning queen of "lesbian music." Aside from being one of the most talented musicians around, she never did the things that the music industry expects. As Grand Ole Opry legend Roy Acuff told her, "You look like a boy, dress like a girl, and sing like a bird."

Dreamed of being a singer

Born Kathryn Dawn Lang in 1961 in Consort, Alberta, Canada, lang was a tomboy-jock. Her javelin throws and volleyball skills notwithstanding, she had other ideas about what she wanted to do. "Everybody knew what my dream was, but nobody ever said anything," she told Mim Udovitch of *Rolling Stone* about her desire to be a singer. "The only thing my mum ever said was, 'If you're going to be onstage, you're going to need braces.'" When her father abruptly left the family when she was twelve, lang felt the sting of abandon she would later sing about. "I was a little bitter," lang confessed to Louise Farr of *Details* about her father leaving. "But it made us independent and I learned to have a healthy view of good-bye."

Soon lang was singing at showers, weddings, and festivals, and later, while studying voice at Red Deer College in Alberta, found inspiration in the spirit of legendary country singer, Patsy Cline. "I heard Patsy Cline for the first time on a K-Tel ad on TV," she reminisced to Farr. "I was sort of a performance artist, and I went into a complete frenzy over country music. I became this woman in cowboy boots, with short hair and cat-eyed glasses, singing Patsy Cline classics and dancing like a disabled turkey." Word began to spread about the girl from Alberta who claimed to have been Cline in a past life but who was singing songs far differently than Cline ever had—or anyone else for that matter.

Released first album

In 1982 lang formed a backup band, the Reclines, and after recording and releasing an album on the independent Bumstead label, 1984's *A Truly Western Experience,* toured Canada. The album and tour brought lang's special blend of "cowpunk" country music to a wider audience; it was successful enough to take her across the border to America.

> **"I became this woman in cowboy boots, with short hair and cat-eyed glasses, singing Patsy Cline classics and dancing like a disabled turkey."**

At a 1985 performance at New York's Bottom Line, lang was seen by Seymour Stein, the chief of Sire Records who had signed Madonna, the Pretenders, the Talking Heads, and the **Ramones** (see entry). Stein was so impressed with what he heard, he signed lang to the label, giving Sire its first country act. Later that year, lang won the Juno Award, Canada's version of the Grammys, as Most Promising Female Vocalist.

More pure country

With a major label behind her, lang set out to incorporate more pure country into her sound to widen her appeal. With the help of Ben Mink, her co-writer and producer, whom she met in 1985, lang began to write songs with less humor and more heart. One of those songs, "High Time for a Detour," appeared on lang's 1987 album and Sire debut, *Angel With a Lariat.* Recorded in London and produced by British rockabilly guitarist

lang, an artist in many musical genres

confessed to Udovitch. "Tons and tons and tons of reverb, 150 milliseconds on everything."

Invited to Nashville, Tennessee

Though the album didn't get much radio airplay, it came to the attention of the folks in Nashville. Lang was invited to sing at the legendary Grand Ole Opry. Following a rendition of Roy Orbison's "Crying," she received a standing ovation. It was clear, however, that the country music capital didn't know what to make of the androgynous-looking singer with the smart, torchy twang. She also appeared on a television show celebrating Orbison's music with **Elvis Costello** (see entry) and **Bruce Springsteen** (see entry) and recorded a duet of "Crying" with Orbison that earned them both a Grammy.

New versions of country classics

In the summer of 1988, lang released *Shadowland.* The album was produced by Owen Bradley, who had produced all of Patsy Cline's hits almost thirty years earlier. He came out of retirement just to work with lang on this album. None of the songs were written by lang or Mink. Instead, the album featured nostalgic workings of classic country songs, such as Cline's "I'm Down to My Last Cigarette."

The album went gold and won Juno and Canadian Country Music Awards, but Nashville was still suspicious. "She's in some kind of weird place between artsy new wave and country," Robert Oer-

Dave Edmunds, the record was considered a success and received good reviews. For her part, lang was less than satisfied, but the passage of time soothed the harshness of her feelings. "I like that record now, but I hated it for years," lang

Parents Aren't Supposed to Like It

mann, music critic of Nashville's *The Tennesseean,* explained to Nicholas Jennings of *Maclean's.* "The country audience tends to be a little more conservative than that. It's pretty extreme for them to accept."

Torch and twang

The next year lang released an album of mostly lang/Mink originals and had a hit on both the pop and country charts with *Absolute Torch and Twang.* Considered her best country album, it was generally conceded that lang wouldn't make any headway in Nashville with this one either. "This album isn't gonna win her any points in Nashville or with country-radio programmers," Holly Gleason wrote in her review for *Rolling Stone,* "but it shows what country music, when intelligently done, can be." The album also earned lang her second Grammy for Best Female Country Vocalist.

Interview with The Advocate

Two years later while doing interviews to promote her album, *Ingenue,* lang admitted to *The Advocate* that she was a lesbian, sparking another wave of controversy and propelling her, unwillingly, into the role of spokesperson. And while every article, interview, and review of *Ingenue* mentioned the new-found fact, the album's music was still good enough to get through the focus on lang's personal life. Gone were the country overtones of the past, replaced by threads of cabaret music and melodies that were unabashedly pop. "Tasteful lounge music with some modern twists," Nicholas Jen-

Militant vegetarian?

In 1990 lang had her first experience with un-music related controversy when she filmed a "Meat Stinks" commercial for People for the Ethical Treatment of Animals (PETA). Though the spot never aired, a furor in her hometown and other cities tied to the meat industry loudly assailed lang as a militant vegetarian. Some radio stations refused to play her music, The "Home of k.d. lang" sign outside of Consort was defaced and eventually taken down, and lang was forced to cancel a concert in response to protesters.

nings wrote in *Maclean's,* "*Ingenue* promises to take the gifted vocalist to even greater heights of popularity." lang did reach greater heights, selling 2.5 million copies worldwide and receiving a Best Female Pop Vocal Grammy for "Constant Craving," a lush tale of unrequited love.

Even Cowgirls Get the Blues

Ingenue was followed by the soundtrack for the film, *Even Cowgirls Get the Blues,* an even larger departure from lang's beginnings marked by the addition of disco and rhythm-and-blues-type grooves. lang took this formula a step further on her 1995 studio album *All You Can Eat,* which went gold but failed to match either the commercial or critical acclaim of *Ingenue.*

"I've always been one for melding genres together," she told Jeremy Helligar of *People Weekly,* "but I think that's because I'm really honestly interested in, and have been influenced by, such a broad spectrum of music that it can't help but come out that way."

In 1996 lang received the prestigious Order of Canada award, an honorary award given to outstanding Canadians. For the future, lang seemed to be moving toward a more jazz-influenced sound with her 1997 album, *Drag*.

Selected Awards

Grammy Award, Best Performance by a Duo for "Crying" with Roy Orbison, 1988.

Grammy Award, Best Female Country Vocalist, 1990.

Grammy Award, Best Female Pop Vocal for "Constant Craving," 1993.

Juno Awards: Most Promising Vocalist of the Year, 1985; Country Female Vocalist of the Year, 1987; Country Female Vocalist of the Year, Female Vocalist of the Year, 1989; Country Female Vocalist of the Year, 1990; Album of the Year, Producer of the Year, Songwriter of the Year, 1993.

Order of Canada Award, 1996.

Creative Integrity Award from Los Angeles Gay and Lesbian Center, 1997.

Selected Discography

A Truly Western Experience (Bumstead), 1984.

Angel with a Lariat (Sire), 1987.

Shadowland (Sire), 1988.

Absolute Torch and Twang (Sire), 1989.

Ingenue (Sire), 1992.

Even Cowgirls Get the Blues (Sire), 1994.

All You Can Eat (Sire), 1995.

Drag (Sire), 1997.

Further Reading

Garr, Gillian A., *She's A Rebel: The History of Women in Rock & Roll,* Seal Press, 1992.

Lemon, Brendan, "Virgin Territory," *The Advocate,* June 12, 1992.

Ali, Lorraine, "k.d.lang (interview)," *Rolling Stone,* November 30, 1995, p.40.

Johnson, Brian D., "A Lighter Side of lang," *Maclean's,* November 6, 1995, p.68.

Walters, Barry, "All You Can Eat," *Rolling Stone,* November 16, 1995, p.112.

Contact Information

Sire Records
75 Rockefeller Plaza
New York, NY 10019

Web Sites

http://www.kdlang.com

http://www.wbr.com/kdlang

Parents Aren't Supposed to Like It

ALANIS MORISSETTE

Canadian singer/songwriter
Born June 1, 1974, in Ottawa, Ontario, Canada

In the mid-1990s, many critics were looking for women performers as a reaction to the testosterone-fueled Seattle grunge-rock bands like **Nirvana**, **Pearl Jam**, and **Soundgarden** (see entries), who were prevalent early in the decade. Female artists as varied as **Liz Phair**, **Tori Amos**, and Courtney Love's **Hole** (see entries) had attained varying levels of success with young audiences.

When Alanis Morissette's debut album, *Jagged Little Pill*, was released in the summer of 1995, her frank and rebellious style immediately connected with listeners. Her single, "You Oughta Know," exploded onto radio. By October, *Jagged Little Pill* topped the *Billboard* charts, making Morissette the first Canadian to have a number one album in the United States. The album went on to sell more than fifteen million copies worldwide in less than two years, making it the seventh best-selling album of all time. All the more amazing was the fact that Morissette's success occurred before she was twenty-two.

"I want to walk though life instead of being dragged through it." –Alanis Morissette

In the beginning

Born and raised in Ottawa, Canada, Alanis Morissette was one of three children in the family of Alan Morissette and Georgia Feuerstein (she has an older brother named Chad and a twin brother named Wade). She loved dancing and acting when she was young. She began playing the piano at age six and wrote her first songs at age nine. When she was ten, Morissette got a part on the Nickelodeon cable network's show *You Can't Do That on Television*. She's also played a budding rock singer in a movie with future *Friends* star Matt LeBlanc and had a part on a short-lived sitcom entitled *Just One of the Girls* (starring Corey Haim) for Fox-TV in 1993.

Using the money she had earned from her acting work and with the help of a friend of the family who was in the music business, Morissette recorded her first single at the age of eleven. The song was called "Please Stay with Me" and was independently released on Lamor Records (established by her parents). The song was not a hit by any means, but it got some airplay on Canadian radio stations and attracted the attention of MCA Publishing in Toronto, Canada. They signed her to a publishing agreement at the age of fourteen, which in turn landed her a recording contract with MCA Records (Canada).

Promising pop star

Her first Canadian album, the dance/pop-based *Alanis*, sold over 100,000 copies in Canada (platinum status) and earned her a Juno (Canada's equivalent to the Grammy) as Most Promising Female Artist of 1991. Her young age and style resulted in comparisons with American counterparts Debbie Gibson and Tiffany. She toured with the novelty rapper, Vanilla Ice, and recorded a follow-up album, *Now Is the Time,* which took her music in a more pop/soul direction, with more emphasis on ballads. After her sophomore effort sold only half as well as her debut, she relocated from her native Ottawa to the more exciting city of Toronto. When her career temporarily stalled, she moved to Los Angeles, California, to take the sitcom part.

While in Los Angeles, she met with local writers and producers in hopes of giving new life and energy to her musical career. Nothing really clicked until she met Glen Ballard through a publishing contact. Ballard, already well-known for his writing and production work with artists such as Wilson Phillips, Paula Abdul, and Michael Jackson, was impressed by Morissette's talent and motivation. Morissette came to think of Ballard as her "spiritual brother," and the two of them settled into his home studio and hammered out the songs that would make up the breakthrough album. With them collaborating on the music and Morissette penning the lyrics, they began recording demos, sometimes completing a song a day. She said, "I wrote some of the songs and woke up the next day not even remembering I'd done them—almost like a stream-of-consciousness. It was a very unfettered [free], spiritual experience." After the demos were completed, Ballard took the tapes around to the major record companies, but they all rejected the project.

I see right through you

After a few months a demo tape fell into the hands of Guy Oseary, the twenty-one-year old A & R (artists & repertoire) chief for Maverick Records, a label owned by pop megastar Madonna. Maverick was impressed by the tape, and they asked Morissette to perform for a group of label executives at Ballard's home studio. She was soon signed to Maverick in late 1994.

Her experiences in the music 'biz' were the inspiration for the severe "Right Through You," in which she scolds a nameless record company executive for taking her less than seriously, even mispronouncing her name. In the lyric's punch line she sings, "Now that I'm Miss Thing / Now that I'm a zillionaire / You scan the credits for your name / And wonder why it's not there." In view of the album's success, those words may seem like sweet revenge, but when she wrote them, she was nearly broke. She told *Rolling Stone,* "I laugh now when I sing the song ... [because] when I wrote those words, I was the furthest thing in the world from it."

You oughta know

The song selected to introduce Morissette to the world was "You Oughta Know." It showcased the album's traits: gritty production; funky beats; and soaring, raw, emotional, dynamic vocals. It also stirred up controversy over its lyrical content. The song's story, a blistering retelling of a conversation with an ex-lover, went into occasionally explicit detail. Morissette also worked in a few insults for the man's current partner.

Geoffrey Darby, one of Morissette's Nickelodeon directors, told *People Weekly,* "When I first heard 'You Oughta Know,' I thought, '*That* came out of the mouth of our sweet little girl?'" Some critics knocked the song as being simply shock-for-the-sake-of-shock (mainly because it contained an obscene word), but the listening public was riveted by her impassioned delivery. Propelled by guest appearances of Flea and Dave Navarro of the **Red Hot Chili Peppers** (see entry), there was no mistaking the singer of this song was seriously upset about something.

Sales of *Jagged Little Pill* exploded, and within five months of its release it was certified as having sold four million copies, in the process making Morissette the first Canadian female to score a number one album on the U.S. charts. By February 1996 it was certified platinum (sale of one million copies in the United States) six times over.

Follow-up singles "Hand in My Pocket," "Ironic," "You Learn," and "Head Over Feet" continued the pattern: simple (but not simplistic) lyrics that allowed the listener to feel that Morissette was telling them her deepest thoughts and music that borrowed from influences as diverse as rock, dance, hip-hop, and folk.

You learn

After the release of *Jagged Little Pill,* Morissette assembled a live band and embarked on an extensive world tour that saw her grow from small clubs to selling out amphitheaters in rapid succession. Along the way she picked up a slew of fans, numerous unofficial pages on the World Wide Web, many awards from the Grammys to the Junos, and inevitably, some backlash against her success.

Some people had a problem with her occasionally strident and affected vocal style, while others complained that there wasn't enough "depth" to her lyrics. The criticisms were only a minor annoyance when compared to the fact that in late 1996, *Jagged Little Pill* surpassed Whitney Houston's 1985 debut album to become the top-selling album by a female of all time.

In early 1997, Morissette was in the studio recording a second album for release later in the year.

Selected Awards

Grammy Awards: 1) Album of the Year, for *Jagged Little Pill,* 2) Best Rock Album, for *Jagged Little Pill,* 3) Best Rock Song, for "You Oughta Know," (songwriting award shared with Glen Ballard), 4) Best Female Rock Vocal Performance, for "You Oughta Know," 1996.

Juno Awards: 1) Most Promising New Female Artist, 1991, 2) Best Album, 3) Best Single, 4) Best Female Vocalist, 5) Best Songwriter, 6) Best Rock Album, 1996.

Select Discography

Alanis (MCA Canada), 1990.

Now Is the Time (MCA Canada), 1992.

Jagged Little Pill (Maverick/Reprise), 1995.

Further Reading

"Coming of Age," *People Weekly,* March 4, 1996, p. 45.

Grills, Barry, *Ironic: Alanis Morissette, The Story,* Quarry Press, 1997.

Rogers, Kalen, *The Story of Alanis Morissette,* Omnibus Press, 1996.

Wild, David, "Alanis Morissette Profile," *Rolling Stone,* November 2, 1995, p. 40.

Contact Information

c/o Maverick Records
8000 Beverly Blvd.
Los Angeles, CA 90048

Web Site

http://www.repriserec.com/Alanis

Sinead O'Connor

Irish folk-rock singer and songwriter
Born December 12, 1966, in Glenageary, Ireland

"I can't be put in any category, and that freaks people out." –Sinead O'Connor

"No one can dispute that O'Connor has an astonishing voice," wrote Christopher John Farley in *Time*. Indeed, with one of the most glorious voices in pop music, Sinead O'Connor carries on the long Irish vocal tradition of sad, romantic, and sometimes angry songs. Yet the outspoken singer/songwriter brings a perspective that makes her emotionally and vocally dramatic—but that can, does, and will offend. "O'Connor has a revelatory [serving to reveal] voice," explained Jeff Giles in *Newsweek*. "Still, there are a lot of people who believe she was put on this earth just to get on their nerves." O'Connor's outspokenness, together with her shaved head, have often distracted the media's attention from her music.

The frightened child

In 1992, O'Connor revealed that her mother—a Valium addict—had abused her physically, verbally, emotionally, and sexually. The singer grew up completely frightened. "All I could do was ask God to help me," O'Connor told Janice C. Simpson in a *Time*

O'Connor performing at the Grammy Awards in 1989

Her first album release in 1989, *The Lion and the Cobra,* sold well and achieved gold record certification the same year as its debut. But it was O'Connor's second album that established the singer as a revered pop music star. Released in 1990, *I Do Not Want What I Have Not Got* sold six million copies and reached number one on music charts in every major industry market. It won a Grammy for Best Alternative Music Performance, which O'Connor declined to accept.

O'Connor's next album in 1992, however, showed a remarkable turn in her popularity. *Am I Not Your Girl?* a collection of standards, sold only 250,000 copies. This left reviewers and the music industry wondering if these low sales were a direct result of O'Connor's behavior on a segment of the television show *Saturday Night Live.*

While appearing on the program in 1992, O'Connor tore up a picture of Pope John Paul II, claiming that the Vatican and the Roman Empire caused the destruction of the world. Believing that the Catholic Church controlled lives of people everywhere, she held the Vatican responsible for domestic violence and child abuse throughout the world, including her own. O'Connor, who revealed that she had two abortions, also opposed the right-to-life policies of the Catholic Church.

interview. "And he did, by giving me my voice."

Success as a singer

O'Connor began singing publicly at age fourteen for the wedding of a teacher.

Exiled from the mainstream

The backlash from her statements and actions was severe. The National Broadcasting Company received more than 3,000 complaints—a record number—regarding her behavior on *Saturday Night Live,* causing the show to issue a lifetime ban on O'Connor. Fans at a subsequent Bob Dylan concert booed O'Connor from the stage during a performance at Madison Square Garden in New York. Radio stations stopped playing her material; demonstrations occurred outside of O'Connor's concerts; and the National Ethnic Coalition Organization destroyed copies of the singer's recordings, donating money to charities for each album or CD that the public brought to be destroyed.

A year later, O'Connor attempted suicide by taking sleeping pills with vodka. Then in 1994 she entered a rehabilitation clinic for drug and alcohol abuse. That same year the singer released her *Universal Mother* album, filled with family-related songs reflecting her pain and recovery from the abuse at the hands of her mother. The private, uncommercial recording was more successful than her previous one, debuting in the Top 40. "Listening to these songs," wrote Giles, "you can't help but think that if O'Connor is permanently exiled from the mainstream, it'll be our loss."

In 1995—after continued controversy regarding such wide and varied topics as the U.S. national anthem (which she refused to allow to be played at one of her concerts) and materialism in the music industry (one reason she gave for refusing a Grammy)—O'Connor promised not to speak with the media again. So far, she has kept her vow.

O'Connor and the Grammys

At the Grammy Awards ceremonies in early 1991, O'Connor became the first artist in Grammy history to refuse an award. Connor had received four nominations on the strength of her album, I Do Not Want What I Have Not Got. Prior to the show, she had issued an announcement that she would not attend the ceremonies, nor would she accept any awards. When the album won the Best Alternative Music Award, O'Connor remained true to her word and declined the award. Shortly afterwards on Arsenio Hall's late-night TV talk show, she explained her actions, "I've said that if I win, I won't accept it and I wouldn't want it near me. As far as I'm concerned, it represents everything I despise about the music industry."

Nearly two years later, O'Connor answered the question for Time: "O.K., shall I tell you why I wouldn't do the Grammys? I wanted to voice my objection to the use of the music business as a means of controlling information and of honoring artists for material success rather than artistic expression or the expression of truth, which I consider to be the job of artists." O'Connor did attend the MTV and American Music Awards that year. In 1989, she performed "Mandinka" at the Grammy ceremonies, having been nominated for Best Female Vocalist.

Selected Awards

Grammy Award nomination, Best Female Vocalist, 1989.

MTV Video Music Awards: 1) Best Video of the Year, 2) Best Female Video, and 3)

Best Post-Modern, all for "Nothing Compares 2 U," 1990.

Billboard Music Awards, Top Worldwide Single, for "Nothing Compares 2 U," 1990.

BRIT Awards, Best International Female Artist, 1991.

Grammy Awards, Best Alternative Music Performance, Vocal or Instrumental, for *I Do Not Want What I Have Not Got,* 1991 (award refused).

Rolling Stone Readers' Picks: 1) Artist of the Year, 2) Best Female Singer, 3) Worst Female Singer, and 4) Best Album for *I Do Not Want What I Have Not Got,* 1991.

Rolling Stone Critics' Picks: 1) Artist of the Year, 2) Best Female Singer, 3) Best Singer, and 4) Best Album, 1991.

Hollywood Women's Press Club, Sour Apple Award, 1991.

Selected Discography

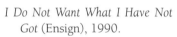

The Lion and the Cobra (Ensign), 1987.

I Do Not Want What I Have Not Got (Ensign), 1990.

Am I Not Your Girl? (Ensign), 1992.

Universal Mother (Ensign), 1994.

Further Reading

Farley, Christopher John, "Singing to a Silent Harp," *Time,* November 7, 1994, p. 87.

Giles, Jeff, "No Forgiving, No Forgetting," *Newsweek,* October 10, 1994, p. 70.

Light, Alan, "Sinead Speaks," *Rolling Stone,* October 29, 1992, pp. 50-53+.

Simpson, Janice C., "'People Need a Short, Sharp Shock,'" *Time,* November 9, 1992, pp. 78-79.

Contact Information

Ensign/Chrysalis Records
3300 Warner Blvd.
Burbank, CA 91510

Web Site

http://www.telebyte.nl/~bobbink/sinead/sinead.htm

Parents Aren't Supposed to Like It

Joan Osborne

American singer/songwriter

Born July 8, 1965, in Louisville, Kentucky

What appeared to be Joan Osborne's overnight success was actually the result of years of working the New York rock and blues bar circuit, two independent CD releases, and a major label debut that languished for months before her hit single, "One of Us," propelled her to stardom. In fact, three years passed from the time *Rolling Stone* magazine hailed her as a "new face" to watch until her debut album *Relish* was released. Following its release, *Relish* sold nearly three million copies, garnered extensive media coverage, and received seven Grammy nominations. Not bad for a girl from Anchorage, Kentucky, whose first time onstage was initiated by a dare.

From Kentucky to New York

One of six children born to Jerry Osborne, a building contractor, and his wife Ruth, a seamstress, Joan never dreamed of a life in music. "In that place," she told *People Weekly* about her hometown of Anchorage, Kentucky, "it would have seemed an unrealistic, pretentious ambition." Instead, she kept her singing as a private pas-

"Well, if this is something you would like to have happen, what's the thing you can make happen on your own? You're not going to wait around for someone to discover you, that's for chumps."

sion. Although she found role models in rhythm and blues singers like Etta James and Tina Turner, it had more to do with attitude than singing. "These black divas had a real sexiness and playfulness about them," she told Chris Willman of *Entertainment Weekly,* "which seemed to me almost like this feminist ideal."

Finding a creative outlet in filmmaking and realizing a desire to see the world outside of Kentucky, Osborne went off to attend New York University's prestigious film school in the early 1980s. Her interest immediately focused on documentary filmmaking, but her aspiring career in that field was soon effectively nipped in the bud.

Osborne had stored all her films at the apartment of a friend. When her friend's apartment building was demolished, so were her films. Around the same time, after stopping in a blues bar with some friends, Osborne was encouraged to go onstage and sing a song. After a heartfelt reading of Billie Holiday's "God Bless the Child" blew away the room, the piano player suggested she come back the next week.

Soon, there were more open mike nights, then regular club dates and a loyal following. In 1990 she won the New York Music Award for Best Unsigned Artist. A year later she released a live CD entitled *Soul Show* on her own Womanly Hips label, a typical act of Osborne's self determination. "I think I had the idea that some larger success might happen for me at some point," she confessed in her Mercury biography. "I was very conscious of thinking about it in terms of,

'Well, if this is something you would like to have happen, what's the thing you can make happen on your own? You're not going to wait around for someone to discover you, that's for chumps.'"

Relish

Blue Million Miles, a Womanly Hips EP, followed in 1993. In 1994 she signed to Mercury's Blue Gorilla label and began recording songs for her major label debut album, *Relish,* which was released in March 1995. The album featured Osborne's bluesy voice singing over a pop-rock backing on original as well as cover songs. "On top of all the lyrical and musical strengths of *Relish,* Osborne is a highly resourceful singer who isn't afraid to take risks," Ron Givens proclaimed in *Stereo Review.* "As far as I'm concerned, the next Joan Osborne album simply cannot get here soon enough." Many shared Givens's point of view, although conservative religious groups blasted Osborne for singing, "What if God was one of us / just a slob like one of us," on her hit song, "One of Us." The line didn't deter record buyers or the Grammy nominating committee, however, and Osborne became a bona fide star even though she didn't take home a Grammy.

Osborne spent most of her post-*Relish* time touring. She also traveled to India to study qawwali, an ancient form of Indian singing, whose most famous practitioner, Nusret Fateh Ali Khan, offered Osborne his tutorial assistance. She also returned to her former craft of filmmaking by directing the video for her song, "St. Teresa." In late 1996 Osborne and

Mercury released *Early Recordings,* a compilation of songs from her out-of-print independent releases, *Soul Show* and *Blue Million Miles.* She then headed into the studio to record her widely anticipated follow-up to *Relish.*

Selected Awards

New York Music Award for Best Unsigned Artist, 1990.

"One of Us," 1996 Grammy Award nominee for Record of the Year and for Song of the Year.

Relish, 1996 Grammy Award nominee for Album of the Year and for Best New Artist.

"St. Teresa," 1996 Grammy Award nominee for Best Rock Vocal, Female.

"Spider Web," 1997 Grammy Award nominee for Best Rock Vocal, Female.

Selected Discography

Soul Show (Womanly Hips), 1991.

Blue Million Miles (Womanly Hips), 1993 (EP).

Relish (Blue Gorilla/Mercury), 1995.

Early Recordings (Womanly Hips/Blue Gorilla/Mercury), 1996.

Further Reading

Billboard, January 14, 1995, p. 3.

"Coming of Age," *People,* March 4, 1996, p. 44.

Moses, Paul, "'One of Us,' Dad Listens to Daughter," *Commonweal,* June 14, 1996, p. 9.

Newsweek, January 22, 1996, p. 60.

Powers, Ann, "Holy Roller," *Rolling Stone,* March 21, 1996, p. 44.

Us, April 1996, p. 64.

Willman, Chris, "Saint Joan," *Entertainment Weekly,* February 2, 1996, p. 34.

Contact Information

Mercury Records

825 Eighth Ave.

New York, NY 10019

Web Sites

http://www.mercuryrecords.com/mercury/artists/

http://www.rockweb.com/bands/joan

LiZ PHair

American singer and songwriter

Born Elizabeth Clark Phair, April 17, 1967,
in New Haven, Connecticut

Chicago-based singer/songwriter Liz Phair virtually came out of nowhere with her 1993 debut album *Exile in Guyville*. With songs consisting of blunt sexual references on top of catchy guitar rock, the album was intended to be Phair's song-by-song response to the Rolling Stones's 1972 classic, *Exile on Main Street*. The album caused the then-twenty-six-year-old Phair to be hurled into alternative rock's limelight.

Critics raved about the honesty of Phair's songwriting; she was named runner-up "artist of the year" by both *Rolling Stone* and *Spin*. In addition, *Exile in Guyville* topped the annual *Village Voice*'s jazz and pop critics' poll, making Phair the first woman to win since Joni Mitchell's *Court and Spark* album won in 1974. Phair followed with 1994's *Whip-smart*—which featured the hit "Supernova"—and the EP (extended play) *Juvenalia* in 1995. Since then she's been spending her time with her husband and new baby, born in December 1996.

Adopted daughter

Born April 17, 1967, in New Haven, Connecticut, she was adopted at birth by John and Nancy Phair. "I was always told that I was adopted," she told Jon Pareles of the *New York Times*. "It hasn't been a major issue, but it's probably a strong underlying issue, in a quiet way.... It makes me feel a little bit detached from everything and at the same time it makes me free ... to pursue my identity according to my instincts." After spending the first part of her life in Cincinnati, the Phairs moved to the affluent Chicago suburb of Winnetka in 1976. At a young age Phair showed a talent for visual art, pursuing it while growing up, then majoring in it at Oberlin College in Ohio.

Following her graduation in 1989 from Oberlin, Phair bounced around, first to San Francisco and then Boston, until she returned to her parent's home in Winnetka in January 1991. Although she had been writing songs on guitar and piano since grade school, she hadn't considered herself a songwriter until a friend in San Francisco encouraged her to make a tape of her songs.

Returning to her childhood bedroom in Winnetka with her guitar and four-track tape recorder, Phair recorded a trio of homemade tapes she called *Girly Sound*. The tapes began to circulate around the Chicago music scene and in a typical act of bold confidence, Phair called up the independent Matador Records to see if they wanted to release her songs on an album. Matador co-owner Gerard Cosloy had just read a review of a *Girly Sound* cassette in a punk fanzine and liked the six-song tape Phair sent in, so he offered her a $3,000 advance. With that, Phair headed into the studio to record a single, which eventually developed into the eighteen-song *Exile in Guyville*.

Exile in Guyville

Guyville was heralded as one of the best records of the year, selling more than 200,000 copies and far exceeding everyone's expectations. Phair had expected to sell about 3,000 copies, and Cosloy of Matador would have been happy with sales of 5,000. When it came time to tour in support of the record, Phair's stage fright got the best of her, forcing her to cancel the tour after a few dates. Never able to gel with the band she hired, Phair instead went back to the studio to record the follow-up to *Guyville, Whip-smart*. Spurred on by the radio-friendly single, "Supernova," sales of the second album were good, although critical response failed to match that of her debut. Phair did return to the stage, though, performing a series of solo shows in support of *Whip-smart*.

In 1995 Phair released an EP called *Juvenalia*, made up of songs from Phair's *Girly Sound* era. Also that year, Phair married Jim Stasauskas, a video editor she met on the set of her first video. In December 1996 she gave birth to their son, James Nicholas. Due to her new marriage and pregnancy, Phair was out of the public eye for quite a while, a situation she liked. "I just want to make records, make videos, make the artwork for the records and occasionally perform in my hometown," she admitted to Robert Hilburn of the *Los Angeles Times.* "That would be my ideal. I prefer to be reclusive and private about my creation and then, once I'm finished, present it to people: 'Here is my work. Now you can critique it and do what you want.'" A new album by Phair is expected in August 1997.

Selected Awards

Village Voice Jazz and Pop Music Critics Poll, Best Album, for *Exile in Guyville,* 1994.

Rolling Stone critics poll, Best New Female Vocalist and runner-up Artist of the Year, 1994.

Spin, runner-up Artist of the Year, 1994.

Grammy nomination, Best Rock Vocal, Female, for "Don't Have Time," 1996.

Selected Discography

Exile in Guyville (Matador Records), 1993.

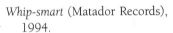

Whip-smart (Matador Records), 1994.

Juvenalia (Matador Records), 1995.

Further Reading

Dunn, Jancee, "That Girl," (Liz Phair interview, cover story), *Rolling Stone,* October 6, 1994, p. 42.

"Liz Phair (The 25 Most Intriguing People of the Year)," *People Weekly,* December 26, 1994, p. 94.

Los Angeles Times, March 5, 1995, p. C3.

Pareles, Jon, "Liz Phair: Blunt Rock," *New York Times Magazine,* October 2, 1994, p. 38.

Raphael, Amy, *GRRRLS: Viva Rock Divas,* St. Martin's Griffin, 1996. (Contains a chapter on Liz Phair.)

Contact Information

Matador Records
676 Broadway, 4th Fl.
New York, NY 10012

Web Sites

http://www.wavefront.com/~lazlo/liz

http://www.is.co.za/andras/music/l

http://www.matador.com

http://members.aol.com/guyville/index.html

LOU REED

Influential rock singer/songwriter and guitarist

Born Louis Firbank, March 2, 1952,
in Freeport, Long Island, New York

While the 1960s flower children had a rock n' roll poet in Bob Dylan, the 1970s New York punks had their own street poet musician in Lou Reed. He started his long musical journey in the 1960s' first-ever art rock band, the Velvet Underground. Being the main songwriter and vocalist for the band helped pave the way for his music, and many Reed "classics" came out of this era. After the Velvet Underground's demise, Lou Reed's successful solo career took off. He penned and recorded numerous solo albums that became his version of the great American novel. Setting urban poetry over simple music, Reed managed to capture the gritty feel of his hometown, New York City. The stark imagery of the city can be found in his songs. He transformed rock n' roll songwriting by writing about various social taboos such as drug addiction ("Heroin"), sexual deviance, and street life ("Walk on the Wild Side"). No subjects were off limits to him.

His experimentation with all styles of music from rhythm and blues (R & B), glam rock, punk, and just plain noise caused some critics, unsure of what he'd do next, to label his music simply

"It's the music that kept us all intact, kept us from going crazy." –Lou Reed

"Lou Reed music." With a music career that has lasted through three decades, Lou Reed has made a name for himself as one of the most influential figures in rock n' roll.

Rock n' roll animal

Native New Yorker Lou Reed was born Louis Firbank in 1942 and raised on Long Island. He became interested in music as a teenager and at seventeen succumbed to the evilness of rock n' roll. At least, that's what his parents thought when his severe mood swings and bizarre behavior threatened to disrupt their lives. They sent him off to a mental hospital for treatment. The shock treatment was much worse than the original problem, and the effects of it left a permanent mental scar that would remain with him forever.

He began writing and playing with a band called The Shades, before he went off to Syracuse University. At college he studied journalism, creative writing, and poetry and played in bar bands. It was the discussions he had there about sex, drugs, and torn romance that he turned into early song lyrics. Composing the conversations to the accompaniment of electric guitars and tribal drum beats was the next step. While he was at school, his love and appreciation of jazz surfaced in a radio show called "Excursion on a Wobbly Rail," named after a song by jazz pianist Cecil Taylor.

Lou found work as a songwriter for Pickwick Records, writing and recording low budget records that were sold at supermarket racks. It was easy work for an experienced writer, and he cashed in. A dance song he wrote, "The Ostrich," was recorded by the Primitives and almost became a hit single at the time.

Cult status

He met John Cale at a party in 1964, and the two decided to form a band. Bringing in bassist Sterling Morrison and original drummer Angus MacLise (who was replaced by Maureen Tucker in 1965), they formed the musical enigma known as the Velvet Underground. There is a saying about the Velvet Underground that "only a thousand people listened to the group during its career, but every one of the thousand formed a band." The first ever "art" rock band of the 1960s turned into underground rock icons by influencing so many musicians after them. The Velvets achieved cult status but saw little mainstream success. Releasing four albums in five years, the band broke up before they accomplished what they should have.

The Velvet Underground could "do a lot of things a lot of ways," Reed says of the band. This was evident in their diverse musical direction, combining three chord rock with wayward melodies, experimental noise, spoken word pieces, and even country and western. They performed "art," and thanks to pop artist Andy Warhol, The Velvets became the darlings of the New York underground scene. The eccentric Warhol acted as a mentor to the band, and at his urging they added German chanteuse Nico to the fold.

With the artist's influence and backing, they were able to put on avant-garde shows like the "Exploding Plastic Inevitable." It was the opposite pulls of art versus commerce that caused the band to part ways with Warhol, and they disbanded soon after in 1970. In 1993, they reunited briefly for concerts and an album. The Velvet Underground finally received the recognition they deserved in 1996, when they were inducted into the Rock N' Roll Hall of Fame.

Walking on the wild side

After the Velvets broke up, Reed got a job as a typist for two years. "My mother always told me, 'You should take up typing. It gives you something to fall back on.' And she was right!," he recalled for *Rolling Stone.* He continued writing poetry and songs while he pondered his next move. In 1972, he signed a deal with RCA Records and released his self-titled solo debut *Lou Reed.*

"What kind of repressive culture would ban a song?"

It was his second effort that left Lou Reed's musical mark. *Transformer,* produced by **David Bowie** (see entry), featured Reed's first and only chart hit (it reached number sixteen), "Walk on the Wild Side." Delivered in Reed's trademark deadpan voice, the song was pure street poetry in motion. With its memorable bass line and sexual connotations, it caught the seedy element of New York nightlife, and Reed's vocals made it into an unforgettable song. It was banned from the BBC and U.S. airwaves for its references to prostitutes, junkies, and

Lou Reed in Brussels, Belgium, 1974

cross-dressers, causing Reed to comment, "What kind of repressive culture would ban a song?" Another track, "Satellite of Love," also became a rock classic. Years later, the Irish supergroup **U2** (see entry) exposed it to a new generation of fans as a part of their "ZOO-TV" tour. A larger than life video image of Reed appeared onscreen behind them "singing" along with the band.

Another major standout in Reed's solo work was the album, *New York.* It showcased his renewed vitality and continued fondness for the Big apple. "[Writer William] Faulkner had the South, [Irish novelist James] Joyce had Dublin, I've got New York," Reed said.

Life is like . . .

He reunited briefly with old Velvet Underground bandmate, John Cale, for a series of shows. The death of Andy Warhol, their mentor, in 1987 led the two to write songs together again in tribute to their late friend. This collaboration brought about the 1990 album *Songs for Drella.*

With death being the "Great Motivator," Reed reflected on the losses all around him on 1992's *Magic and Loss.* Surprisingly the songs here are more upbeat than depressing. That was Reed's way of dealing with the emotions and grief that accompanied the deaths of friends, heroes, and old bandmates. He also returned to his first love, poetry, and finally published his writings in the book, *Between Thought and Expression.*

In 1994, the solace in his personal life returned. After two divorces, Reed finally found his soulmate in performance artist/musician, Laurie Anderson. Anderson not only fulfilled his personal void, she became his musical companion, too.

The two recorded a spoken-word duet that appeared on her album, *Bright Red.*

A brief cameo appearance and cut on the soundtrack to the movie *Blue in the Face* came next. In 1996 he signed with Warner Bros. (which was Laurie Anderson's label, too) and released *Set the Twilight Reeling,* an album that was recorded entirely at his home studio, with all of the songs written on a computer. The late 1990s seemed to bring no sign of stopping for Reed. "I've become completely well-adjusted to being a cult figure," he says. "I'm a cult figure, but I sell some records, too."

Selected Awards

Best New Poet Award from Council of Small Literary Magazines, 1977.

Rock N' Roll Animal certified gold, 1978.

Knight of the French Order of Arts and Letters, 1992.

Selected Discography

With the Velvet Underground (on MGM/Verve, except where noted):

The Velvet Underground & Nico, 1966.

White Light/White Heat, 1967.

The Velvet Underground, 1969.

Loaded (Cotillion), 1970.

The Velvet Underground Live at Max's Kansas City (Atlantic), 1972.

1969: The Velvet Underground Live (Mercury), 1974.

VU (Polydor), 1985.

Another View (Polydor), 1986.

Live MCMXCIII (Sire), 1993.

Peel Slowly and See (Polydor Chronicles), 1995.

Solo Releases: (On RCA, except where noted)

Lou Reed, 1972.

Transformer, 1973.

Berlin, 1973

Rock N' Roll Animal, 1974.

Sally Can't Dance, 1974.

Lou Reed Live, 1975.

Metal Machine Music, 1975.

Coney Island Baby, 1976.

Walk on the Wild Side: The Best of Lou Reed, 1977.

Rock and Roll Heart (Arista), 1976.

Street Hassle (Arista), 1978.

Take No Prisoners (Arista), 1979.

The Bells (Arista), 1979.

Growing Up in Public (Arista), 1980.

Rock and Roll Diary, 1967-80 (Arista), 1980.

The Blue Mask, 1982.

Legendary Hearts, 1983.

New Sensations, 1984.

Mistrial, 1986.

New York (Sire), 1989.

Magic and Loss (Sire), 1992.

Set the Twilight Reeling (Warner Bros.), 1996.

Further Reading

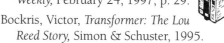

Baker, Ken, "Reloaded," *People Weekly,* February 24, 1997, p. 29.

Bockris, Victor, *Transformer: The Lou Reed Story,* Simon & Schuster, 1995.

Fricke, David, "Lou Reed: The Rolling Stone Interview", *Rolling Stone,* May 4, 1989.

Helliger, Jeremy, "Set the Twilight Reeling," *People Weekly,* March 11, 1996, p. 22.

Norris, Chris, "Lou Reed" (interview), *New York,* March 11, 1996, p. 40.

Rogers, Ray, "Lou Reed" (interview), *Interview,* March 1996, p. 86.

Spin, September 1995.

Contact Information

c/o Warner Brothers Records
75 Rockefeller Plaza
New York, NY 10019

Web Site

http://www.geocities.com/WestHollywood/3660/loureed.html

http://www.geocities.com/Paris/LeftBank/2800/lou.html

inDEX

Italic type indicates volume numbers;
boldface type indicates featured entries and their page numbers;
(ill.) indicates photographs.

231 (ill.), **232-236**, 239, 271, 400; *3:* 614, 655
Bowie, David, with Nine Inch Nails *1:* 91; *2:* (ill.) 231
Bowman, Steve *3:* 557
Boxley, James Hank *2:* 393
A Boy Named Goo *1:* 58
The Boys *3:* 507
Boyz in the Hood (film and song) *2:* 332, 339, 361, 362
Boyz II Men *3:* 503, **511 (ill.) 512-514**
Bradley, Owen *3:* 636
Break A Dawn *3:* 526
Breakdancing *2:* 277
Bridge School benefit concerts *1:* 207
Brill, Dmitry *2:* 283-285
Brion, Jon *3:* 613
Bristol (England) Sound *2:* 299-301
Brit Pop *2:* **219-222**, 238, 255
British press *1:* 39
British new wave music *1:* 154; *2:* 253
British Invasion *3:* 543
Broadus, Calvin (see Snoop Doggy Dogg)
Brodsky Quartet *2:* 245
The Brown Album *1:* 133
Brown, Andre *2:* 331
Brown, Bobby *3:* 503, **516 (ill.) 517-519**
Brown, James *2:* 276, 304; *3:* 502, 503
Brown, Mark (see Brown Mark)
Brown Mark *3:* 529
Brown, Rex "Rocker" *3:* 491
Brown, Vincent *2:* 382, 383
"Bruise Violet" *1:* 18
Brutal Truth *3:* 468
Bryan, Mark *3:* 572
Bryson, David *3:* 556
Buchignani, Paul *1:* 9
Buck, Peter *1:* 154
Buckley, Jeff *3:* 441 (ill.), 442, **443 (ill.), 444-445**
Buckley, Tim *3:* 442
Budd, Harold *2:* 297
Buddhism *2:* 231
Buffalo Springfield *1:* 204
Bullet *2:* 427
"Bullet in the Head" *1:* 135
Bulletproof *2:* 414
Bumstead records *3:* 635
Burrell, Stanley Kirk (see Hammer)

Burton, Cliff *3:* 486, 487
Burton, James *2:* 244
Busby, Jheryl *3:* 513
Bush *2:* 222, **237 (ill.), 238 (ill.), 239-240**
Bush, Dave *2:* 256
Bush, George *2:* 340
Bustin' Records (label) *2:* 350, 352, 353
Busy Bee *2:* 372
Butcher Brothers *1:* 188
Butler, Bernard *2:* 270, 272
The **Butthole Surfers** *1:* 3, **33 (ill.), 34 (ill.), 35-36**
The Buzzcocks *1:* 139; *2:* 253
The Byrds *2:* 221; *3:* 543

C

Caine, Michael *2:* 272
Cajun music *2:* 243
Cale, John *3:* 654, 656
Calhoun, William *3:* 480
Calire, Mario *1:* 200
Cameron, Matt *1:* 118, 172, 173
Campbell, Sterling *1:* 170
Campbell, Tevin *3:* 503, **520 (ill.) 521-523**
Cantrell, Jerry *1:* 11 (ill.), 12, 14
Capitol Records *3:* 484
Captain Beefheart *2:* 222
Carey, Mariah *2:* 277; *3:* 513
Caroline Records *1:* 163
The Cars *2:* 277
Cash, Johnny *1:* 194
The Castilles *3:* 597
Cauty, Jimmy *2:* 295, 296
Cave, Nick *2:* 222
CBGB's *1:* 139
CBS/Columbia Records *3:* 598
Cease, Jeff *3:* 546
Censorship and freedom of speech issues *1:* 62, 76, 79; *2:* 310, 361, 368, 369, 394-395, 399; *3:* 655-656
Chamberlin, Jimmy *1:* 164 (ill.), 165, 167
Chapel Hill, North Carolina *1:* 4
Chapman, Tracy *3:* 439 (ill.), 441, 442, **446 (ill.), 447-450**
Charles, Ray *3:* 501 (ill.), 502
Cheap Trick *2:* 277
Cheeba, Eddie *2:* 304

Chemical Brothers *2:* 278, **280-282**
Cherone, Gary *3:* 468
Cherry, Nenah *2:* 300
Chic *2:* 276, 308
Chicago, Illinois , *1:* 165, 188
Childress, Ross *3:* 553
Chilli *3:* 536
Chipperfield, Sheila *2:* 256
Christianity *2:* 291
Christianne F *2:* 233
Christian Right *2:* 292, 293
The Chronic *2:* 336
Chrysler Corporation *3:* 600
Chuck D *1:* 27; *2:* 305, 362, 374, 392 (ill.), 394-396, 408
"Cinnamon Girl" *1:* 204
Civil rights movement *3:* 439
Clarke, Gilby *3:* 477
The Clash *1:* 1, 60, 139, 154; *2:* 219, 225, 308
Clash of the Titans tour *1:* 13
Classical music *2:* 245
Claypool, Les *1:* 130 (ill.), 131-133
Clayton, Adam *1:* 190, 191, 192 (ill.)
Clearmountain, Bob *3:* 476
Clemmons, Clarence *3:* 598
Clifford Ball *3:* 589
Cline, Patsy *3:* 635
Clink, Mike *3:* 474, 476
Clinton, Bill *1:* 193; *2:* 315
Clinton, George *1:* 149; *2:* 276, 285; *3:* 503, 541
Clockers (film) *2:* 396
Clouser, Charlie *3:* 499
Cobain, Kurt *1:* 49, 50, 65-67, 94, 96 (ill.), 97, 98, 175, 206, 208; *2:* 238; *3:* 573
Cobra Verde *3:* 570
Codling, Neil *2:* 272
Coed rock *1:* 196
Coffey, King *1:* 36
Collective Soul *3:* 543, **552 (ill.), 553-555**
Colley, Dana *1:* 81, 82
Colling, Bootsy *3:* 507
Collins, Judy *3:* 440
Colt, Johnny *3:* 546
Columbia Records *3:* 444
Colvin, Douglas *1:* 138
Combs, Sean "Puffy" *2:* 310, 388-390, 424, 426, 428
"Come Out and Play" *1:* 108
Comedy, musical *1:* 20
Comess, Aaron *3:* 595
The Commodores *2:* 404

Mizell, Jason "Jam Master Jay" *2:* 404, 405, 408
Moby *2:* 279, **291 (ill.), 292-294**
Molina, Ralph *1:* 204
Monie Love *2:* 310
"Monkey Wrench" *1:* 51
Monster *1:* 157
Monsters of Rock Festival *3:* 475, 487, 491
Moon, Chris *3:* 529
Moon Records *1:* 185
Moore, LeRoi *3:* 585
Morello, Tom *1:* 134 (ill.)
Morissette, Alanis *1:* 151; *3:* 611 (ill.), 613, **639 (ill.), 640-642**
Morphine *1:* **81 (ill.), 82-83;** *3:* 550
Morris, Nathan *3:* 511, 512
Morris, Wanya *3:* 511, 512
Morrison, Sterling *3:* 654
Morrison, Van *3:* 541, 542
Morrissey *2:* 221, **260-264**
Moshing *2:* 277, 279
Mother Love Bone *1:* 85, 118
Mother's Milk *1:* 149
Motley Crue *3:* 467
Motown *2:* 243; *3:* 504
Motown Records *2:* 2763: 506, 512, 513
Mouth of Rasputin *3:* 566
Moyet, Alison *2:* 300
Mr. Crowes Garden *3:* 546
MTV Unplugged *1:* 14, 98, 118; *2:* 376, 379; *3:* 441
MTV *1:* 2, 13; *2:* 221, 222, 376, 379, 407; *3:* 441, 459, 467, 498
Mudhoney *1:* **84 (ill.), 85-86,** 95
Mueller, Karl *1:* 170
Mullen, Larry, Jr. *1:* 190
Multimedia images *1:* 193
Murmur *1:* 154
Murphy, Daniel *1:* 170
Music 4-Life *2:* 357
Mustaine, Dave *3:* 482 (ill.), 483-484, 486
My Aim Is True *2:* 220, 241
"My Boy Lollipop" *1:* 184
My Brother the Cow *1:* 85
Myers, Dwight A. *2:* 356
The Mynah Birds *1:* 204

N

Nadirah *2:* 315

"Name" *1:* 57
Napalm Death *3:* 468
Nastanovich, Bob *1:* 111
Nasty Ness *2:* 416
National Ethnic Coalition *3:* 645
National Institute on Drug Abuse *3:* 560
Natural Born Killers (film) *1:* 90
Naughty Gear *2:* 384
Naughty by Nature *2:* 307, 323, **382 (ill.), 383 (ill.), 384-386,** 408
Navarro, Dave *1:* 76, 77, 126, 151; *3:* 641
Nazz *2:* 231
Nelson, David Jordan, Jr. *2:* 305
Nelson, Prince Rogers (see Prince)
Nemesister *1:* 18
Nettwerk Records *3:* 456
Neurotic Outsiders *3:* 478
Nevermind *1:* 4, 54, 95, 97
New Edition *2:* 277, 369; *3:* 516, 517, 519
New Jack City (film) *2:* 369
New Jack Swing *2:* 277, 358
New Jill Swing *3:* 505, 524, 535
New Order *1:* 2; *2:* 221
New Orleans, Louisiana *3:* 603
New Power Generation *3:* 528, 531, 532
New School Punk *1:* 105
The New Style *2:* 384
New wave *1:* 1, 72, 142; *2:* 277
New York City dance scenes *2:* 284
Newsted, Jason *3:* 487
Next Plateau Records, Inc. *2:* 411
Nico *3:* 654
Nieve, Steve *2:* 243
Nine Inch Nails *1:* 3, 79, **87 (ill.), 88, 89 (ill.), 90-92;** *2:* 234
1960s rock music *2:* 275
Nirvana *1:* 2, 4, 5, 49-51, 54, 66, 84, **93 (ill.), 94-95, 96 (ill), 97-100,** 115, 175; *2:* 222, 238, 240
No Code *1:* 121
No Depression *3:* 607

No Doubt *1:* **101 (ill.), 102-104,** 185; *2:* 279
No Limit label *2:* 311
No Need to Argue *1:* 39
Nosebleeds *2:* 260
Nothing Records *1:* 78, 90
Nothing's Shocking *1:* 76
Notorious B.I.G. *2:* 310, **387 (ill.), 388-391,** 424, 426, 428
Novoselic, Kris *1:* 5, 94, 99
Nowell, Brad *1:* 182
NPG (New Power Generation) *3:* 528, 531, 532
NWA *2:* 305, 310, 332, 333, 339, 360, 361, 362, 419

O

Oakes, Richard *2:* 270, 272
Oasis *2:* 221, 227, 228, 238, **265 (ill.), 266 (ill.), 267 (ill.), 268-269,** 281
O'Brien, Brendan *1:* 150
Ochs, Phil *3:* 439
O'Connor, Sinead *2:* 253, 256; *3:* 614, **643 (ill.), 644-646**
Odelay *1:* 3, 24, 26, 28
O'Donnell, Roger *2:* 249, 250
Offspring *1:* **105 (ill.), 106 (ill.), 107-110**
Ohio Players *2:* 276
Oje, Baba *2:* 313
Old school punk *1:* 146, 183
Old school rap *2:* 372, 375
Olliver, Ian *2:* 258
Onassis, Blackie *1:* 187
One Hot Minute *1:* 151
One Little Indian *3:* 624
Onyx *2:* 408
Operation Ivy *1:* 145, 146, 185
The Orb *2:* 279, **295 (ill.), 296-298**
Orbison, Roy *3:* 599, 636
The Organisation *2:* 288
Orioles *3:* 502
O'Riordan, Caitlin *2:* 243
O'Riordan, Dolores *1:* 37 (ill.), 38-41
Osborne, Joan *3:* 615, **647 (ill.), 648-649**
Osbourne, Ozzy *3:* 465, 466
Oseary, Guy *3:* 641
Osman, Mat *2:* 270
Osterberg, James Jewell (see Iggy Pop)

Parents Aren't Supposed to Like It